SIGN R

(signs used in t~~~~ and ~~~~)

Good footpath - - - - - - - - - - - - - - - -
(sufficiently distinct to be followed in mist)

Intermittent footpath -·- -·- -·- -·-·-·-
(difficult to follow in mist)

Route recommended
but no path ··>·····················>·····
(if recommended one way only, arrow indicates direction)

Wall ∞∞∞∞∞∞∞∞∞∞∞   **Broken wall** ∘∘∘∘∘∘∘∘∘∘∘∘∘∘∘∘

Fence ++++++++++++++   **Broken fence** ''''''''''''''''''''''''

Marshy ground ⸜⸝⸜⸝⸜⸝   **Trees** 🌲🌲🌲🌲

Crags ⸜⸝⸜⸝⸜⸝   **Boulders** ◇◇◇◇◇

Stream or River ∿∿∿∿∿∿∿→
(arrow indicates direction of flow)

Waterfall ⌣⌣⌣←   **Bridge** ∿∿≍∿∿

Buildings ▪▪▪   **Unenclosed road** ∷∷∷∷∷∷∷∷∷∷∷

Contours (at 100' intervals)
                              ·····1900·····
                              ···1800·····
                              ·1700·····

Summit-cairn ▲   **Other** (prominent) **cairns** △

The Best of Wainwright

The Best of Wainwright

A Personal Selection
by Hunter Davies

FRANCES LINCOLN

Frances Lincoln Limited, 4 Torriano Mews, Torriano Avenue, London NW5 2RZ
www.franceslincoln.com

The Pictorial Guides to the Lakeland Fells published by Frances Lincoln 2003
This anthology published by Frances Lincoln 2004

Publisher's Note

This book contains unamended pages from A. Wainwright's Pictorial Guides. The maps
and descriptions of walks reproduced here were correct, to the best of A. Wainwright's
knowledge, at the time of first publication in the 1950s and 1960s, but footpaths and
features such as cairns and waymarks may have changed since then. Walkers are strongly
advised to check with an up-to-date map when planning a walk. They are also advised
to take sensible safety precautions when out on the fells.

Printed and bound in Singapore

A CIP catalogue record is available for this book from the British Library.

ISBN 978 0 7112 2463 6

9 8 7

List of Illustrations

A. Wainwright: a self-portrait

Introduction

I picked up my first book by Wainwright in the mid 1970s when we had a holiday home at Caldbeck, in the Northern Fells of Lakeland. I found his *Northern Fells* in a bookshop, not realising at first it was part of a series. I noticed it contained maps and routes for climbing High Pike, the main fell behind our cottage, so I thought that would be handy, especially when I saw it included details about the old mines and quarries which we'd been coming across all the time but weren't sure what they were. The Ordnance Survey maps didn't give much information about them. I thought what fun, what an extra incentive – taking my children on these walks, we can follow Wainwright's routes and also look for interesting minerals. Off we went.

Over the next ten years, we walked every fell in *The Northern Fells*. We kept a record of these walks, with the initials of who had done what and when, on a large piece of green drawing paper which we kept pinned by the fireplace, an honours board for ourselves, and of course to show off to every visitor. When young, the children used to fight to see who was first on a summit and cry if they got beaten. We'd have to bribe the older ones with mint cake to hold back. Until, of course, they refused to come any more: boring, all this walking.

On our own, my wife and I, we would try to work out all-day walks from Wainwright, through the Northern Fells, linking fells together. We once walked right across, taking in Skiddaw, a walk which lasted ten hours. We ended up in Keswick where we stuffed our faces in Maysons – and then we got a taxi back, which, of course, is cheating.

We told everyone how brilliant Wainwright was, how accurate, how artistic, how informative. Many people said, 'Who? Never heard of him. Who is he?' But there were others who said, 'What took you so long? We've known about Wainwright for years.' But of course they didn't know about Wainwright, the person, any more than we did.

I could have done with a bit of help, when I first came across his books, to explain what he was on about, how to read and appreciate his methods. It does take a while to get the hang of it, although *in situ*, with book in hand, doing the walk on the page in front of you, it all makes sense, as we very quickly found.

But I would have liked to have known something about him, the background to his life and his books, why he had done them the way he had. It wouldn't have made the books better, but it would have added to the pleasure, increased the understanding.

When I picked up that first book, I wasn't sure if Wainwright was alive or dead. If dead, I wondered if he had died decades ago, before the war – perhaps he might even be Victorian, some amateur enthusiast who had left his little notebooks behind, judging by the way the pages were presented in his own hand.

I never knew, in all those early years, that he was alive and well and living not far away from us in Cumbria. Or that he had a proper job, which was nothing to do with writing and walking. I didn't know what he looked like either. I soon discovered, of course, that there were other guides in the series, which we went on to use, but in none of them did his photograph appear, nor any biographical information.

Like most Wainwright fans, I referred to him simply as 'Wainwright' or 'AW', which was how he signed off at the end of each book. I never knew what the 'A' bit stood for as he never revealed it in his guide books, although later on he made a joke about it, when thousands of people were asking the same question. He said no, it wasn't Aloysius.

The object of this book is to offer a little help to newcomers to Wainwright and also to people who might recently have fallen in love with the Lake District but perhaps haven't got around to reading his books, or the books about him. It's meant to serve as an introduction, a taster of his style, his methods, and explain something of what he was like, what he was on about.

Wainwright wrote over fifty books, but it's just seven which really concern us here, plus an eighth, *The Outlying Fells of Lakeland*, which covers the lower fells.

Wainwright's seven books in the series which he called 'A Pictorial Guide to the Lakeland Fells' are, in my opinion, the best work he ever did. In them, he covers 214 fells, from which I have chosen seventeen – plus one fell from *The Outlying Fells*. Many Wainwright disciples who have read every book, climbed every mountain, memorised every word, will doubtless have their own totally different favourites.

My choice was based on several factors. I wanted to pick two or three from each of the seven books, to get a geographical spread across the Lake District, so wherever you happen to be staying, there should be one near you to have a go at. But the main criteria are his. When he had finally finished the project, he revealed which were his own favourite fells and his best summits. These twelve fells happen to include the best known, best loved, most popular and also the biggest – the ones every Lakeland lover wants to get under their belt, to boast about. The household-name mountains, names known at least in most British households, could not really be omitted.

I have also included a few smaller, lesser-known ones, which Wainwright also loved, which give an insight into his character and style and which are fun to climb. On your holiday, or even in your lifetime, you might have space and time and the legs for only a

3

handful of Wainwright walks. These, then, are the eighteen I think you should try, should experience, or failing that, at least read and contemplate, in order to sample the range of his walks, his style, his humour, his art.

I've written a little introduction to each walk, taking you through various aspects of his work, his motives, his methods, his genius. I do think he was a genius – in his field. What he produced in his Pictorial Guides were works of art, masterpieces which no one had done before and no one has done since, not in quite the same way.

Wainwright revolutionised the art of guide books to the Lake District, bringing an original eye to the problem of getting down on a one-dimensional piece of paper the multi-faceted emotions and the possibilities and perspectives of a Lakeland climb, however modest. What he brought was an artist's eye, in words and pictures, and also a craftsman's, in his designs and layout.

I can see his Pictorial Guides being used, and admired, for ever, as long as the fells are there and people have the breath to want to climb them. For both the newcomer and the converted, there is an added pleasure in Wainwright – that of studying him by the fireside, enjoying his art and expertise without actually going anywhere. You can either contemplate what you might do soon, once you have got up the energy or the rain stops, or recollect in tranquillity deeds already done, fells conquered, paths trodden, revisiting views and sensations still lurking in the mind's eye.

A Brief Biography

Wainwright was born on 17 January 1907 in Blackburn, Lancashire, the youngest of four children, and he was christened Alfred. So now you know. His father was a stone mason who was unemployed for long periods, and also a drunk, for sometimes quite long periods, but his mother was god-fearing and hard-working and she brought up her four children in decent, respectable if rather poverty-stricken conditions.

They rented a terrace house, two-up two-down, with no inside bathroom or lavatory, surrounded by the cotton mills. A knocker-up could be heard walking down the street at five each morning, knocking with a stick at the upper windows to waken the mill workers. Then the sound of clogs could be heard on the cobble-stones as the mill girls in their shawls rushed to work.

Wainwright, as it's easier to call him – even now the use of Alfred seems strange, if not rather impertinent – went to the local elementary school where he was good at maths, English and drawing. At thirteen, he left school and got a job with the local council as an office boy on fifteen shillings a week. It was a sign of success and social status: coming from an artisan's family, yet managing to become a white-collar worker, if on the lowest possible rung. He started in the Borough Engineer's department but after three years moved to the office of the Borough Treasurer, as he was told that the chances of advancement there would be better. To do so, he had to study for exams, doing them in his spare time, taking correspondence courses in order to become a municipal accountant. It took him almost ten years, sitting all the various examinations, turning himself almost into a recluse, until he was qualified.

In the office, he used to produce little home-made magazines to amuse the other clerks and trainees sitting at their tall desks.

He did all the drawings and wrote the stories and jokes, most of them poking fun at their superiors. They were surprisingly well produced. Several of his colleagues were so impressed by his art-work that they kept copies for the rest of their lives, long after they had forgotten all the jokes and references.

Wainwright got married in 1931 to Ruth Holden, a member of the same Congregational church in Blackburn. She worked as a cot-ton weaver in a local mill. She appears to have been his very first girlfriend and he later gave the impression, rather ungallantly, that that was really why he had married her. They had one son, Peter.

After two or three years, he realised the marriage had been a mis-take. He had improved himself professionally, rising from the same working-class background as Ruth to become a qualified account-ant, but he seemed to feel he had left her behind socially and intel-lectually. He began going on long walks and holidays, around Lancashire and then further afield, without her. In a way it was a form of escape from his unhappy marriage, keeping out of the house for days on end, coming home late, exhausted.

He also took a keen interest in Blackburn Rovers, his local football team, whom he always supported. During his long years of study, he had little spare time or money, but by the late 1930s he had more leisure time and in 1939, with some friends from the office, he founded Blackburn Rovers Supporters Club, of which he was in turn Hon. Treasurer and Hon. Secretary. In 1940, he helped organise a coach trip to Wembley for the war-time Cup Final between Blackburn and West Ham. (Rovers were beaten 0:1.)

He never took Ruth with him to games, but through the Supporters Club he met quite a few young women – girls from his office, the wives of other fans – which he enjoyed greatly. Football served as another escape, to get him out of the house, use up his energies, forget his unhappy marriage.

There was no possibility of a divorce, not at that time, not in his position in local government, where appearances and respectability mattered so much. In 1939, he secretly wrote a fictionalised account of his marriage, which he showed no one. It confirms that he was physically trying to exhaust himself by all the walking, hoping to subjugate his sexual and emotional needs. He keeps seeing a fantasy woman, someone he will one day meet, and even perhaps already has, who comes to him when he is dreaming or half asleep, talking to him, stroking his hand. But of course it was all in his mind.

Wainwright made his first visit to the Lake District with a cousin in 1930 and they climbed Orrest Head. It was his first-ever Lakeland climb and as he looked around at the mountains, almost all name-less to him at this stage, he immediately fell in love. 'I was utterly enslaved by it. I gazed in disbelief at the loveliness around me. I never knew there could be so much colour and charm in landscape.'

In 1938, during his annual holidays, he did a two-week walking tour along the eastern flank of the Pennines to Hadrian's Wall, returning to Settle by the west side. He walked on his own, and on his return he wrote an account of it. It was his first attempt at a proper, full-length work. He let three friends from his office read it, and then it was put in a drawer and forgotten for many years.

In 1941, Wainwright achieved his life's ambition when he secured a job as an accountancy assistant in Kendal in the Borough Treasurer's department. It was at a lower level than he had been in Blackburn and he took a cut in salary. Through the job he found accommodation in a council house at 19 Castle Grove, and he moved there with his wife and eight-year-old son, Peter. During the war, he was busy in Kendal on various government enterprises, such as helping organise 'Holidays at Home'.

In 1948, he became Borough Treasurer of Kendal, a position which he held until his retirement. As befitted his new and exalted position, he bought a plot at the end of Kendal Green on the edge of town, where his house was built. He then set himself the task of knocking the garden into shape. He gave himself eight years, but had finished it in two.

In his spare moments from work, and from gardening, at weekends and holidays, he was out walking. He still did nothing with Ruth, took her nowhere, hardly talked to her, while she stoically endured their sterile marriage.

In 1952, aged forty-five, Wainwright created another self-imposed task for himself. He worked out a plan to spend the next thirteen years, which would take him close to the age of retirement, writing about all the Lakeland fells which by now he knew intimately from his mostly solitary walks.

'I was working for my own pleasure,' so he wrote later, 'and enjoying it hugely. I was gathering together all my notes and drawings and a host of recollections and putting them in a book so that when I became an old man I could look through them at leisure, recall all my memories, and go on fellwalking in spirit long after my legs had given up.'

He maintained he never thought of publication, not when he first began. He was writing his notes purely for himself to read in his fireside years, but I suspect the hope or fantasy of some sort of publication was lurking at the back of his mind very early on. All the same, there is no doubt the whole project was undertaken for his own pleasure, to keep him active and occupied for the next thirteen years.

Before he had finished Book One, he had decided he would like to have his handiwork published after all – but he wanted to do it himself. He didn't trust desk-bound publishers in London, who knew nothing of fellwalking. He had spent so long writing and creating the book his way, that he preferred to have the book printed exactly as he had penned it.

He was helped by a colleague, Henry Marshall, Borough Librarian of Kendal. He had been brought up in the East End of London and, like Wainwright, had deliberately chosen to come to Kendal in order to enjoy walking and living in the Lake District. Wainwright assumed Marshall would know more about books than he did, being the Librarian. He did have lots of contacts in the local book-selling and printing world.

They found a local printer, Sandy Hewitson of Bateman and Hewitson, a jobbing printer, who mainly produced leaflets for the Council and other bodies. In the event, the actual printing of the book was done by Westmorland Gazette, a bigger firm with more machinery, which had recently taken over Bateman and Hewitson. When Harry Firth, Printing Manager of Westmorland Gazette, saw Wainwright's artwork, he was amazed. 'I couldn't believe one man had hand-drawn every page. I don't think anybody since the days of the monks had ever produced a completely hand-written book.' Sandy Hewitson was equally impressed and agreed to defer payment until the book started to sell.

Although Westmorland Gazette was the printer, Sandy Hewitson was the front man who dealt with the client, which is why his firm's name went on the early books as being the printer. Henry Marshall's name appeared as publisher, and the author as A. Wainwright.

Before publication, Wainwright got Bateman and Hewitson to print 2,000 leaflets advertising his forthcoming book. On one side of the leaflet was an order form, giving Henry Marshall's home address. The other side gave information about the book and stated that 'the author is Alfred Wainwright of Kendal'. At some time, just before publication, however, Wainwright had second thoughts. He not only omitted his first name but cut out the reference to Kendal. Thus no one ever knew his full name or where he lived.

On publication, Wainwright and Henry Marshall went round

This is to announce the publication of a book
that is quite out of the ordinary

• Primarily it is a book for fellwalkers, for those who know
the fells intimately and for those who know them but little •
It is a book for all lovers of Lakeland
It is a book for collectors of unusual books

It is the first volume of a series under the title of
A PICTORIAL GUIDE TO THE LAKELAND FELLS

This first volume is
BOOK ONE : THE EASTERN FELLS
describing the Helvellyn and Fairfield groups

Hand printed throughout, with 500 illustrations
(drawings, maps and diagrams) in its 300 pages
it represents an original idea in the making of books

• The author is *Alfred Wainwright* of Kendal

Its price is twelve shillings and sixpence
Copies are obtainable from bookshops in Lakeland,
or by post (for sixpence more) from HENRY MARSHALL
LOW BRIDGE, KENTMERE, WESTMORLAND

Flyer (left) and order form (below) for the first of the Pictorial Guides

THE EASTERN FELLS

ORDER FORM

The book will be addressed
exactly in accordance
with the particulars
you state alongside
BLOCK LETTERS, PLEASE

Name ....
Address ....
....
....
....

This form should be sent
with a remittance for 13s
to
HENRY MARSHALL
LOW BRIDGE
KENTMERE
WESTMORLAND

Cheques may be made payable to H. MARSHALL

local bookshops trying to solicit orders. They contacted colleagues in other council offices in the Lake District, asking them to help spread the word. They put on a little display of Wainwright's drawings from the book in a shop window in Ambleside (now the 'Home of Football'), bought some advertising in the magazine *Cumbria* and sent out copies for review in local newspapers. Quite professional really, when you consider that Wainwright later refused to have anything to do with the unsavoury world of selling and promotion.

Book One was published in May 1955. A rail strike upset deliveries for a while but during the summer the book started to sell and they were able to make the printer a first payment. The first fan letters arrived. In July, there was even one from a gentleman in Chicago, sending an order to Marshall for the next six books, wanting them sent to him the moment they were published. By the end of the year, almost all of the first 2,000 copies had been sold and they ordered a reprint of 1,000 copies in February 1956. By this time, Wainwright had paid off the printer in full. The bill was £950 for those first 2,000 copies. Wainwright had only been able to pay £35 up front, which was the limit of his savings.

Wainwright was by then well into Book Two and planning Book Three, leaving Marshall to deal with orders and deliveries. As each book came out, the number of advance orders for the next one increased. By the time Book Five appeared in 1962, Book One had been reprinted eight times, Book Two five times, Book Three nine and Book Four eight. The total in print was by then 40,000. Quite an achievement for a little local printing firm with no sales force, no marketing, no publicity department and all the paperwork, including invoices, handled by Wainwright and Marshall from home.

In 1963, Wainwright suddenly dispensed with Marshall. Book Six, and all subsequent Wainwright books, and new editions of the earlier ones, no longer carried the name of Henry Marshall as

Wainwright and Henry Marshall with the 'unknown woman'

publisher. He was replaced by the Westmorland Gazette. Without telling Marshall, Wainwright had done a deal with the Gazette to take over all the paperwork from then on.

Wainwright and Marshall had no legal agreement. Nothing had been written down on paper. There was little Marshall could do about it, but he was greatly saddened that all his hard work over the previous years now appeared to count for little. In later years, Wainwright seemed to wipe Marshall from his mind and tried to give the impression that they had never been close friends anyway.

In my biography of Wainwright which first appeared in 1995, I included a photograph of Wainwright and Marshall, the only snap I could find of them together. They were on a hill, which I couldn't identify, but I assumed it must be near Kendal. It was proof that at some time they must have gone on walks together. Beside them was a woman, whom I could not identify either. I simply described her in the caption as 'an unknown woman'.

Not long ago, out of the blue, I got a letter from her, a Mrs Mary Helps, telling me exactly about the day in question, and all about her meeting with Wainwright and Marshall.

In June 1954 she was on her honeymoon on the isle of Skye, staying in a hotel at Sligachan. Also there on holiday was Mr Wainwright, his friend Mr Marshall and a third man, whose name she can only remember as Colin. The three men had set out one day to climb Sgurr nan Gillean but only one of them, Colin, had succeeded.

The following day, in perfect weather conditions, we ourselves set off to climb the mountain and on our way across the glen overtook Mr Wainwright and Mr Marshall, disappointed at their failure the previous day and determined to succeed on this, their second attempt.

We proceeded on our way, reached the col and left our rucksacks there and scrambled up the final ascent. It was a memorable achievement. We then returned to the ridge and were having our lunch when Mr Wainwright and Mr Marshall appeared. We were able to reassure them that the final ascent was possible and offered to escort them ourselves. The four of us reached the summit successfully and then it was that my husband took the photograph. They were, of course, delighted to get there and declared it was the highlight of their holiday.

On the way down, they told us that they were just beginning to discover the delights of fell walking in the Lake District.

Subsequently, we sent them a copy of the photograph and a few months later Mr Marshall wrote to tell us that he had published Mr Wainwright's first guide, *The Eastern Fells*, and would we like a copy. And so we have it – a first edition, with an accompanying note from the author – now one of our treasured possessions.

Their encounter with Wainwright is interesting because it shows that he and Marshall were friendly enough to have taken a holiday together. It indicates, as we know from other sources, that he never claimed to be an expert climber. And it reveals that in 1954 you could leave your rucksack, containing your lunch, out on an open mountainside and return to find nobody had scoffed the food.

The seventh and final Pictorial Guide to the Lakeland Fells came out in 1966, bang on schedule, just as Wainwright had planned thirteen years previously. He next wrote *Fellwanderer*, which gave some background to the Pictorial Guides without revealing much that was personal.

The *Pennine Way Companion* was published in 1968, three years after Tom Stephenson's route up the backbone of England was opened. In 1973, *A Coast to Coast Walk* was published and became perhaps the most celebrated of Wainwright's books. There were other guide books and sketchbooks including, in 1974, *The Outlying Fells of Lakeland*, a companion volume to the Pictorial Guides.

In 1957, Wainwright met Betty McNally, who had separated from her husband, with whom she had been living in Dublin. When the marriage broke down in 1952, she had returned to England, and was living in Kendal with her two daughters. She had been educated at Casterton School, near Kirkby Lonsdale, still a well-regarded Cumbrian boarding school for girls, whose previous pupils, although in earlier premises, had included the Bronte sisters. That was a chance meeting, but they met again in 1965, when Betty was forty-three. After a long and complicated and mainly clandestine friendship and courtship, they were eventually married in 1970, two years after his divorce from Ruth, who had finally thrown in the towel and walked out of the marriage just three weeks before Wainwright retired as Borough Treasurer in 1967. Wainwright was sixty-three when he and Betty married, and it turned out to be a long and incredibly happy and fulfilling marriage. Betty Wainwright proved to be committed to animal welfare, as Wainwright was himself. She was also a strong woman, with her own opinions – and an excellent driver.

I met both of them for the first time in 1978 at their home in Kendal Green. I hadn't imagined it would be a modern, suburban house, expecting something olde and rural, perhaps a cottage on the fells, but it did have a view of Kendal Fell from the back.

I rather tricked Wainwright into seeing me, saying I would never use anything I might write about him in a newspaper. Despite the growing fame of his books, he was still declining all requests for interviews, had not appeared on television, refused all signing sessions or anything which smacked of personal publicity. I was writing a book about the area, walking round the whole of the Lake District, talking to interesting people, and I wanted to include him. Fortunately, he knew a book on similar lines I had done, about walking Hadrian's Wall, which helped, and he agreed to see me.

Wainwright was then aged seventy-one, tall and well built with a mass of thick white hair, rather pebbly strong glasses and a soft Lancashire accent. The furniture was a bit chintzy, lots of cats around, no sign of affluence, although by then his books were enormous sellers.

During our meeting, I congratulated him on the success of his Pennine Way guide which, in ten years, had now reached the 100,000 sales mark, so the Westmorland Gazette, still his publisher, had told me. He started bemoaning the recent increase in the price of beer because, in the book, in a mad, generous moment, he had said that anyone who finished the walk and got to Kirk Yetholm could have a pint on him at the Border Hotel. 'Back in 1968, beer was only 1s 6d a pint. Now it's four shillings. It's quite shocking.' He'd recently been sent a bill for £400 – but he didn't regret it: 'If you've walked 270 miles, a free pint is a nice thing to have at the end.'

When Betty came home, I learned that she had been hanging some of his illustrations, drawings for a book about 19th-century

Kendal, for an exhibition at Abbot Hall, Kendal. When I heard that the drawings were for sale, I went back with her and bought three of them, priced at £10 each. Which I still have.

I got out my cheque book and was writing the cheque to A.W. … when Betty stopped me. She asked me to write the cheque to Animal Rescue, Cumbria. What I didn't know until then, and what very few people were aware of, was that he was giving away all his income from his books to an animal charity and refuge which he and Betty were creating.

In 1985, the Westmorland Gazette discovered to their astonishment that the total sales of the Pictorial Guides were about to reach one million copies. They decided some sort of celebration was in order and announced that the purchaser of the one-millionth copy would be rewarded with a free holiday at the Langdale Time Share and a meal for two with Wainwright himself.

The one-millionth book off the presses was a copy of Book Six. They marked it in a special way, so any reader would spot it, and in due course it formed part of an order despatched to a bookshop just outside Manchester. Wainwright then realised what he had let himself in for. 'I don't want to eat with strangers,' he said. So he and the Gazette's General Manager, Andrew Nichol, went to the bookshop and found the book, still unsold. They bought it, without saying anything to the bookshop, and took it back to Kendal.

The Gazette then changed the terms of the prize, omitting the promise of a meal with Wainwright. This time the one-millionth book went out to a bookshop in Keswick, Chaplin's. Chaplin's did their best to advertise the one-millionth copy – and I have in my collection of Wainwright memorabilia the poster they put up in their window. They did not know, originally, they had the precise copy, but they were now publicising the existence of the prize.

However, no one ever turned up to claim the prize. I have a

Reward for the buyer of the one-millionth copy of Wainwright's Pictorial Guides

sneaking suspicion that Wainwright himself went in and bought the one-millionth copy, took it home and cut it up.

In 1983, Wainwright agreed to write a large-format illustrated book about fellwalking, with photographs by Derry Brabbs, for the London publisher Michael Joseph. The reason for his agreeing to do this book was simple – he was trying to raise the money to establish a proper sanctuary for Animal Rescue, and the monetary advance proved irresistible. Other titles followed and they became huge bestsellers. Even more surprisingly, Wainwright then started a television career, appearing in a series of BBC TV walking programmes, accompanied by Eric Robson. At the age of eighty in 1987, he had emerged as a TV star. Much to his fury, he found himself being recognised all over the country. Some of his older fans, brought up on the Pictorial Guides, who had always admired his anti-publicity, anti-personal-fame attitudes, were a little perturbed and disappointed. He didn't really like doing it himself, but it was all for a good cause – to make more money for his beloved animal refuge, Kapellan.

He received quite a few honorary degrees, but refused more than he accepted. In 1986, after years of turning down approaches from BBC's 'Desert Island Discs', he agreed to go on and be interviewed by Sue Lawley. 'He always did have an eye for a good pair of legs,' said Andrew Nichol of the Westmorland Gazette, who drove him to the studio. But Wainwright laid down two conditions. He refused to go to London and said Sue Lawley had to come to Manchester. And he got Andrew Nichol to promise to take him to Harry Ramsden's for chips after the recording.

By his eighties, Wainwright's eyes had begun to grow weak, making it harder for him to draw and read, but he still managed to follow the progress of Blackburn Rovers by listening to the radio.

In an interview recorded for Border Television just before Christmas 1990, he said, 'I live in a world of mists, but by closing my eyes, I can see a thousand walks as clearly as when I first walked them. Memory is going to be a great comfort to me.'

Just over two weeks later, his heart gave out and he died on 20 January 1991, three days after his eighty-fourth birthday. He died peacefully, knowing that Betty would carry out his wishes and scatter his ashes on one of his favourite fells.

1 | Orrest Head

The Outlying Fells of Lakeland

Best to begin the 'Best' at the beginning, where Wainwright himself began, although no one would ever claim that Orrest Head is one of the finest or most famous fells and it is so low that it didn't even make the Pictorial Guides. It's little more than a stroll, handy to get to, easy to climb, still very popular, a pleasant little fell which serves as a perfect introduction for any visitor to the Lake District.

Orrest Head is at the edge of Lakeland's biggest town, Windermere. You can step straight out from the station and start walking towards it. The railway is still going, the end of the branch line which connects to the main line at Oxenholme. Orrest Head can be tackled by all walkers of any age and experience and yet it is very rewarding, giving stunning views of lake and mountains for very little effort. The harder, handsomer stuff, from his seven Pictorial Guides to the fells, will come next. Make the most of the easy going.

Wainwright's description of Orrest Head in *The Outlying Fells of Lakeland*, which was published after the seven main Pictorial Guides, is fairly brief, just four pages, and is not as detailed or with as many illustrations and maps as in the Guides, but it gives a taste of his style.

In this book, he was aiming at walkers who, because of age or health, were not quite up to the high fells, wanting something milder, lower and less exhausting. He chose fifty-six fells, all inside the National Park, but mainly on the outskirts, in the foothills of the major mountains. He called the book 'a late bonus for old-age pensioners who have enjoyed the fells in years gone by and are reluctant to put away their boots and call it a day'. His drawings on the back of the book's dust jacket poke gentle fun at the walkers he was writing for.

When he first saw Orrest Head in 1930, Wainwright was a young man of twenty-three. He took the bus from Blackburn to Kendal with his cousin, Eric Beardsall, then caught the local bus to Windermere. They had no boots, just stout shoes, no waterproofs and little money, but they did have a week's holiday from their council offices.

As they walked up the slopes of Orrest Head, which had been recommended as a local viewpoint, Wainwright passed some large houses with big gardens and thought how wonderful it must be to live in a house with a garden. One of the reasons he was so stunned by the beauty and the views when he reached the top was that, until then, his life had been surrounded and circumscribed by back-to-back houses and dark, satanic mills. In the view ahead of him 'there were no big factories and tall chimneys and crowded tenements to disfigure a scene of supreme beauty. My more prosaic cousin went to sleep in the warm grass. I forgot his existence. I felt I was some other person; this was not me. I wasn't accustomed or entitled to such a privilege. I didn't belong. If only I could, sometime! Those few hours on Orrest Head cast a spell that changed my life.'

They stayed that night in a cheap bed-and-breakfast in Windermere, then next day set out to explore further afield. They got to Ullswater having climbed up to High Street – Wainwright being attracted by its name and its Roman associations. The following day they climbed Helvellyn. When they got to Keswick that evening, they booked into a B&B in Stanger Street, totally soaked through, water dripping from every protuberance. They worried that the landlady might not let them in, but not only did she dry all their clothes, giving them a set of her husband's to wear in the meantime, but when they got back the following evening, they found she had ironed all their clothes, ready for them.

The kindness of strangers, almost as much as those first glimpses

Drawings for the back of the dust jacket of The Outlying Fells of Lakeland

of the beauty of the Lake District, stayed in Wainwright's mind for many years, making him determined to return.

Today, climbers have something new to look out for and enjoy when they reach the top of Orrest Head, along with the excellent views across to Scafell Pike and the Langdales. There is a panoramic plaque, erected in 2000 by Windermere Parish Council and other local bodies, which commemorates Wainwright's work. Its main headline reads: 'That day on Orrest Head changed my life.'

Orrest Head
783'
400 feet of ascent

from WINDERMERE
RAILWAY STATION
2½ miles
2 hours
by the route described

1 mile : 1 hour
there and back direct

from the north

Orrest Head, for many of us, is "where we came in" — our first ascent in Lakeland, our first sight of mountains in tumultuous array across glittering waters, our awakening to beauty. It is a popular walk, deservedly, for here the promised land is seen in all its glory. It is a fitting finale, too, to a life made happy by fellwandering. Dare we hope there will be another Orrest Head over the threshold of the next heaven?

The way to Orrest Head is announced by a large signboard, which proclaims its unrivalled views and states that it is a twenty minutes' walk to the top. It is the leftmost of three drives that leave the main road near the bus stops opposite the railway station, and is a tarmac strip initially. Almost at once a footpath goes off to the left: ignore this, keeping ahead and climbing gradually in a series of loops and bends. When a farm is reached the path becomes rough; further, it divides into three branches: take the one on the right by a wall to reach and enter a fenced lane with many seats. This leads to a kissing gate; in the wall alongside is a memorial tablet to Arthur Henry Heywood, whose family gave Orrest Head for public enjoyment. Through the gate, and clear of trees at last, the view-indicator on the summit is seen on the left and soon reached. There is a choice of seats — iron, wood, stone and grass — from which to admire the fine view and reflect that, once upon a time, you too could have done this climb in twenty minutes just like that signboard said. Never mind. You've had a good innings.

Return the same way, or, if a longer alternative route is preferred, leave the rocky top by a path heading north to a quiet byroad, which follow left to join the A.592 road (to Troutbeck) but without actually setting foot on it go through a gate on the left (public footpath sign), whence a good path leads forward into a wood and continues very pleasantly past some handsome residences amid noble trees, rejoining the outward route only a few paces from the starting point: in fact along the path ignored earlier.

There is a plan afoot to re-align the A591 through the woods below Orrest. If this comes to pass (which heaven forsend!) the start and finish of this walk will also need re-routing.

MAP

The view indicator on the summit

THE VIEW

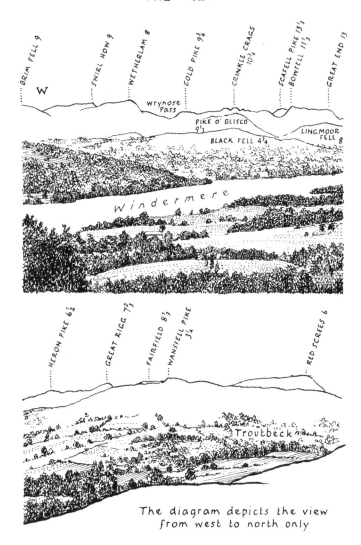

BRIM FELL 9
W
SWIRL HOW 9
WETHERLAM 8
COLD PIKE 9¾
Wrynose Pass
CRINKLE CRAGS 10¼
SCAFELL PIKE 13½
BOWFELL 11½
GREAT END 13
PIKE O' BLISCO 9½
BLACK FELL 4¼
LINGMOOR FELL 8

Windermere

HERON PIKE 6½
GREAT RIGG 7½
FAIRFIELD 8½
WANSFELL PIKE 3¼
RED SCREES 6

Troutbeck

The diagram depicts the view
from west to north only

THE VIEW

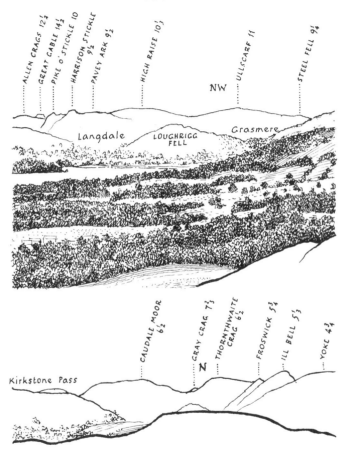

ALLEN CRAGS 12¼
GREAT GABLE 14½
PIKE O'STICKLE 10
HARRISON STICKLE 9½
PAVEY ARK 9½
HIGH RAISE 10¾
NW
ULLSCARF 11
STEEL FELL 9¼

Langdale
LOUGHRIGG FELL
Grasmere

CAUDALE MOOR 6½
GRAY CRAG 7¾
N
THORNTHWAITE CRAG 6½
FROSWICK 5¾
ILL BELL 5¾
YOKE 4¾

Kirkstone Pass

The thick line is the outline of the summit rocks.

The figures accompanying the names of fells
indicate distances in miles.

Summit seats and litter, which occur in profusion,
and the view indicator, are omitted.

2 | Dove Crag

Book One: The Eastern Fells

Dove Crag was the first fell Wainwright drew and described for the first book in his Pictorial Guide series, *The Eastern Fells*. He settled down to work on 9 November 1952, knowing he had only another 213 fells to go and thirteen years in which to complete them.

It is not known why he started with this fell. It would have been easier and handier, living in Kendal, to have begun with one of the fells much nearer to his house, in what he had already decided would be Book Two, *The Far Eastern Fells*. But Dove Crag was fairly convenient all the same. He was able to get a bus along the main road from Kendal through Windermere to Ambleside. The ascent from Ambleside was the first page he completed. This was the more

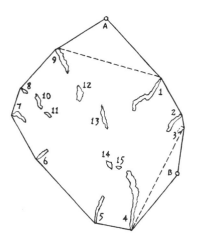

1 : *Ullswater*
2 : *Hawes Water*
3 : proposed *Swindale Resr*
4 : *Windermere*
5 : *Coniston Water*
6 : *Wast Water*
7 : *Ennerdale Water*
8 : *Loweswater*
9 : *Bassenthwaite Lake*
10 : *Crummock Water*
11 : *Buttermere*
12 : *Derwent Water*
13 : *Thirlmere*
14 : *Grasmere*
15 : *Rydal Water*
A : *Caldbeck*
B : *Longsleddale (church)*

The natural boundaries of the Lakeland fells

frequently used route to the summit, although Wainwright preferred the climb from Patterdale. On Dove Crag 4 he says it gives a 'much more interesting and intimate approach'.

His division of the project, and of the Lakeland fells, into seven separate parts was his own idea. Traditionally, the most common division of the Lake District is into two parts – north and south, with the boundary being Dunmail Raise. Each part does have a separate culture, accent, history, but of course Wainwright was not thinking about social or cultural aspects. His concern was about climbing the fells.

Lakeland, roughly speaking, is circular. Wordsworth likened its shape to a wheel, with the lakes and valleys radiating from the centre like spokes, which is neat. This circular shape was reflected by the National Park Authority when it laid out the boundaries of the

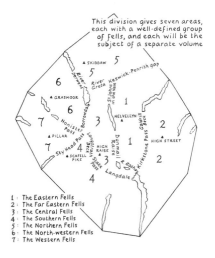

The division of the Lakeland fells into seven areas

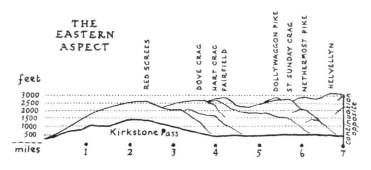

Outline of the Eastern Fells, viewed from the east

Lake District National Park in 1951 – England's largest national park, covering 866 square miles. Wainwright followed the basic shape, but stuck to the high ground, ignoring the lower parts towards the west coast. Having decided his extremities, he drew a series of straight lines, connecting them together. Inside he identified seven major lumps or groups of fells and decided they would make the basis of seven separate sections. The diagrams he drew to explain his approach are shown on pages 26 and 27.

The pages explaining Wainwright's approach to classifying and defining the fells were repeated at the front of each Pictorial Guide, along with an introduction to the area of fells that particular book covered. He included diagrams there too. Running across the top of this page is half of his diagram showing the shape and elevation in feet of the Eastern Fells in their eastern aspect – as they appear when viewed from the east.

Wainwright's definition of a Lakeland fell was, first, height. In Book One, his cut-off point was around 1400 ft but in later books it was nearer the 1000-ft mark. Which was why he could never have included Orrest Head, at only 783 ft, in the Pictorial Guides.

Secondly, a fell had to have an individual quality, be an entity in its own right, not part of another, with its own ascents and summit.

In Dove Crag, his first fell, he established the format he was going to use. He started with a brief general description and opening illustration of the fell in question, its Natural Features, Map, Ascents, the Summit, Views from the top and Ridge Routes (if there were any).

He didn't reveal much about himself at this stage. That came later. The writing is staid, informative, workmanlike, a bit amateurish in places, as on Dove Crag 4, the Ascent from Patterdale, where he writes about 'soft loveliness'. But these were his first pages and he was not yet into his stride, still to find his true voice and own style.

It was apt and appropriate that the first outing held by the Wainwright Society – formed in 2002 – took place on 9 November 2002 to Dove Crag. It was fifty years exactly to the day when and where it all began.

Dove Crag

2603'

from Dovedale

Patterdale •

Hartsop •

▲ FAIRFIELD

DOVE ▲ CRAG

RED SCREES ▲

• Grasmere

Ambleside
•

MILES

0   1   2   3   4

The lofty height that towers so
magnificently over Dovedale is
indebted for its name to a very
impressive vertical wall of rock
on its north-east flank: the crag
was named first and the summit
of the parent fell above, which
officially is considered unworthy
of any title and is nameless on
the Ordnance Survey maps, has
adopted it by common consent.

NATURAL FEATURES

Dove Crag is a mountain of sharp contrasts. To the east, its finest aspect, it presents a scarred and rugged face, a face full of character and interest. Here, in small compass, is a tangle of rough country, a maze of steep cliffs, gloomy hollows and curious foothills gnarled like the knuckles of a clenched fist, with the charming valley of Dovedale below and the main crag frowning down over all. Very different is its appearance from other directions. A high ridge runs south, with featureless grass slopes flowing down from it to the valleys of Rydale and Scandale. The fell is a vertebra of the Fairfield spine and is connected to the next height in the system, Hart Crag, by a lofty depression.

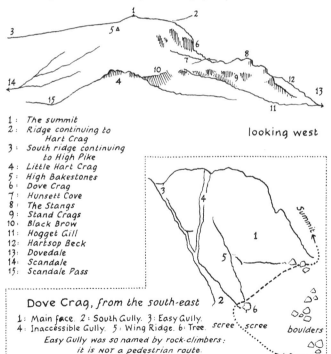

looking west

1: The summit
2: Ridge continuing to Hart Crag
3: South ridge continuing to High Pike
4: Little Hart Crag
5: High Bakestones
6: Dove Crag
7: Hunsett Cove
8: The Stangs
9: Stand Crags
10: Black Brow
11: Hogget Gill
12: Hartsop Beck
13: Dovedale
14: Scandale
15: Scandale Pass

Dove Crag, from the south-east

1: Main face. 2: South Gully. 3: Easy Gully.
4: Inaccessible Gully. 5: Wing Ridge. 6: Tree.
Easy Gully was so named by rock-climbers: it is NOT a pedestrian route.

MAP

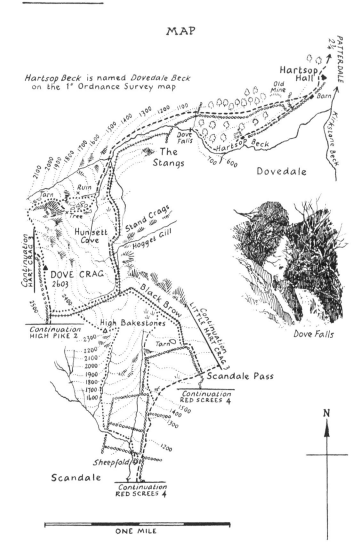

Hartsop Beck is named Dovedale Beck on the 1" Ordnance Survey map

PATTERDALE 24

Hartsop Hall

Old Mine

Barn

Kirkstone Beck

Dove Falls

Hartsop Beck

700 600

Dovedale

1100 1200 1300 1400 1500 1600 1700 1800 1900 2000 2100

The Stangs

Tarn

Ruin ×

× Tree 1850

Hunsett Cove

Stand Crags

Hogget Gill

Continuation HART CRAG 1

▲ DOVE CRAG 2603

2500 2400

Continuation HIGH PIKE 2

Black Brow

Continuation LITTLE HART CRAG 3

High Bakestones

△ 2300

Tarn

Scandale Pass

2200 2100 2000 1900 1800 1700 1600

Continuation RED SCREES 4

1500 1400 1300

1200

Sheepfold

Scandale

Continuation RED SCREES 4

Dove Falls

N

ONE MILE

ASCENT FROM PATTERDALE
2,200 feet of ascent: 5 miles from Patterdale village

DOVE CRAG

HART CRAG

Scandale Pass

Black Brow

2400
2300
2200
2100

grass

~Tarn

awkward crossing

Hunsett Cove.

Scree

1800

Ruin

1600

Stand Crag

The Stangs

1400
1300
1200
1100

1100
1000
900
800

falls

Hogget Gill

1000

700

Old mine

Barn

600

PATTERDALE 2¾

←— Scandale Pass 1½ ←—

Kirkstone Beck

Hartsop Hall

Brothers Water

looking south-west

The route passing along the base of the crag involves rough scrambling but the scenery is very impressive. A shorter variation by the ruined hut is easier but steep. *Both are dangerous in bad conditions:* then, the detour by the wire fence is a safe and practicable alternative.

An easier but longer way (not shown in the diagram) is to proceed by Caiston Glen to the top of Scandale Pass, there turning right. *(for map see Little Hart Crag 3)*

It is believed that Hunsett Cove was once the crater of a volcano. Huge boulders litter the Cove, many having gardens of lush vegetation on their massive tops. Some of these blocks have been artificially detached: there are evidences of former quarrying operations nearby. The Cove is grand territory for the explorer; and for those hardy souls who like to spend occasional nights amongst the fells there is abundant shelter available in the many holes and caves formed by the boulders.

Hazel nuts are profuse in this wood in October

Dove Crag is most often ascended from Ambleside on the popular tour of the 'Fairfield Horseshoe' — but the climb from Patterdale, by Dovedale, is far superior: it gives a much more interesting and intimate approach, the sharp transition from the soft loveliness of the valley to the desolation above being very impressive.

ASCENT FROM AMBLESIDE
2500 feet of ascent : 5 miles

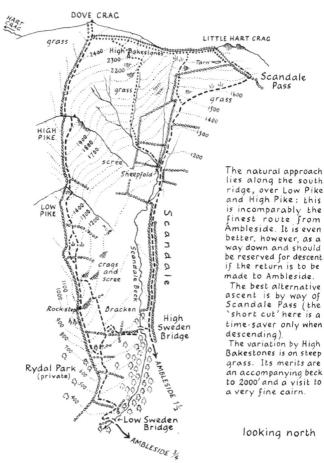

HART CRAG

DOVE CRAG

LITTLE HART CRAG

grass

2400
2300
2200

High Bakestones

Tarn

Scandale Pass

grass
1600
1500
1400
1300

HIGH PIKE

grass

1900
1800
1700

scree

1200

Sheepfold

LOW PIKE

1400
1300
1200

Scandale

crags and scree

Scandale Beck

Rock step

Bracken

High Sweden Bridge

1100
1000
900
800
700

Rydal Park (private)

600

500
400

AMBLESIDE 1½

←Low Sweden Bridge

AMBLESIDE ¾

The natural approach lies along the south ridge, over Low Pike and High Pike: this is incomparably the finest route from Ambleside. It is even better, however, as a way down and should be reserved for descent if the return is to be made to Ambleside.

The best alternative ascent is by way of Scandale Pass (the 'short cut' here is a time-saver only when descending).

The variation by High Bakestones is on steep grass. Its merits are an accompanying beck to 2000' and a visit to a very fine cairn.

looking north

Dove Crag cannot be seen from Ambleside, but rising from the fields north of the town is its clearly-defined south ridge, offering an obvious staircase to the summit.

THE SUMMIT

The actual top of the fell is a small rock platform crowned by a cairn, twenty yards east of the crumbling wall crossing the broad summit-plateau. It is of little distinction and there is nothing of interest in the immediate surroundings.

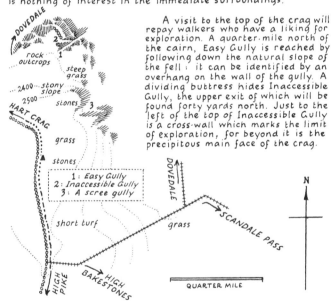

A visit to the top of the crag will repay walkers who have a liking for exploration. A quarter-mile north of the cairn, Easy Gully is reached by following down the natural slope of the fell: it can be identified by an overhang on the wall of the gully. A dividing buttress hides Inaccessible Gully, the upper exit of which will be found forty yards north. Just to the left of the top of Inaccessible Gully is a cross-wall which marks the limit of exploration, for beyond it is the precipitous main face of the crag.

1: Easy Gully
2: Inaccessible Gully
3: A scree gully

QUARTER MILE

DESCENTS: All routes of ascent may be reversed for descent but the way down into Dovedale by the base of the crag is very rough. The High Bakestones route to Scandale is not recommended.

In mist, whether bound for Ambleside or Patterdale, the wall should be followed south, soon turning left along the fence for Patterdale via Dovedale or Scandale Pass. *Direct descents to Dovedale from the summit must not be attempted.*

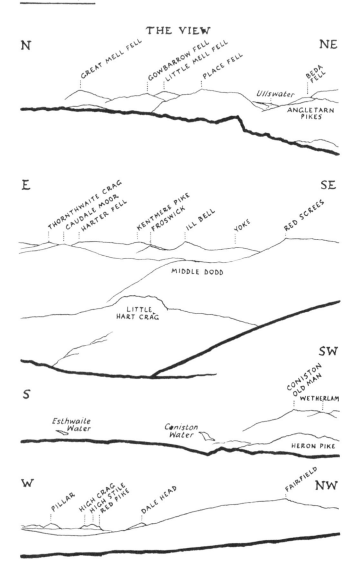

THE VIEW

THE VIEW

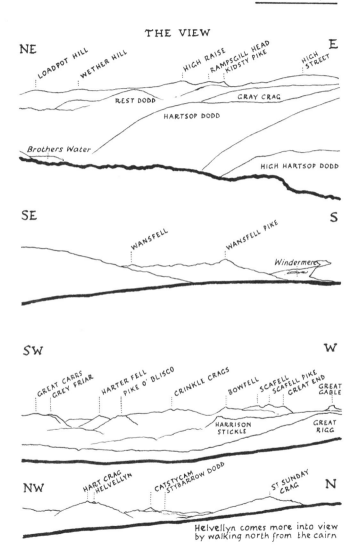

Helvellyn comes more into view
by walking north from the cairn

RIDGE ROUTES

To HART CRAG, 2698': ¾ mile : NW
Depression at 2350'
350 feet of ascent

An easy walk. Hart Crag is not safe in mist.

A faint grass path accompanies the wall to
the depression; beyond, the wall ends at a
cluster of rocks. A track, plain at first, goes
steeply up the stony breast of Hart Crag and
becomes indistinct on the grass at the top.

HART CRAG

2400

2300

2400

2500

N

QUARTER
MILE

DOVE
CRAG

To HIGH PIKE, 2155': 1 mile : S
Slight depression
Only a few feet of ascent

*One of the easiest miles in
Lakeland; grass all the way.
Perfectly safe in mist.*

Follow the wall south; an
intermittent path keeps a
few yards to the left of it.

DOVE
CRAG

2500

2400

2300

2200

2100

2000

N

QUARTER
MILE

HIGH
PIKE

To LITTLE HART CRAG
2091': 1¼ miles
S then ENE and SE
Minor depressions
200 feet of ascent

*Rough grass; may be marshy
in places. Little Hart Crag is
dangerous in bad conditions.*

Follow first the wall south
and then the wire fence: it
approaches within 200 yards
of the summit before turning
down towards Scandale Pass.

N

DOVE
CRAG

2500
2400
2300
2200
2100

2000

High Bakestones

LITTLE HART
CRAG

HALF A MILE

*The cairn on
High Bakestones*

This beautifully-built 8'
column, commanding a
view of Scandale, is one
of the finest specimens
on these hills. It is more
than a cairn. It is
a work of art and
a lasting memorial
to its builder.

Dovedale, from the top of Easy Gully

3 | St Sunday Crag

Book One: The Eastern Fells

Wainwright worked with a steel mapping pen, a ruler, a pencil, rubber and a bottle of Indian ink. The blank pages on which he worked were exactly the same size as the pages as they appeared in his Pictorial Guides, and as they appear here. Perhaps if he had worked on bigger sheets of paper his eyes might not have grown so tired over the years with all the fiddly, detailed work he had set himself.

He prided himself on his handwriting and his drawings were immaculate, no mistakes, no crossings-out. His account books and ledgers from his days as Kendal's Borough Treasurer, and before that in Blackburn, testify to the quality of his work. He maintained that accounts should be presented as works of art in themselves.

He was doing it for himself, so he imagined when he started out, and therefore dispensed with any notion of printer's type of any sort being inserted later. All headlines and numbers, as well as the contents of each page, were done in his own fair hand. He decided not to number the pages, as such, which has proved somewhat confusing to newcomers to Wainwright's books, used to normal printery pagination. Instead, he numbered in order the pages devoted to each mountain, then started numbering again with the next one. The mountains themselves appear in the books in alphabetical order.

There is no index at the end of the books, so you can't turn to the back and look up the page number of the mountain you fancy climbing. Instead, inside the front cover and at the beginning of each book, he lists in alphabetical order all the fells included. In the latter list the fells are also numbered in descending order of altitude, and a map opposite shows where the fells are (see pages 42 and 43). All very logical. And easy to use, once you've got the hang of it.

With most printed books, publishers try to begin a new chapter or section on a right-hand page. However, Wainwright always began with a spread and ended on a spread, as will be seen with the ten pages he devoted to St Sunday Crag. This was the format he followed throughout the seven guides. It meant that he had spreads available for large maps (see Helvellyn 7 and 8) and spreads for Views (see Dove Crag 7 and 8). If his plan for a fell ran to an odd number of pages, he would insert a full-page illustration to even things up (see Dove Crag 10).

On St Sunday Crag 2, Natural Features, he has a chunk of writing, 27 lines in length, which displays many of the stylistic rules and arrangements he followed. Admire how neat it is, how well ordered, almost as if it had been done by the latest computer. Note how straight and regular the lines are at either side.

When he started work on Book One, he decided to justify his words on the left-hand side only – meaning the words were aligned at the left but were jagged on the right, which is how a normal handwritten letter looks, or something typed on an old-fashioned typewriter. A printer, however, normally justifies pages of print on both sides, squaring them up.

Halfway through Book One, after eight months, Wainwright decided he would justify his lines on both sides. He scrapped the hundred or so pages he had done thus far and began again.

He also decided, right from the beginning, never to break a word at the end of a line, refusing to add a hyphen because a word didn't fit, putting the rest of the word on the next line. Nowhere in any of the seven books does he use a hyphen at the end of a line. He also manages, on most occasions, to avoid widows, the printing term for a word on its own at the end of a paragraph. That's another reason why those 27 lines of Natural Features look so remarkably neat.

Wainwright was clearly fond of St Sunday Crag, which he

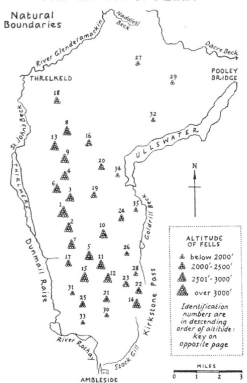

THE EASTERN FELLS

Natural
Boundaries

River Glenderamackin

Naddles/ Beck

Dacre Beck

THRELKELD

POOLEY
BRIDGE

27

29

St John's Beck

18

8

13   16

9

ULLSWATER

32

20

34

4

6   3   19

1

24   35

2   10

Goldrill Beck

7

5   26

17   11

15   11

28

12

31   23   22

25   21

14

33   30

N

THIRLMERE

Dunmail Raise

Kirkstone Pass

ALTITUDE
OF FELLS

& below 2000'

& 2000'-2500'

& 2501'-3000'

& over 3000'

*Identification
numbers are
in descending
order of altitude:
key on
opposite page*

River Rothay

Stock Gill

AMBLESIDE

MILES

0   1   2   3

*Map of the
Eastern Fells*

describes as a 'fine mountain', and impressed by its regular shape and the ridge routes. It makes it into my selection of his Best for those reasons, and because of Grisedale Tarn, one of my favourite tarns. I have to admit I also included it because of one of his illustrations.

In his view of Ullswater (St Sunday Crag 8), a woman appears in the foreground. He never included a female figure in any other

THE EASTERN FELLS

Each fell is the subject of a separate chapter

The Eastern Fells in descending order of altitude

pages of his Guides. She is seen from the back, wearing what looks like a 1930s bob-style haircut and a frock. He never revealed who she was, but office colleagues from his days in Blackburn have told me that it was a woman called Betty Ditchfield, a secretary to the Borough Treasurer. Wainwright admired her from afar and developed a passion for her, but nothing ever came of it.

Saint Sunday Crag 2756'

Glenridding
Patterdale
▲ HELVELLYN
ST SUNDAY
CRAG ▲
Hartsop
▲ FAIRFIELD

MILES
0 1 2 3 4

from Ullswater

NATURAL FEATURES

The slender soaring lines of St Sunday Crag and its aloof height and steepness endow this fine mountain with special distinction. It stands on a triangular base and its sides rise with such regularity that all its contours assume the same shape, as does the final summit-plateau. Ridges ascend from the corners of the triangle to the top of the fell, the one best-defined naturally rising from the sharpest angle: this is the south-west ridge connecting with Fairfield at Deepdale Hause. A shorter rougher ridge runs down northeast to Birks. Due east of the top is a subsidiary peak, Gavel Pike, from which a broadening ridge falls to Deepdale. A fringe of crags, nearly a mile in length, overtops the Grisedale face, which drops nearly 2000 feet in height in a lateral distance of half-a-mile: in Lakeland, only Great Gable can show greater concentrated steepness over a similar fall in altitude. The south-east face is also steep but less impressive, and the easy slopes to the north-east break into foothills before dropping abruptly to valley-level in Patterdale: these slopes are the gathering grounds of Coldcove Gill, the main stream.

Every walker who aspires to high places and looks up at the remote summit of St Sunday Crag will experience an urge to go forth and climb up to it, for its challenge is very strong. Its rewards are equally generous, and altogether this is a noble fell. Saint Sunday must surely look down on his memorial with profound gratification.

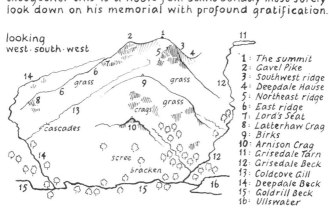

looking
west·south·west

1: The summit
2: Gavel Pike
3: Southwest ridge
4: Deepdale Hause
5: Northeast ridge
6: East ridge
7: Lord's Seat
8: Latterhaw Crag
9: Birks
10: Arnison Crag
11: Grisedale Tarn
12: Grisedale Beck
13: Coldcove Gill
14: Deepdale Beck
15: Goldrill Beck
16: Ullswater

NATURAL FEATURES

St Sunday Crag has an imposing appearance from whatever direction it is seen, an attribute rare in mountains. From Ullswater and from Grisedale its outline is very familiar; less well known (because less often seen) is its fine eastern aspect.

SUMMIT

GAVEL
PIKE

LORD'S
SEAT

LATTERHAW
CRAG

The East Ridge, from Dubhow

There is a glimpse, often unnoticed, of the lofty east ridge soaring high above Deepdale, from the roadway near Bridgend. A much better view is obtained from Dubhow, nearby on the old cart-track across the valley.

Cascades, Coldcove Gill

Summit of Gavel Pike

MAP

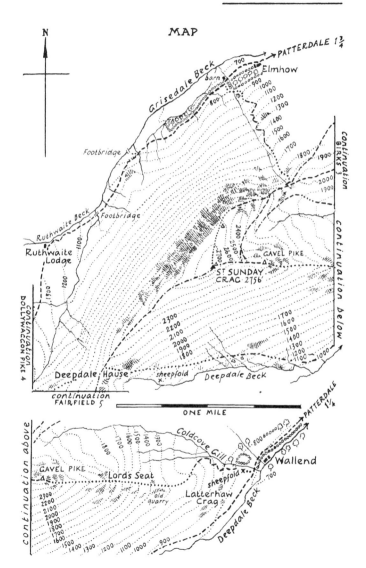

N

PATTERDALE 1¾

Grisedale Beck

barn
Elmhow

700
800
900
1000
1100
1200
1300
1400
1500
1600
1700
1800
1900
2000
1900

continuation BIRKS 3

continuation below

Footbridge

Ruthwaite Beck

Footbridge

1100

1200

1500

Ruthwaite Lodge

continuation DOLLYWAGGON PIKE 4

GAVEL PIKE

2700
2600
2500
2400

ST SUNDAY CRAG 2756

2300
2200
2100
2000
1900
1800

1700
1600
1500
1400
1300
1200
1100
1000

Deepdale Hause

sheepfold

Deepdale Beck

continuation FAIRFIELD 5

ONE MILE

continuation above

Coldcove Gill

800 700 600 500

PATTERDALE 1¼

Wallend

sheepfold

1800
1700
1600
1500
1400
1300

GAVEL PIKE

2300
2200
2100
2000
1900
1800
1700
1600
1500
1400
1300

Lords Seat

old quarry

Latterhaw Crag

1200 1100 1000 900

700

Deepdale Beck

ASCENT FROM PATTERDALE
2300 feet of ascent : 3 miles (4 by East Ridge)

looking
south·west

ST SUNDAY CRAG

GAVEL PIKE

East Ridge

DEEPDALE HAUSE

2700
2600 △
2500
2400
2300
2200
Lord's 2100
Seat 2000
1900
1800
1700
1600
1500

Latterhaw
Crag

Coldcove Gill

ruin x↑

BIRKS

grass

grass

bracken

Black Crag

Trough
Head

stile

1300

Hag Beck

1200

900

bracken

GRISEDALE TARN

The Elmhow
zig-zag, once
the popular route,
has now fallen
from favour. It
is useful only
for descent
in mist

scree
bracken

Thornhow
End

1100
1000
900
800

barn

Elmhow

Grisedale Beck

Glemara
Park

ARNISON
CRAG

scree

Wallend

bracken

Deepdale Beck

Deepdale Hall

bracken

Further details
of Arnison Crag
and Birks will
be found in
the separate
chapters on
those fells.

gate

Mill Moss

church

gate

900
800

Patterdale

KIRKSTONE ←

Bridgend

The *easiest* route (not depicted) follows
Deepdale to its head at Deepdale Hause,
then ascends the southwest ridge. Apart
from a short sharp pull on to the Hause
there is no steep climbing. There are
intimate views of the crags of Fairfield

The popular route is *via* Thornhow End and the western
flank of Birks (in clear weather it is better to proceed
over the top of Birks). The Trough Head route is easier
but dull. The east ridge is an interesting alternative
and technically the best line of ascent.

ASCENT FROM GRISEDALE TARN
1000 feet of ascent : 1¾ miles

looking north-east

ST SUNDAY CRAG

2700
2600
2500
2400
2300
2200
2100
2000
1900

Birkhouse Moor

Griesdale

Deepdale
Hause

FAIRFIELD

1700
1800
1500 PATTERDALE

HELVELLYN

Grisedale
Beck

1800

DUNMAIL
RAISE

Grisedale Tarn

GRASMERE

The traverse from
the tarn to Deepdale
Hause is rough: there
is no path, but there is
need of one, and some
public-spirited hiker
with nothing better to do
would serve his fellows
well by stamping
out a track and
cairning it.

St Sunday Crag is commonly and correctly regarded
as the preserve of Patterdale, yet it is interesting to
note that the summit is less than three miles from
the Keswick-Ambleside road at Dunmail Raise : it
may be ascended easily and quickly from here. And
from Grasmere *via Tongue Gill.*   In either case, the
first objective is Grisedale Tarn.

St Sunday Crag
from Grisedale Tarn

THE SUMMIT

The summit hardly lives up to the promise of the ridges: it is merely a slight stony mound set on the edge of a plateau — a pleasant place of mosses and lichens and grey rocks, but quite unexciting. Two cairns adorn the top, and there is also a well-built column of stones a quarter of a mile away across the plateau to the north.

Gavel Pike has a much more attractive summit than the main fell: here are bilberries and heather and natural armchairs among the rocks of the tiny peaked top, and splendid views to enjoy. A delectable place for (packed) lunch!

NORTH-EAST RIDGE

Best viewpoint for Ullswater

grass

big gully

North cairn

crags

N

stones

2400
2500
2600
2100

GAVEL PIKE

EAST RIDGE

saddle

grass

HALF A MILE

SOUTH-WEST RIDGE

DESCENTS: The royal way down to Patterdale is by the northeast ridge, traversing the flank of Birks and descending the steep woodland of Glemara Park — a delightful walk with charming views. Other routes are very inferior. For Grisedale Tarn, use the southwest ridge to Deepdale Hause, thence slanting over rough ground to the tarn, which is in view.

In bad conditions, the danger lies in the long line of crags on the Grisedale face, this fortunately being preceded by steep ground which serves as a warning. For Patterdale, the path from the saddle is safest. To find Deepdale Hause in mist, leave the top with the two cairns in line behind.

Ullswater
from the
north-east ridge

RIDGE ROUTES

To FAIRFIELD, 2863' : 1½ miles : SW then S
Depression at 2150' : 750 feet of ascent
A simple descent followed by rough scrambling

A very pleasant stroll down the
south-west ridge, on grass, leads
to the depression of Deepdale
Hause. From here, Cofa Pike
looks quite formidable, but
a plain path climbs steeply
up the stony slope to the
interesting crest of the
Pike. A loose scree slope
is then climbed to the
grassy shoulder above
and the summit-cairn
is just beyond. *In
mist, Fairfield is a
dangerous place to
strangers.*

To BIRKS, 2040' : 1¼ miles : NE
Minor depressions : 50 feet of ascent
An easy walk with delightful views

Cross the tilted summit-plateau
to the north cairn; beyond,
the north-east ridge goes
down to a col, whence a
level grassy path leads
on to Birks.

The view from the north cairn

GREAT MELL FELL

LITTLE MELL FELL

COWBARROW FELL

BIRK FELL

PLACE FELL

GLENRIDDING DODD

BIRKHOUSE MOOR

BIRKS

THE VIEW

Principal Fells

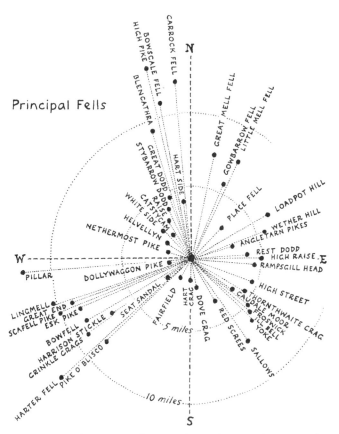

The walker who reaches the summit eagerly expecting to see the classic view of Ullswater from St Sunday Crag will be disappointed — he must go to the bristly rocks at the top of the north-east ridge for that. The lake makes a beautiful picture also from the saddle leading to Gavel Pike. Helvellyn is a fine study in mountain structure, and the best aspect of Fairfield is seen, but these two fells restrict the view. The High Street range, however, is well seen.

Lakes and Tarns

NE : *Ullswater*
E : *Angle Tarn*

4 | Helvellyn
Book One: The Eastern Fells

There are only four mountains in the Lake District over 3000 ft – Scafell Pike, Scafell, Helvellyn and Skiddaw. Mere pimples compared to the Himalaya or mountains in America or elsewhere in Europe, but they are big enough to fall off and get lost on, and they are all exceedingly popular. These are the ones which British people want to have climbed, to notch up as an achievement.

Helvellyn is considered by many experts as the finest of the four, for its brilliant views and exciting approaches to the summit. In his final summing up at the end of Book Seven, Wainwright names Striding Edge on Helvellyn – a narrow spine of rock some 900 ft long – as the first of his six best places for 'a fellwalker to be (other than summits) because of their exciting situations'. Elsewhere he calls the ascent from Patterdale via Striding Edge 'The finest way of all to the top of Helvellyn, a classic ascent recorded and underlined in the diaries of all fellwalkers in Lakeland and giving newcomers and novices a thrilling first taste of real mountaineering'.

Unlike Scafell, Helvellyn is also relatively easy to get to. Wordsworth managed to climb it at the age of seventy, despite the fact that he was continually moaning about his health.

Wainwright's coverage of Helvellyn is the most extensive and detailed of all the fells in Book One. He excels himself, thinking of ways to get across the full grandeur, explore all the possibilities, cover all the approaches. He lists all the Western and Eastern Approaches (Helvellyn 9 and 10, 13 and 14) and includes graphs showing the heights as you ascend, a device he does not use elsewhere in the Pictorial Guides.

He adds the odd personal note – 'Who cut this strange path?' (Helvellyn 12). On the Ascent from Patterdale, he notices that the path is being eroded by boots. Fifty years later, erosion on some Lakeland paths caused by walkers' boots is much worse – and there are those who say that the Blessed Wainwright is greatly to blame for this. On the other hand, since his day, the Lake District is being conserved and paths protected and saved far more professionally than they were in the past.

The 26 pages devoted to Helvellyn are extremely informative. Wainwright even included a short section on the monuments to be found on the fell, which always intrigue Lakeland fellwalkers when they come across them, wondering about their history.

The aeroplane monument he mentions commemorates one of the most bizarre events in Lakeland history. On 22 December 1926, a pilot from Lancashire decided to fly to the Lake District and try to land on the top of Helvellyn. He and his companion managed it, somehow, then realised they needed proof of their stunt. How could they get it? They decided to ask the next person arriving on the top to take their photograph. He turned out to be a professor from Birmingham University, who duly obliged. They got back in their plane, taxied slowly down the slope, with the professor watching, convinced they were never going to make it and would disappear over the edge, but they took off, with a struggle, and flew off safely. Idiots, or heroes, depending on your point of view.

It's a stunt which has not been repeated, not in that form, at least. Today, however, you do see paragliders hovering over many Lakeland mountains, one person somehow hanging on to what appears to be a mini parachute, often taking off or landing on extremely high slopes. I don't think Wainwright would have approved of having his solitary walk interrupted by a stranger dropping out of the sky right in front of him. I bet he would have refused to take their photograph.

Helvellyn

3118'

from the south-west ridge of St Sunday Crag

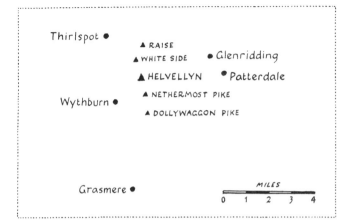

Legend and poetry, a lovely name and a lofty altitude combine to encompass Helvellyn in an aura of romance; and thousands of pilgrims, aided by its easy accessibility, are attracted to its summit every year. There is no doubt that Helvellyn is climbed more often than any other mountain in Lakeland, and, more than any other, it is the objective and ambition of the tourist who does not normally climb; moreover, the easy paths leading up the western flanks make it particularly suitable for sunrise expeditions, and, in a snowy winter, its sweeping slopes afford great sport to the ski parties who congregate on these white expanses. There are few days in any year when no visitor calls at the wall-shelter on the summit to eat his sandwiches. It is a great pity that Helvellyn is usually ascended by its western routes, for this side is unattractive and lacking in interest. From the east, however, the approach is quite exciting, with the reward of an extensive panorama as a sudden and dramatic climax when the top is gained; only to the traveller from this direction does Helvellyn display its true character and reveal its secrets. There is some quality about Helvellyn which endears it in the memory of most people who have stood on its breezy top; although it can be a grim place indeed on a wild night, it is, as a rule, a very friendly giant. If it did not inspire affection would its devotees return to it so often?

NATURAL FEATURES

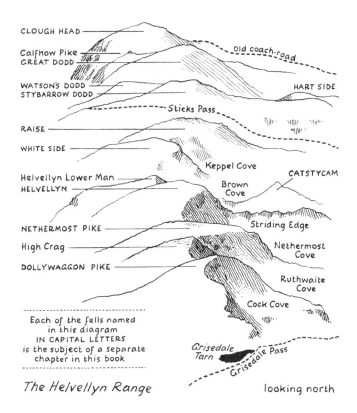

CLOUGH HEAD

Calfhow Pike
GREAT DODD

WATSON'S DODD
STYBARROW DODD

Old coach-road

HART SIDE

Sticks Pass

RAISE

WHITE SIDE

Keppel Cove

CATSTYCAM

Helvellyn Lower Man
HELVELLYN

Brown
Cove

NETHERMOST PIKE

Striding Edge

High Crag

Nethermost
Cove

DOLLYWAGGON PIKE

Ruthwaite
Cove

Cock Cove

Each of the fells named
in this diagram
IN CAPITAL LETTERS
is the subject of a separate
chapter in this book

Grisedale
Tarn

Grisedale Pass

The Helvellyn Range

looking north

The altitude of these fells and the main connecting ridges
is consistently above 2500 feet from Dollywaggon Pike (2810')
to Great Dodd (2807') except for the depression of Sticks Pass,
which is slightly below. This is the greatest area of high fells
in Lakeland, and the traverse of the complete range from south
to north (the better way) is a challenge to all active walkers.
(As a preliminary canter, strong men will include the Fairfield group,
starting at Kirkstone Pass and reaching Grisedale Tarn over the tops
of Red Screes, Little Hart Crag, Dove Crag, Hart Crag and Fairfield)

NATURAL FEATURES

The Helvellyn range is extremely massive, forming a tremendous natural barrier from north to south between the deep troughs of the Thirlmere and Ullswater valleys. The many fells in this vast upland area are each given a separate chapter in this book, and the following notes relate only to Helvellyn itself, with its main summit at 3118' (the third highest in Lakeland) and a subsidiary at 3033'.

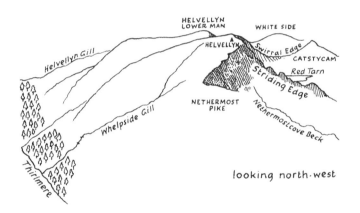

looking north·west

Helvellyn is a high point on a high ridge and therefore is substantially buttressed by neighbouring heights, the connecting depressions, north and south, being relatively slight. Westwards, however, after a gentle incline from the summit the slope quickens and finally plunges steeply down to Thirlmere, the total fall in height being nearly half a mile in a lateral distance of little more than one mile. This great mountain wall below the upper slopes is of simple design, consisting of two broad buttresses each bounded by swift·flowing streams and scarred by broken crags and occasional scree gullies. The base of the slope is densely planted with conifers.

continued

NATURAL FEATURES

continued

The smooth slopes curving up from the west break abruptly along the ridge, where, in complete contrast, a shattered cliff of crag and scree falls away precipitously eastwards : here are the most dramatic scenes Helvellyn has to offer. From the edge of the declivity on the summit Red Tarn is seen directly below, enclosed between the bony arms of Swirral Edge on the left and Striding Edge on the right. Swirral Edge terminates in the grassy cone of Catstycam, a graceful peak, but Striding Edge is all bare rock, a succession of jagged fangs ending in a black tower. The Edges are bounded by deep rough hollows, silent and very lonely. Beyond the Edges is the bulky mass of Birkhouse Moor, Helvellyn's long east shoulder, a high wedge separating Grisedale and Glenridding and descending to the lovely shores of Ullswater.

Striding Edge

Early writers regarded Striding Edge as a place of terror; contemporary writers, following a modern fashion, are inclined to dismiss it as of little account. In fact, Striding Edge is the finest ridge there is in Lakeland, for walkers — its traverse is always an exhilarating adventure in fair weather or foul, and it can be made easy or difficult according to choice. The danger of accident is present only when a high wind is blowing or when the rocks are iced : in a mist on a calm day, the Edge is a really fascinating place.

Swirral Edge

Helvellyn from Red Tarn

MAP

continuation on next page

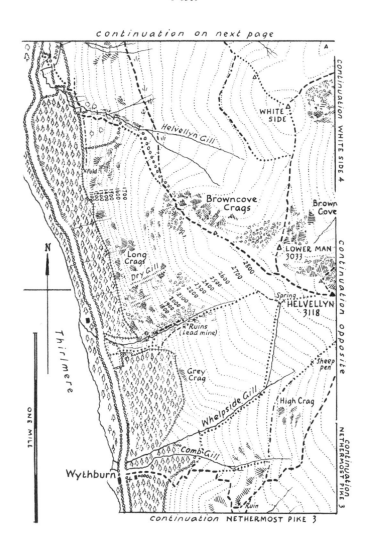

continuation NETHERMOST PIKE 3

MAP

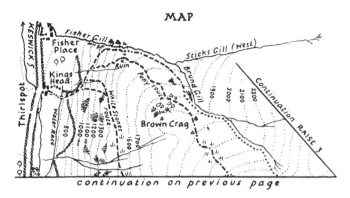

continuation on previous page

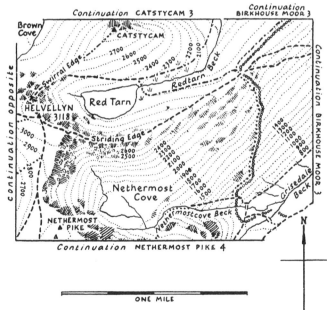

ONE MILE

THE WESTERN APPROACHES

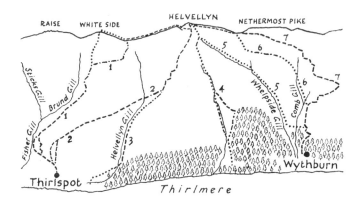

1 : The old pony-route : The original, longest and easiest route. The path is now becoming intermittent owing to disuse. This is the route indicated on the Ordnance Survey and Bartholomew's maps, but it is unnecessary to pass over the summit of White Side.

2 : The 'White Stones' route : The usual and popular way up from Thirlspot, originally marked by whitewashed stones (now a dim grey). Steep initially and midway, and marshy in places. Inexplicably this path, although long in use, is not shown on the published maps.

3 : via Helvellyn Gill : A more pleasant start to Route 2, but it is unremittingly steep for 2,000 feet. Dry underfoot. The correct start from the road is doubtful, and possibly involves a mild trespass: aim for the bridge in the field (over the water-race) and the plantation wall.

4 : via the old lead mine : The shortest way to the top from the road, taking advantage of a breach in the plantation. Very steep and rough for 2,200 feet. This is not a recognised route, and is not attractive. Solitary walkers with weak ankles should avoid it.

5 : via Whelpside Gill : A good route on a hot day, with water close almost to the summit. Rough scrambling in the gill. No path.

6 : via Comb Gill : A route of escape from the crowds on the popular Birk Side path. Steep up by the gill, but generally easy walking most of the way, on grass. No path, but a shepherd's track is helpful if it can be found.

7 : The 'Wythburn' route, via Birk Side : One of the most popular ways up Helvellyn, and the usual route from Wythburn. Good path throughout. Steep for the first mile, then much easier. This is the route indicated on the published maps.

These routes are illustrated on pages 11 and 12 following

THE WESTERN APPROACHES

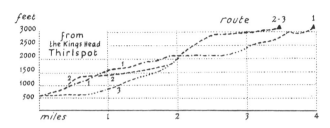

feet
route 2-3 1

from
the Kings Head
Thirlspot

miles

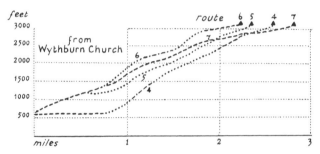

feet
route 6 5 4 7

from
Wythburn Church
6

miles

Helvellyn Gill

In mist:

Route 1 is very difficult to follow.

Route 2 is fairly clear, but the divergences from Route 1 at 900' and 1000' are not distinct.

Route 3 is safe but is not easy to locate.

Route 4 is safe but seems even rougher in mist.

Route 5 is safe if the gill is kept alongside.

Route 6 is better avoided.

Route 7 is the best of all, the path being distinct throughout its length.

Whelpside Gill

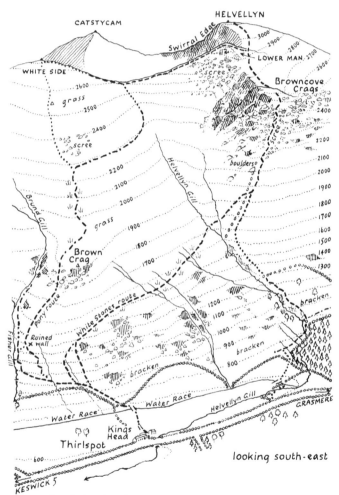

ASCENT FROM THIRLSPOT
2600 feet of ascent : 3½ - 4 miles

looking south-east

See Helvellyn 9 for details of the routes illustrated

ASCENT FROM WYTHBURN
2550 feet of ascent : 2¼-2¾ miles

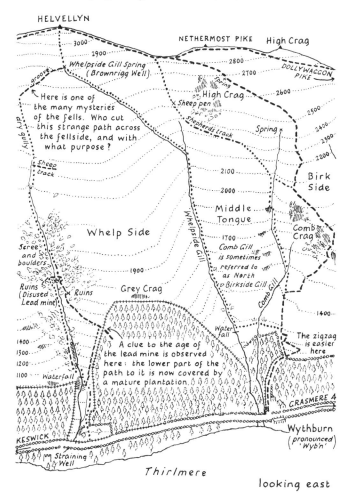

HELVELLYN

3000

2900

NETHERMOST PIKE   High Crag

Whelpside Gill Spring
(Brownrigg Well)

2800

DOLLYWAGGON PIKE

2700

← Here is one of
the many mysteries
of the fells. Who cut
this strange path across
the fellside, and with
what purpose?

High Crag
✗ Sheep pen

2600

Shepherds track

Spring ✗

2500

2400

2300

2200

dry gully

groove

Sheep
track

Birk
Side

2100

2000

Middle
Tongue

Comb
Crag

Whelp Side

Whelpside Gill

1700
Comb Gill
is sometimes
referred to
as North
Birkside Gill

Scree
and
boulders

1900

Grey Crag

Comb Gill

Ruins ←
(Disused
Lead mine)

↳ Ruins

Water
fall

1400

The zigzag
is easier
here

1400
1300
1200
1100   Waterfall

↳ A clue to the age of
the lead mine is observed
here : the lower part of the
path to it is now covered by
a mature plantation.

KESWICK

↓ Straining
↓ Well

CRASMERE 4

Wythburn
(pronounced)
'Wyb'n'

Thirlmere

looking east

See Helvellyn 9 for details of the routes illustrated

THE EASTERN APPROACHES

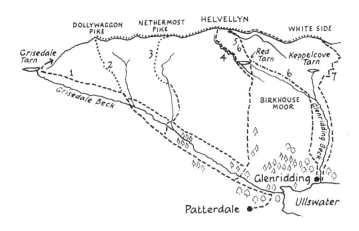

1 : *via* Grisedale Tarn : A long easy walk on a good path, with
     only one steep section. An interesting and pleasant route, which
     can be improved by following the edge of the escarpment between
     Dollywaggon Pike and the summit, instead of the path.

2 : *via* Ruthwaite Cove and Dollywaggon Pike : A very fine
     route for the more adventurous walker, cutting off a big corner
     of Route 1 — but the variation is steep and pathless.

3 : *via* Nethermost Cove and Nethermost Pike : A twin to
     Route 2, with a steep enjoyable scramble. Not for novices.

4 : *via* Striding Edge : The best way of all, well known, popular,
     and often densely populated in summer. The big attraction is an
     airy rock ridge, very fine indeed. Good path throughout.

5 : *via* Red Tarn and Swirral Edge, from Patterdale : An
     easier variation finish to Route 4, marshy by Red Tarn, ending in
     a good scramble up a steep rock staircase.

6 : *via* Red Tarn and Swirral Edge, from Glenridding : An
     easy walk, marshy in places, finishing with a good scramble up a
     steep rock staircase. Path intermittent but not difficult to follow.

7 : The old pony-route *via* Keppel Cove : The original route
     from Glenridding, now little-frequented but still quite distinct.
     A long but easy and interesting walk.

Routes 4 to 7 are illustrated on pages 15 and 16 following.
For routes 1, 2 and 3, the diagrams on Dollywaggon Pike 5
and 7 and Nethermost Pike 6 respectively, will be helpful.

THE EASTERN APPROACHES

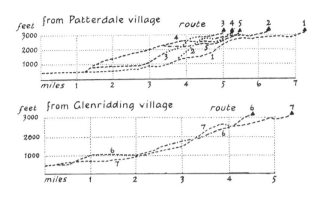

In mist:

Route 1 is easy to follow every inch of the way.
Routes 2 and 3 should be avoided absolutely.
Route 4 is safe for anyone already familiar with it.
Route 5 is safe, but there will be uncertainty near Red Tarn.
Route 6 is safe if Redtarn Beck is kept alongside to the tarn.
Route 7 is distinct except on the short south slope of White Side.

The summit, from Striding Edge

ASCENT FROM PATTERDALE
2700 feet of ascent : 5 miles

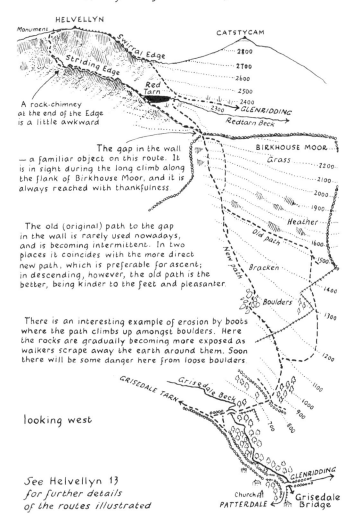

HELVELLYN

Monument

CATSTYCAM

Swirral Edge

Striding Edge

A rock-chimney
at the end of the Edge
is a little awkward

Red
Tarn

2800
2700
2600
2500
2400
2300 → GLENRIDDING
Redtarn Beck

The gap in the wall
— a familiar object on this route. It
is in sight during the long climb along
the flank of Birkhouse Moor, and it is
always reached with thankfulness

BIRKHOUSE MOOR

Grass

2200
2100
2000
1900

The old (original) path to the gap
in the wall is rarely used nowadays,
and is becoming intermittent. In two
places it coincides with the more direct
new path, which is preferable for ascent;
in descending, however, the old path is the
better, being kinder to the feet and pleasanter.

Heather

Old path

1600

New path

1500

Bracken

1400

Boulders

1300

There is an interesting example of erosion by boots
where the path climbs up amongst boulders. Here
the rocks are gradually becoming more exposed as
walkers scrape away the earth around them. Soon
there will be some danger here from loose boulders.

1200

1100

GRISEDALE TARN

Grisedale Beck

1000

900

800

700

looking west

Church
PATTERDALE ←

GLENRIDDING
→

Grisedale
Bridge

*See Helvellyn 13
for further details
of the routes illustrated*

ASCENT FROM GLENRIDDING
2750 feet of ascent : 4½ or 5½ miles

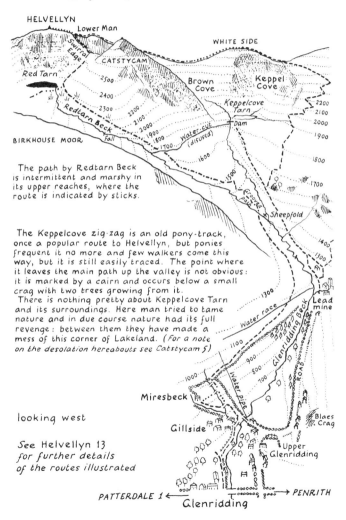

HELVELLYN
Lower Man
Swirral Edge
WHITE SIDE
CATSTYCAM
Red Tarn
2500
2400
2300
Redtarn Beck
Fall
2200
2100
2000
1900
1800
1700
Brown Cove
Keppel Cove
Keppelcove Tarn
Dam
Water-cut (disused)
1600
BIRKHOUSE MOOR
2200
2100
2000
1900
1800
1700
1600
1500
Crooked Pah
Sheepfold

The path by Redtarn Beck
is intermittent and marshy in
its upper reaches, where the
route is indicated by sticks.

The Keppelcove zig-zag is an old pony-track,
once a popular route to Helvellyn, but ponies
frequent it no more and few walkers come this
way, but it is still easily traced. The point where
it leaves the main path up the valley is not obvious:
it is marked by a cairn and occurs below a small
crag with two trees growing from it.
There is nothing pretty about Keppelcove Tarn
and its surroundings. Here man tried to tame
nature and in due course nature had its full
revenge : between them they have made a
mess of this corner of Lakeland. (For a note
on the desolation hereabouts see Catstycam 5)

1400
1300
1300
Lead mine
Water race
1100
1000
900
800
700
Glenridding Beck
ROAD
Water pipe
Blaes Crag
Miresbeck

looking west

Gillside

See Helvellyn 13
for further details
of the routes illustrated

Upper Glenridding

PATTERDALE 1 ← → PENRITH
Glenridding

ASCENT FROM GRASMERE
3050 feet of ascent : 6½ miles from Grasmere Church

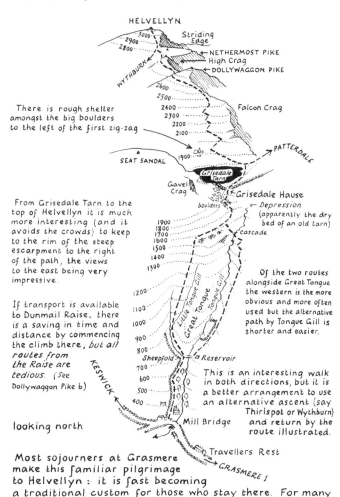

HELVELLYN

Striding Edge

3000
2900
2800

WYTHBURN

← NETHERMOST PIKE
High Crag
← DOLLYWAGGON PIKE

2600
2500
2400
2300
2200
2100

Falcon Crag

There is rough shelter amongst the big boulders to the left of the first zig-zag

SEAT SANDAL

1900

PATTERDALE

Grisedale Tarn

Gavel Crag

Grisedale Hause

From Grisedale Tarn to the top of Helvellyn it is much more interesting (and it avoids the crowds) to keep to the rim of the steep escarpment to the right of the path, the views to the east being very impressive.

boulders

← Depression (apparently the dry bed of an old tarn)

1900
1800
1700
1600
1500
1400
1300

cascade

1200

Of the two routes alongside Great Tongue the western is the more obvious and more often used but the alternative path by Tongue Gill is shorter and easier.

If transport is available to Dunmail Raise, there is a saving in time and distance by commencing the climb there, *but all routes from the Raise are tedious.* (See Dollywaggon Pike b)

1100
1000
900
800

Little Tongue Gill
Great Tongue
Tongue Gill

boulders

Sheepfold ← Reservoir

KESWICK

700
600
500
400

This is an interesting walk in both directions, but it is a better arrangement to use an alternative ascent (say Thirlspot or Wythburn) and return by the route illustrated.

looking north

Mill Bridge

Travellers Rest

GRASMERE 1

Most sojourners at Grasmere make this familiar pilgrimage to Helvellyn : it is fast becoming a traditional custom for those who stay there. For many it serves as a pleasant introduction to the fells.

Helvellyn Lower Man

looking northwest

Helvellyn Lower Man, half a mile northwest of the principal top, occupies a key position on the main ridge, which here changes its direction subtly and unobtrusively. Walkers intending to follow the ridge north may easily go astray hereabouts. The wide path from Helvellyn skirts the Lower Man and continues clearly along a broad spur which appears to be the main ridge, but is not (this is the direct way to Thirlspot, not indicated on Bartholomews' and Ordnance Survey maps); while, being indistinct, the bifurcation to the Lower Man may not be noticed, will not in mist.

Summit of Lower Man

HELVELLYN

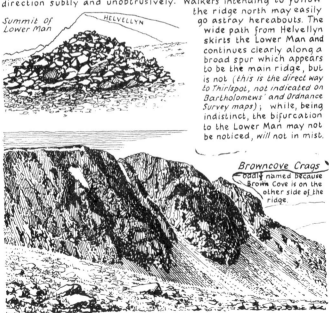

Browncove Crags
oddly named because Brown Cove is on the other side of the ridge.

THE SUMMIT

It might be expected that the summit of so popular a mountain would be crowned with a cairn the size of a house, instead of which the only adornment is a small and insignificant heap of stones that commands no respect at all, untidily thrown together on the mound forming the highest point. It is a disappointment to have no cairn to recline against, and as there is no natural seat anywhere on the top visitors inevitably drift into the nearby wall-shelter and there rest ankle-deep in the debris of countless packed lunches. The summit is covered in shale and is lacking in natural features, a deficiency which man has attempted to remedy by erecting thereon, as well as the shelter, a triangulation column and two monuments. And until many walkers learn better manners there is a crying need for an incinerator also, to dispose of the decaying heaps of litter they leave behind to greet those who follow.

The paths across the summit are wide and so well-trodden as to appear almost metalled: they are unnecessarily and amply cairned.

The dull surroundings are relieved by the exciting view down the escarpment to Red Tarn and Striding Edge below.

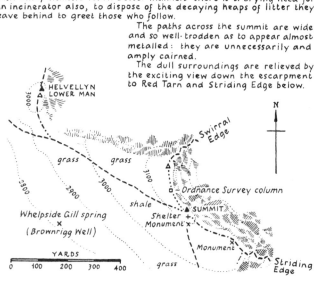

DESCENTS

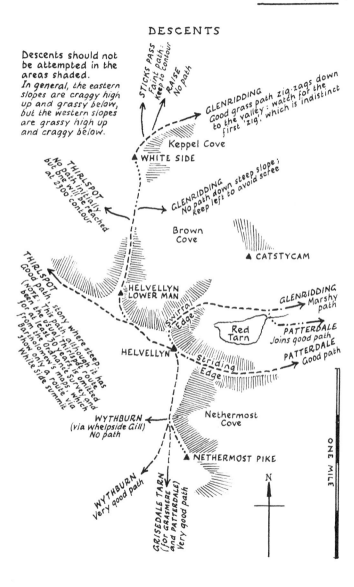

Descents should not
be attempted in the
areas shaded.
In general, the eastern
slopes are craggy high
up and grassy below,
but the western slopes
are grassy high up
and craggy below.

STICKS PASS
Faint path:
Keep to contour

RAISE
No path

GLENRIDDING
Good grass path zig-zags down
to the valley: watch for the
first 'zig', which is indistinct

Keppel Cove

▲ WHITE SIDE

THIRLSPOT
No path initially
but one will be reached
at 2300 contour

GLENRIDDING
No path down steep slope:
keep left to avoid scree

Brown
Cove

▲ CATSTYCAM

THIRLSPOT
Good path: stony where steep, it has
been the usual Thirlspot route
for at least 30 years
(NOTE: This path, although it has
from the Ordnance Survey and
Bartholomew's maps, which
show only a route via
White Side summit

HELVELLYN
LOWER MAN

Swirral Edge

GLENRIDDING
Marshy
path

Red
Tarn

PATTERDALE
Joins good path

HELVELLYN

Striding Edge

PATTERDALE
Good path

WYTHBURN
(via Whelpside Gill)
No path

Nethermost
Cove

▲ NETHERMOST PIKE

N

WYTHBURN
Very good path

GRISEDALE TARN
(for Grasmere
and PATTERDALE)
Very good path

ONE MILE

RIDGE ROUTES

To HELVELLYN LOWER MAN, 3033' : ½ mile : NW

Depression at 2975': 60 feet of ascent

A simple stroll, safe in mist.

Take the Thirlspot path, forking right below the cone of Lower Man. Or, better, follow the edge of the escarpment all the way.

NOTE : *Helvellyn Lower Man stands at the point where the main ridge makes an abrupt and unexpected right-angled turn. Its summit must be traversed for White Side, Sticks Pass or Glenridding.*

- -

To CATSTYCAM, 2917' : 1 mile : NW (200 yards), then NE

Depression at 2600' : 320 feet of ascent

A splendid walk with a fine rock scramble. Safe in mist; dangerous in ice and snow.

200 yards north-west of the top of Helvellyn is a cairn (the Ordnance Survey column is midway), and just beyond, over the rim, is the start of the steep rock stairway going down to Swirral Edge : the descent is less formidable than it looks. Midway along the Edge the path turns off to the right : here continue ahead up the grass slope to the summit.

- -

The Monuments of Helvellyn ⟶

The Gough Memorial

Erected 1890 on the edge of the summit above the path to Striding Edge.

This small stone tablet, 40 yards S of the shelter, commemorates the landing of an aeroplane in 1926. (Playful pedestrians may have hidden it with stones)

The Dixon Memorial 1858

Situated on a platform of rock on Striding Edge overlooking Nethermost Cove (often not noticed)

RIDGE ROUTES

To BIRKHOUSE MOOR, 2350' : 2 miles : ESE then NE

Minor depressions only : 100 feet of ascent

An unpleasant descent on loose scree, followed by an exhilarating scramble along a narrow rock ridge and an easy walk. Dangerous in snow and ice; care necessary in gusty wind ; safe in mist.

Turn down the scree for Striding Edge 30 yards beyond the monument. The Edge begins with a 20' chimney, well furnished with holds : this is the only difficulty. From the rock tower at the far end the path slants across the slope but it is pleasanter to follow the crest.

To NETHERMOST PIKE, 2920'
¾ mile : S then SE

Depression at 2840' : 80 feet of ascent
A very easy walk. Safe in mist.

A broad path leads south to the depression. Here note, *in mist*, that the first few yards of the fork on to Nethermost Pike are not clear: the main path goes on to Wythburn and the unwary walker will go with it. A detour from the track across the flat top of Nethermost Pike is necessary to visit the summit-cairn.

In clear weather a more interesting route follows the edge of the escarpment, the views being very impressive.

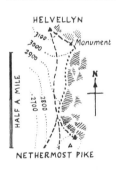

Whelpside Gill Spring
(Brownrigg Well)

Few visitors to Helvellyn know of this spring (the source of Whelpside Gill), which offers unfailing supplies of icy water. To find it, walk 500 yards south of west from the top in the direction of Pillar.

THE VIEW

The figures following the names of fells
indicate distances in miles

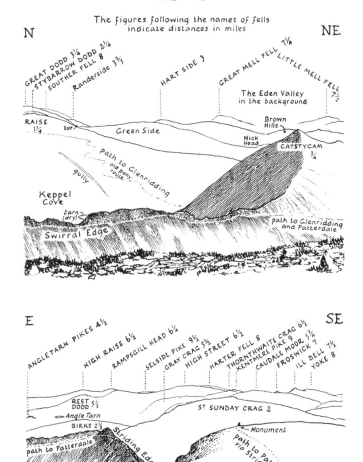

THE VIEW

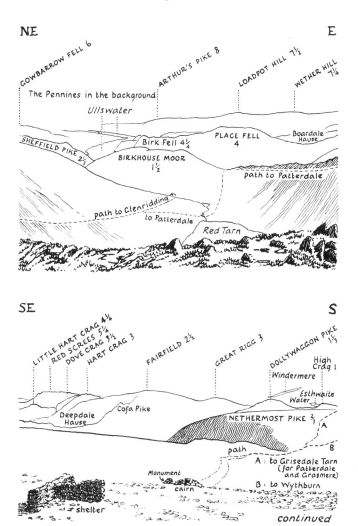

NE   E

COWBARROW FELL 6

The Pennines in the background

Ullswater

ARTHUR'S PIKE 8

LOADPOT HILL 7½

WETHER HILL 7¼

SHEFFIELD PIKE 2½

Birk Fell 4¼

BIRKHOUSE MOOR 1½

PLACE FELL 4

Boardale Hause

path to Patterdale

path to Glenridding

to Patterdale

Red Tarn

SE   S

LITTLE HART CRAG 4½
RED SCREES 5¼
DOVE CRAG 3½
HART CRAG 3

FAIRFIELD 2½

GREAT RIGG 3

DOLLYWAGGON PIKE 1⅓

High Crag 1

Windermere

Esthwaite Water

Deepdale Hause

Cofa Pike

NETHERMOST PIKE ⅔

A

B

path

A : to Grisedale Tarn
(for Patterdale and Grasmere)

B : to Wythburn

Monument

cairn

shelter

continued

THE VIEW

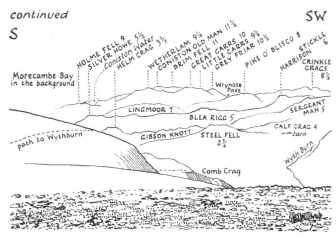

continued

S

SW

Morecambe Bay
in the background

HOLME FELL 9
SILVER HOWE 5½
Coniston Water 3⅓
HELM CRAG 3⅓
WETHERLAM 9½
CONISTON OLD MAN 11½
BRIM FELL 11
GREAT CARRS 10
LITTLE CARRS 9½
GREY FRIAR 10½
PIKE O' BLISCO 8
HARRISON
STICKLE 6
CRINKLE CRAGS 8½

Wrynose Pass

LINGMOOR 7
BLEA RIGG 5
SERGEANT MAN 5

path to Wythburn
GIBSON KNOTT
STEEL FELL 2¾
CALF CRAG 4
→ tarn

Comb Crag

Wyth Burn

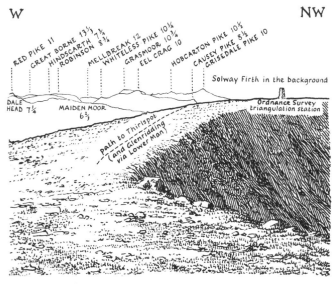

W

NW

RED PIKE 11
GREAT BORNE 13½
HINDSCARTH 7½
ROBINSON 8¾
MELLBREAK 12
WHITELESS PIKE 10½
GRASMOOR 10¾
EEL CRAG 10
HOBCARTON PIKE 10½
CAUSEY PIKE 8½
GRISEDALE PIKE 10

Solway Firth in the background

DALE HEAD 7¼
MAIDEN MOOR 6⅔

Ordnance Survey
triangulation station

path to Thirlspot
(and Glenridding
via Lower Man)

THE VIEW

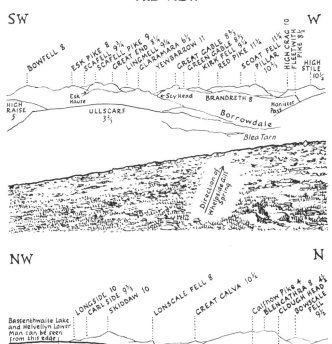

SW

Bowfell 8
Esk Pike 8
Scafell 9¾
Scafell Pike 9
Great End 8½
Lingmell 9¼
Claramara 6½
Yewbarrow 11
Great Gable 8⅔
Green Gable 8½
Kirk Fell 9¼
Red Pike 11½
Scoat Fell 11½
Pillar 10⅔
High Crag 10
Fleetwith Pike 8½
High Stile 10½

W

HIGH RAISE 5
Esk Hause
ULLSCARF 3⅔
← Sty Head
BRANDRETH 8
Borrowdale
Honister Pass
Blea Tarn

Direction of Whiteside Gill Spring

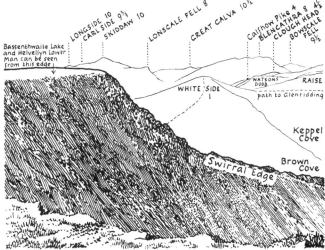

NW

Bassenthwaite Lake and Helvellyn Lower Man can be seen from this edge

Longside 10 9⅓
Carl Side 10
Skiddaw 10
Lonscale Fell 8
Great Calva 10½
Calfhow Pike
Blencathra 8 4½
Clough Head
Bowscale Fell 9½

N

WHITE SIDE
WATSONS DODD
RAISE
path to Glenridding

Swirral Edge

Keppel Cove

Brown Cove

5 | Hallin Fell
Book Two: The Far Eastern Fells

Book One did not have a jacket for its first impression. But Book Two, *The Far Eastern Fells*, had one from the outset. Wainwright had either forgotten to create a jacket for the first book or had decided that, as the books were meant to slip into the pocket, jackets were not necessary. The books were hardback, bound in a sturdy material called Rexine, with the corners slightly rounded, easy to slip into your pocket and not tear your clothes.

When a second printing of Book One was being ordered, Wainwright decided that this time they should have paper dust jackets, as is normal with hardback books. The printer announced that those who had bought the first edition of Book One, jacketless, could come to the Westmorland Gazette's offices in Kendal, or send a stamped addressed envelope, and they would get one free. To their surprise, more people wrote in for the jacket than had bought the first edition of the book. The cult of Wainwright had begun.

Wainwright designed and drew the covers for all seven Pictorial Guides himself – and, again, they were without any printer's type. He drew them in black ink, as usual, then one colour was added by the printer. The colour for the cover of Book One was lime green, Book Two red, Book Three blue, Book Four orange, Book Five brown, Book Six yellow and Book Seven dark green. The Rexine bindings under the dust jackets were similarly varied in colour. Wainwright might have known nothing about printing or publishing when he began, but he was a stickler for neatness and uniformity, even with the minor features most readers don't notice. As, of course, all publishers should be.

In Book Two he lowered the height regulation which I believe he had set for himself. Now he included a few lower fells in his plan for the book. One of these was Hallin Fell, a mere 1271 ft. Clearly it was a fell he loved – he extolled its beauty, its situation, its views of Ullswater and its surprisingly large cairn on the summit. As we will be including most of the big mountains in Wainwright's Best, it's only right and proper and fair to include one or two of the smaller fells which are pretty and easy to climb, such as Hallin Fell.

Wainwright noted that it was popular with day visitors who came by car from Cumbria's major metropolises, such as Penrith and Carlisle. Today, of course, they zoom up from much further afield, from Manchester and Liverpool, thanks to the M6. The attraction of Hallin Fell is just as great today as in the 1950s. As Wainwright neatly put it, 'the rich rewards its summit offers are out of all proportion to the slight effort of ascent'.

Because of its continuing popularity, Hallin Fell is crowded at weekends. Weekdays are a better choice, especially in autumn when the colours are at their best (although that, of course, applies to all Lake District fells).

Hallin Fell

from above Mellguards

Hallin Fell, beautifully situated overlooking a curve of Ullswater and commanding unrivalled views of the lovely secluded hinterland of Martindale, may be regarded as the motorists' fell, for the sandals and slippers and polished shoes of the numerous car-owners who park their properties on the crest of the road above the Howtown zig-zags on Sunday afternoons have smoothed to its summit a wide track that is seldom violated by the hobnails of fellwalkers. In choosing Hallin Fell as their weekend picnic-place and playground the Penrith and Carlisle motorists show commendable discrimination, for the rich rewards its summit offers are out of all proportion to the slight effort of ascent.

HALLIN FELL
● ▲
Sandwick   Howtown

PLACE
FELL ▲   ▲ BEDA
                      FELL

● Patterdale

MILES
0   1   2   3

MAP

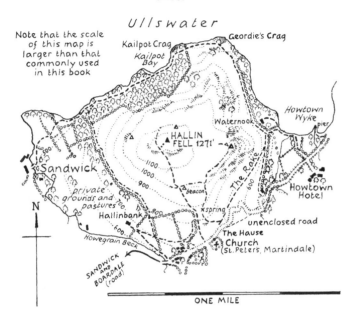

Note that the scale of this map is larger than that commonly used in this book

Ullswater

Kailpot Crag
Geordie's Crag
Kailpot Bay
Waternook
Howtown Wyke
pier
HALLIN FELL 1271'
Sandwick
1100
1000
900
beacon
× spring
The Rake
600
Howtown Hotel
private grounds and pastures
Hallinbank
unenclosed road
600
Howegrain Beck
The Hause
Church
(St. Peters, Martindale)
SANDWICK AND BOARDALE (road)

N

ONE MILE

ASCENTS

There is one royal road to the top: this is the wide grass path leaving the Hause opposite the church, and it can be ascended comfortably in bare feet; in dry weather the short smooth turf is slippery. Another track from the Hause visits the large cairn overlooking Howtown, and offers an alternative route to the top. Incidentally (although this has nothing to do with *fell-walking!*) the lakeside path *via* Kailpot Crag is entirely delightful.

HIGH RAISE RAMPSGILL HEAD THE KNOTT REST DODD GRAY CRAG CAUDALE MOOR LITTLE HART CRAG DOVE CRAG

THE NAB BEDA FELL ANGLETARN PIKES

The Martindale skyline, from the top of Hallin Fell

THE SUMMIT

The man who built the summit-cairn of Hallin Fell did more than indicate the highest point : he erected for himself a permanent memorial. This 12-foot obelisk, a landmark for miles around, is a massive structure of squared and prepared stone. The undulating top of the fell suffers from a rash of smaller, insignificant cairns : they occupy not merely the many vantage-points but even the bottoms of sundry hollows. The top is mainly grassy with bracken encroaching; there is a good deal of outcropping rock.

DESCENTS : The temptation to descend east directly to Howtown should be resisted for the slope above the Rake is rough and unpleasant.
    The easiest way off, and the quickest, is by the path going down to the church on the Hause. *In mist, no other route can safely be attempted.*

The lower reach of Ullswater from the north cairn

THE VIEW

Principal Fells

The bird's-eye view of Ullswater is dramatic, but the classic scene unfolded is an intimate one of green fields and steep fells, the Martindale district, for which this is the best viewpoint. The panorama is good considering the modest elevation.

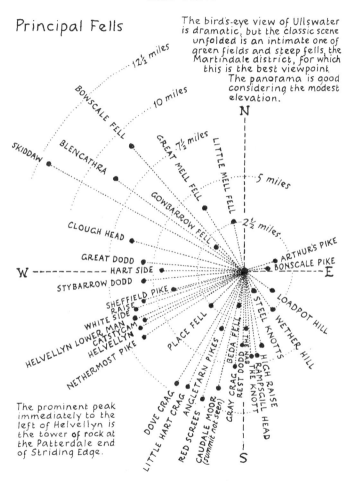

The prominent peak immediately to the left of Helvellyn is the tower of rock at the Patterdale end of Striding Edge.

Lakes and Tarns
WSW to NE : *Ullswater*
(all of the middle and lower reaches)

6 | High Street

Book Two: The Far Eastern Fells

The name High Street must perplex total newcomers to the Lake District, wondering if they might come across a Boots or a Dixons. The name reflects Cumbria's Roman connections, back to a time when the Roman army created a marching route high up across the tops. It was a name that intrigued Wainwright which was one reason why he climbed it during that first week in the Lake District in 1930. The summit of High Street – the highest fell in the Far Eastern Fells – is still called Racecourse Hill, after the locals who used to take their horses up there.

Wainwright also makes High Street one of his top eleven ridge walks. He doesn't arrange these in any order, but I personally would make it my number one ridge walk. So many ridge walks are tough and exhausting, up and then down again, just as you are enjoying the views, loved by macho athletes rather than leisure walkers, but if you stick to the High Street ridge, aiming roughly between Ullswater and Haweswater, once you are up, you are mostly up up up, sailing along, lord of all you survey.

Wainwright waxes lyrical when describing the Natural Features and when he gets to the summit (High Street 10) imagines the Romans and others who have gone the same way over the centuries. Not really like him, in the Pictorial Guides, to stray into cultural or historical fantasies. He is usually more concerned about down-to-earth matters, such as getting up by the best and most interesting ways. For High Street, he singles out the ascent from Mardale, 'the connoisseur's route'.

His words on High Street 2, Natural Features, as almost always with the Natural Features section, are justified each side, but if you peer closely, you can see how he was fiddling the spaces to get

88

things in neatly, square at either end and without hyphens. Eleven lines down, before the word 'Not', and then sixteen lines down, before 'by marching', he has made the gaps much bigger than normal, in order to make things fit.

You need, of course, your best specs to spot such ruses, for the overall effect is still immaculate, with uniform lines, all letters perfect, no ink splodges or corrections. On his original pages, some of which are on show at Kendal Museum, you can detect faint pencil marks, where he has ruled lines, and now and again, though rarely, he has used white erasing ink to blot out a word or line and then written over it. On the whole, however, his original pages which went to the printer were a hundred per cent perfect.

We don't know, of course, how many pages or half-pages he threw away before he was happy with his handiwork. Probably hundreds with each book. Even in his personal letters, notes to friends or fans, he would never send anything scruffy or hastily scrawled. Most things, however humble, were written twice, so that there were no mistakes or rubbings-out in the version that was sent out. It meant that recipients of his letters, even when they were just being sent bread-and-butter replies or a brief note, kept them as little works of art, as I have.

A note from Wainwright

from the north ridge of Branstree

NATURAL FEATURES

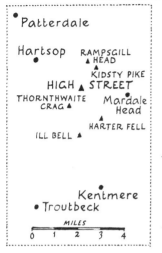

Most of the high places in Lakeland have no mention in history books, and, until comparatively recent times, when enlightened men were inspired to climb upon them for pleasure and exercise, it was fashionable to regard them as objects of awe and terror, and their summits were rarely visited. Not so High Street, which has been known and trodden, down through the ages, by a miscellany of travellers on an odd variety of missions: by marching soldiers, marauding brigands, carousing shepherds, officials of the Governments, and now by modern hikers. Its summit has been in turn a highway and a sports arena and a racecourse, as well as, as it is today, a grazing ground for sheep.

The long whale-backed crest of High Street attains a greater altitude than any other fell east of Kirkstone. Walking is easy on the grassy top: a factor that must have influenced the Roman surveyors to throw their road along it. But High Street is much more than an elevated and featureless field, for its eastern flank, which falls precipitously from the flat top to enclose the splendid tarn of Blea Water in craggy arms, is a striking study in grandeur and wildness; on this side a straight narrow ridge running down to Mardale is particularly fine. The western face drops roughly to Hayeswater. To north and south, high ground continues to subsidiary fells along the main ridge.

The River Kent has its birth in marshes on the south slope but most of the water draining from the fell flows northwards to Haweswater and Hayeswater.

Rough Crag
from
Long Stile

NATURAL FEATURES

The main High Street range
illustrating the complexity of the valley systems

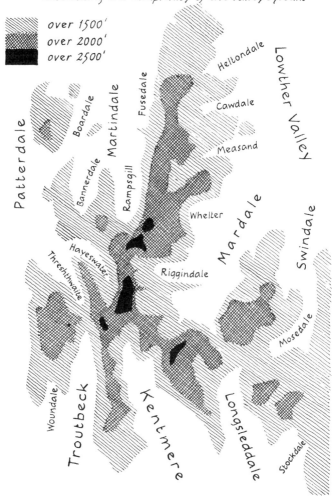

over 1500'
over 2000'
over 2500'

MAP

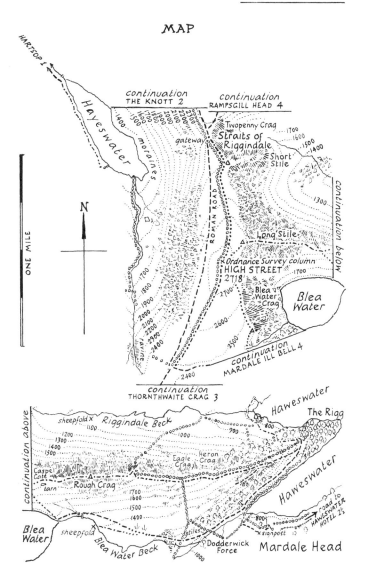

ASCENTS FROM PATTERDALE AND HARTSOP
2450 feet of ascent : 5½ miles from Patterdale
2300 feet of ascent : 3¾ miles from Hartsop

Proceed from the Straits of Riggindale to the summit
not by the wall nor by the Roman Road (which are
dull trudges) but by following the edge of the eastern
face (which has excellent views) until the Ordnance
Survey column comes into sight.

HIGH STREET

RAMPSGILL HEAD

Straits of
Riggindale

ROMAN ROAD

2700
2600
2500
2400
2300
2200

groove

gateway

2500 grass
2400

tarn

THE
KNOTT

2300
2200
2100
2000
1900
1800
1700
1600
1500 moraines
1400

Rampsgill
REST DODD

2200
2100
2000

grass

peat
hags

900

Bannerdale

1900
1800
1700

Satura
Crag

Buck Crag

gate

BROCK
CRAGS

1800
1700
1600

Angle
Tarn

For a diagram
of the ascent
to Angle Tarn
from Patterdale
see Angletarn Pikes 5

PATTERDALE 2

scree gully

Hayeswater

dam

gate

HARTSOP 1

Enterprising pedestrians
approaching from Hartsop
may tackle High Street
direct from the head
of Hayeswater — but
they will not enjoy
the climb, which is
steep, dull, and
overburdened
with
scree.

For a diagram
of the path from
Hartsop to Hayeswater
see The Knott 3

looking south-east

Two good viewpoints, only a few paces from the
path but often missed, are (1) the main cairn on
Satura Crag (view of Bannerdale), and (2) the tarn
on the col below Rampsgill Head (view of Rampsgill)

This is the least exciting approach to High Street; it
is, nevertheless, a very enjoyable walk, with a series
of varied and beautiful views; and the tracking of
the indistinct path, which has many unexpected
turns and twists, is interesting throughout.

ASCENT FROM MARDALE
2050 feet of ascent   3 miles from the road end

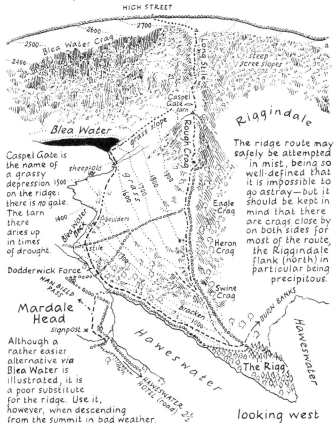

HIGH STREET

2600   2700

2500   Blea Water Crag

2400

Long Stile

steep scree slopes

Blea Water

grass slope

Caspel Gate tarn

Rough Crag

Riggindale

Caspel Gate is the name of a grassy depression 1500 on the ridge: there is *no* gate. The tarn there dries up in times of drought.

sheepfold

grass

1800

1700

1600

1900

Eagle Crag

The ridge route may safely be attempted in mist, being so well-defined that it is impossible to go astray—but it should be kept in mind that there are crags close by on both sides for most of the route, the Riggindale flank (north) in particular being precipitous.

1400

Blea Water Beck

Boulders

Stile

1500

Heron Crag

Dodderwick Force

NAN BIELD PASS

Mardale Head

signpost ✗

Although a rather easier alternative *via* Blea Water is illustrated, it is a poor substitute for the ridge. Use it, however, when descending from the summit in bad weather.

Swine Crag

bracken

1000

BURN BANKS

Hawes water

HAWESWATER HOTEL (road) 2½

The Rigg

Haweswater

looking west

The ridge of Rough Crag and the rocky stairway of Long Stile together form the connoisseur's route up High Street, the only route that discloses the finer characteristics of the fell. The ascent is a classic, leading directly along the crest of a long, straight ridge that permits of no variation from the valley to the summit. The views are excellent throughout.

ASCENT FROM TROUTBECK
2350 feet of ascent : 6 miles

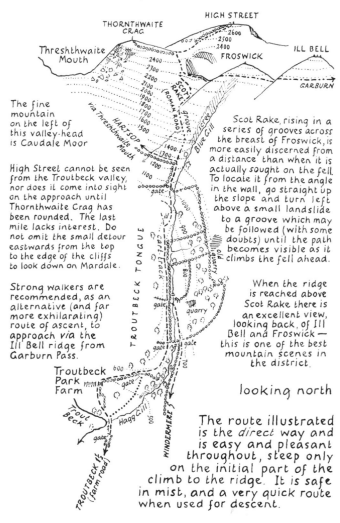

THORNTHWAITE CRAG
HIGH STREET
Threshthwaite Mouth
ILL BELL
FROSWICK
2600
2500
2400
GARBURN
SCOT RAKE (ROMAN ROAD)
2400
2300
2200
2100
2000
1900
1800
1700
1600
1500
1400
1300
1200
1100
HARTSOP via Threshthwaite Mouth
Blue Gill
gate
old quarry
CAT-TRACK
TROUTBECK TONGUE
gate
quarry
gate
gate
Troutbeck Park Farm
600
gate
Trout Beck
Hagg Gill
gate
WINDERMERE
TROUTBECK (farm road)

The fine mountain on the left of this valley-head is Caudale Moor

High Street cannot be seen from the Troutbeck valley, nor does it come into sight on the approach until Thornthwaite Crag has been rounded. The last mile lacks interest. Do not omit the small detour eastwards from the top to the edge of the cliffs to look down on Mardale.

Strong walkers are recommended, as an alternative (and far more exhilarating) route of ascent, to approach via the Ill Bell ridge from Garburn Pass.

Scot Rake, rising in a series of grooves across the breast of Froswick, is more easily discerned from a distance than when it is actually sought on the fell. To locate it from the angle in the wall, go straight up the slope and turn left above a small landslide to a groove which may be followed (with some doubts) until the path becomes visible as it climbs the fell ahead.

When the ridge is reached above Scot Rake there is an excellent view, looking back, of Ill Bell and Froswick — this is one of the best mountain scenes in the district.

looking north

The route illustrated is the *direct* way and is easy and pleasant throughout, steep only on the initial part of the climb to the ridge. It is safe in mist, and a very quick route when used for descent.

ASCENT FROM KENTMERE
2300 feet of ascent
5½ miles via Hall Cove : 6 miles via Nan Bield Pass

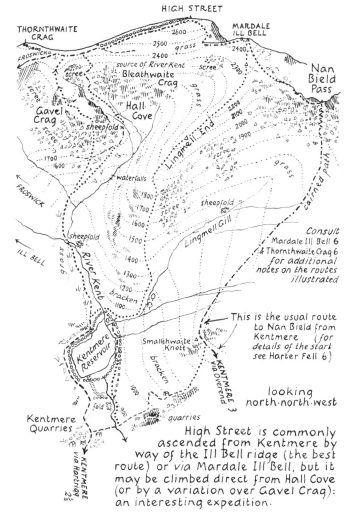

HIGH STREET

THORNTHWAITE CRAG

MARDALE ILL BELL

FROSWICK

2600
2500   grass
2400
source of River Kent
Bleathwaite Crag
scree
2400
2300
grass
scree

Nan Bield Pass

Gavel Crag
scree
sheepfold
Hall Cove
Lingmell End
2200
2100
2000
1900
grass

1700
1600

waterfalls
1800
1700
scree
1600
sheepfold

cairned path

grass

FROSWICK

ILL BELL

sheepfold
grass
River Kent
1500
1400
1300
1200
1100
bracken

Lingmell Gill

Consult
Mardale Ill Bell 6
& Thornthwaite Crag 6
for additional
notes on the routes
illustrated

This is the usual route
to Nan Bield from
Kentmere (for
details of the start
see Harter Fell 6)

Kentmere Reservoir
Smallthwaite Knott
bracken

KENTMERE via Overend 3

looking
north·north·west

Kentmere Quarries
1000
900
quarries
fold

KENTMERE via Hartrigg 2½

High Street is commonly
ascended from Kentmere by
way of the Ill Bell ridge (the best
route) or via Mardale Ill Bell, but it
may be climbed direct from Hall Cove
(or by a variation over Gavel Crag):
an interesting expedition.

High Street 9

Haweswater, from above Long Stile

Hayeswater, from the Roman Road

THE SUMMIT

The summit is barren of scenic interest, and only visitors of lively imagination will fully appreciate their surroundings.   Any person so favoured may recline on the turf and witness, in his mind's eye, a varied pageant of history, for he has been preceded here, down the ages, by the ancient Britons who built their villages and forts in the valleys around; by the Roman cohorts marching between their garrisons at Ambleside and Brougham; by the Scots invaders who were repulsed on the Troutbeck slopes; by the shepherds, dalesmen and farmers who, centuries ago, made the summit their playground and feasting-place on the occasion of their annual meets; by racing horses (the summit is still named Racecourse Hill on the large-scale Ordnance Survey maps).....and let us not forget Dixon of immortal legend, whose great fall over the cliff while fox-hunting is an epic in enthusiasm.

Nowadays all is quiet here and only the rising larks disturb the stillness. A pleasant place, but — to those unfortunate folk with no imagination — so dull!

DESCENTS should be made only by the regular routes. It must be emphasised that there is only one direct way to Mardale — by Long Stile, the top of which is indicated by a cairn. Direct descents into Kentmere may lead to trouble, the best plan being to aim for Nan Bield Pass, in clear weather.

In mist, consult the maps. For Mardale, stick to the crest of Long Stile, but at Caspel Gate turn down *right* to Blea Water. Kentmere is best reached by descending into Hall Cove at a point 100 yards south east of the end of the High Street wall. Avoid the Hayeswater face.

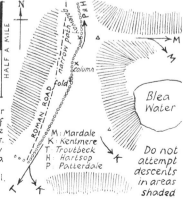

N

HALF A MILE

ROMAN ROAD

narrow path

fold

×column

P & H

△

M: Mardale
K: Kentmere
T: Troutbeck
H: Hartsop
P: Patterdale

M

Blea Water

Do not attempt descents in areas shaded

THE VIEW

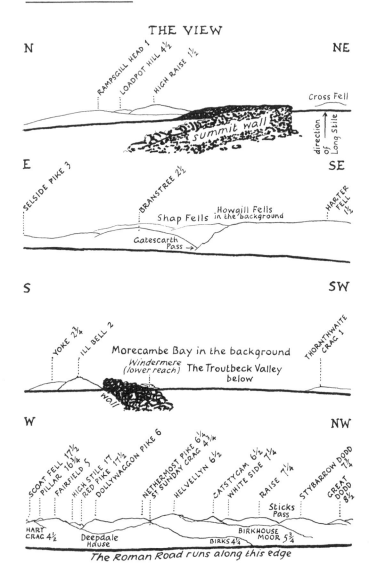

N — RAMPSGILL HEAD 1 — LOADPOT HILL 4½ — HIGH RAISE 1½ — NE

Cross Fell

direction of Long Stile

summit wall

E — SELSIDE PIKE 3 — BRANSTREE 2½ — SE — HARTER FELL 1½

Shap Fells — Howgill Fells in the background

Gatescarth Pass →

S — SW

YOKE 2¾ — ILL BELL 2 — THORNTHWAITE CRAG 1

Morecambe Bay in the background

Windermere (lower reach) — The Troutbeck Valley below

Wall

W — NW

SCOAT FELL 17½ — PILLAR 16¾ — FAIRFIELD 5 — HIGH STILE 17 — RED PIKE 17½ — DOLLYWAGGON PIKE 6 — NETHERMOST PIKE 6¼ — ST SUNDAY CRAG 4¼ — HELVELLYN 6½ — CATSTYCAM 6½ — WHITE SIDE 7¼ — RAISE 7¼ — STYBARROW DODD 7¾ — GREAT DODD 8½

HART CRAG 4½ — Deepdale Hause — BIRKS 4¼ — BIRKHOUSE MOOR 5¾ — Sticks Pass

The Roman Road runs along this edge

THE VIEW

NE   E

The figures following the names of fells
indicate distances in miles

The Pennines in the background

View of Haweswater and Blea Water from this edge

SE   S

KENTMERE PIKE 2½   MARDALE ILL BELL 3¾

Ingleborough

Morecambe Bay
and the Kent Estuary

The Kentmere Valley
below

SW   W

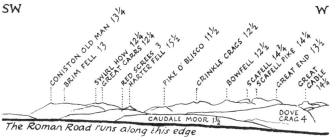

CONISTON OLD MAN 13¾ BRIM FELL 13 SWIRL HOW 12¼ GREAT CARRS 12¼ RED SCREES 3 HARTER FELL 15½ PIKE O' BLISCO 11½ CRINKLE CRAGS 12½ BOWFELL 12½ SCAFELL 14¾ SCAFELL PIKE 14¼ GREAT END 13½ GREAT GABLE 14¼

CAUDALE MOOR 1½   DOVE CRAG 4

The Roman Road runs along this edge

NW   N

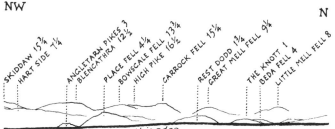

SKIDDAW 15¾ HART SIDE 7¼ ANGLETARN PIKES 3 BLENCATHRA 12½ PLACE FELL 4¼ BOWSCALE FELL 13¾ HIGH PIKE 16½ CARROCK FELL 15¼ REST DODD 1¾ GREAT MELL FELL 9¾ THE KNOTT 1 BEDA FELL 4 LITTLE MELL FELL 8

View of Hayeswater from this edge

RIDGE ROUTES

TO RAMPSGILL HEAD, 2581': 1¼ miles : N then NE
Depression at 2340': 250 feet of ascent
An easy and interesting walk

Follow the edge of the escarpment north to the narrow Straits of Riggindale. Beyond, watch for the divergence to the right from the main path, and bear left when the top of the fell is reached.

TO MARDALE ILL BELL, 2496':
⅘ mile : SE then ESE
Depression at 2350': 150 feet of ascent
An easy walk with fine views

Follow the edge of the escarpment south-east —a cairn en route indicates an excellent view of Blea Water. Incline left when the marshy depression is crossed. In mist, there is likely to be some uncertainty beyond the depression.

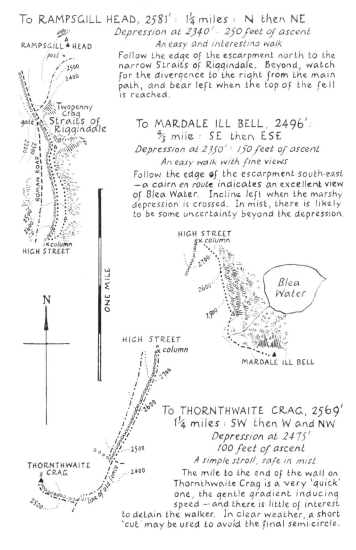

TO THORNTHWAITE CRAG, 2569'
1¼ miles : SW then W and NW
Depression at 2475'
100 feet of ascent
A simple stroll, safe in mist

The mile to the end of the wall on Thornthwaite Crag is a very 'quick' one, the gentle gradient inducing speed —and there is little of interest to detain the walker. In clear weather, a short 'cut' may be used to avoid the final semi-circle.

High Street from Mardale Ill Bell

Blea Water Crag

7 | Eagle Crag
Book Three: The Central Fells

Eagle Crag is one of the top six summits nominated by Wainwright in his summing-up at the end of Book Seven – these are not to be confused with his top six fells. He also lists six fells which have the most exciting situations, including Sharp Edge on Blencathra as one. Then, not in order of merit, he lists eleven fine ridge walks. Since he was so methodical, it is surprising he does not list twelve ridge walks – perhaps it was because he had reached the bottom of the page.

Eagle Crag is not all that well known, not often climbed and, viewed from below, looks pretty difficult, but Wainwright outlined a fairly safe way up which he thought most people could attempt, although he made it clear that it should not be attempted in bad weather.

On Eagle Crag 4, he refers to the fact that a 'substantial wall was not built to be climbed, but it can be negotiated at its upper end, where it abuts against crags, without damage to either party'. Wainwright was a first-class walker, and could keep going for hours, but he was not exactly gifted or talented when it came to rock climbing or any of the more technical manoeuvres involved in tackling the tougher crags, sheerer edges or awkward rock faces.

He does not even appear to have been much good at climbing walls either, according to one of his friends, Harry Griffin, the author, journalist and expert rock climber – but then Harry was always lean and agile while Wainwright was big and burly, over six feet high, with a tendency to put on weight as one of his passions in life was fish and chips. One can, of course, be big and agile, but Wainwright wasn't. Harry had been a Lieutenant Colonel in the Army during the war and had learned rock climbing from the feet and hands of other experts who had gone before. Wainwright, from his humble, urban background, had never had any formal training in how to climb, or what to wear. He just went off and did it.

The joy of the Lake District for Wainwright was the walking, the plodding away on his own, slowly getting up to the top of the fells for the views and the feeling of satisfaction, not to endanger his limbs by deliberately doing the dangerous, macho stuff. He never carried ropes or crampons or any other specialist gear. My sympathies are all with Wainwright.

Peter Wainwright, who sometimes accompanied his father on the fells, confirmed that Wainwright didn't like walls. 'He'd never climb a wall unless he had to,' he told me while I was writing the biography. 'He lacked co-ordination between feet and hands, so we'd walk a hundred yards to find a gate or a stile or even a sheep hole to crawl through.'

Wainwright had a great deal of respect for walls, which, he said on Eagle Crag 4, were not there for ornament, but to keep sheep in the proper place. In fact, he dedicated Book Two to 'THE MEN WHO BUILT THE STONE WALLS which have endured the storms of centuries and remain to this day as monuments to enterprise, perseverance and hard work.' No, walls were not meant to be clambered over.

He obviously had respect for the sheep too, since he dedicated Book Four to 'the hardiest of all fellwalkers, THE SHEEP OF LAKE-LAND'. He chose 'THE MEN OF THE ORDNANCE SURVEY' to dedicate his first book to, 'whose maps of Lakeland have given me much pleasure both on the fells and by my fireside'. Book Three was dedicated to 'THE DOGS OF LAKELAND, willing workers and faithful friends, and an essential part of Lakeland life.'

Book Five was dedicated to 'THE SOLITARY WANDERERS ON THE FELLS', to those who, like himself, were happiest when alone.

BOOK THREE
is dedicated to
those eager explorers of the fells

THE DOGS OF LAKELAND

willing workers and faithful friends,
and an essential part of Lakeland life

The lucky recipients of his dedication to Book Six were 'those unlovely twins, MY RIGHT LEG and MY LEFT LEG', thanking them for never having once let him down.

BOOK FOUR
is dedicated to
the hardiest of all fellwalkers

THE SHEEP OF LAKELAND

the truest lovers of the mountains,
their natural homes
and providers of their food and shelter

Finally, Book Seven was dedicated to 'ALL WHO HAVE HELPED ME', remarkably including thanks to 'my wife, for not standing in my way'.

Eagle Crag

1650'
approx.

- Rosthwaite
- Stonethwaite
  ▲ ▲ ULLSCARF
EAGLE CRAG

  ▲ HIGH RAISE

MILES
0   1   2   3

from Stonethwaite Beck

MAP

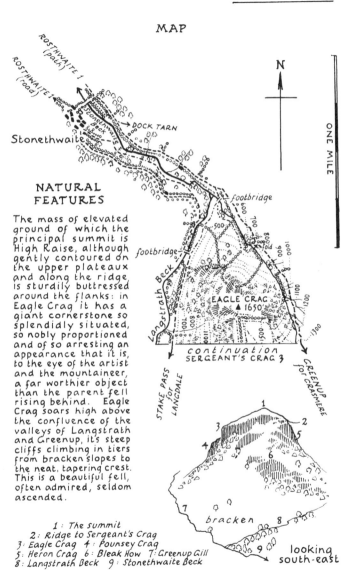

N

ONE MILE

ROSTHWAITE (path)
ROSTHWAITE (road)

DOCK TARN

Stonethwaite

footbridge

footbridge

fold

EAGLE CRAG
▲ 1650

continuation
SERGEANT'S CRAG 3

STAKE PASS
for LANGDALE

GREENUP
for GRASMERE

NATURAL FEATURES

The mass of elevated
ground of which the
principal summit is
High Raise, although
gently contoured on
the upper plateaux
and along the ridge
is sturdily buttressed
around the flanks: in
Eagle Crag it has a
giant cornerstone so
splendidly situated,
so nobly proportioned
and of so arresting an
appearance that it is,
to the eye of the artist
and the mountaineer,
a far worthier object
than the parent fell
rising behind.   Eagle
Crag soars high above
the confluence of the
valleys of Langstrath
and Greenup, it's steep
cliffs climbing in tiers
from bracken slopes to
the neat, tapering crest.
This is a beautiful fell,
often admired, seldom
ascended.

bracken

looking
south-east

1 : The summit
2 : Ridge to Sergeant's Crag
3 : Eagle Crag   4 : Pounsey Crag
5 : Heron Crag   6 : Bleak How   7 : Greenup Gill
8 : Langstrath Beck   9 : Stonethwaite Beck

ASCENT FROM STONETHWAITE
1300 feet of ascent : 2 miles

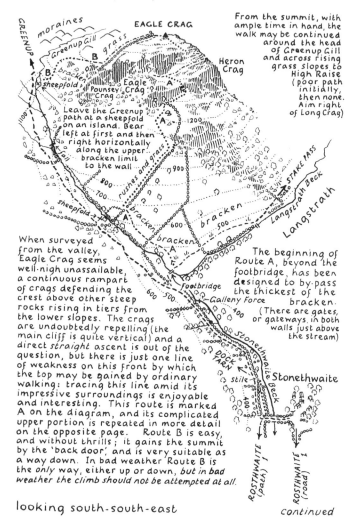

GREENUP

moraines

Greenup Gill

EAGLE CRAG

grass

B

bracken

B

sheepfold

Eagle
Pounsey Crag
Crag

Heron
Crag

Leave the Greenup
path at a sheepfold
on an island. Bear
left at first and then
right horizontally
along the upper
bracken limit
to the wall

1100

'A'

1200

'A'

800

700

rushes and grass

900

sheepfold

'A'

bracken

600

bracken

500

STAKE PASS

Langstrath Beck

Langstrath

bracken

'A'

footbridge

600

500

Galleny Force

400

DOCK TARN

Stonethwaite Beck

stile

Stonethwaite

400

From the summit, with
ample time in hand, the
walk may be continued
around the head
of Greenup Gill
and across rising
grass slopes to
High Raise
(poor path
initially,
then none.
Aim right
of Long Crag)

The beginning of
Route A, beyond the
footbridge, has been
designed to by-pass
the thickest of the
bracken.
(There are gates,
or gateways, in both
walls just above
the stream)

When surveyed
from the valley,
Eagle Crag seems
well-nigh unassailable,
a continuous rampart
of crags defending the
crest above other steep
rocks rising in tiers from
the lower slopes. The crags
are undoubtedly repelling (the
main cliff is quite vertical) and a
direct straight ascent is out of the
question, but there is just one line
of weakness on this front by which
the top may be gained by ordinary
walking: tracing this line amid its
impressive surroundings is enjoyable
and interesting. This route is marked
A on the diagram, and its complicated
upper portion is repeated in more detail
on the opposite page.   Route B is easy,
and without thrills; it gains the summit
by the 'back door', and is very suitable as
a way down. In bad weather Route B is
the only way, either up or down, but in bad
weather the climb should not be attempted at all.

ROSTHWAITE (path) 1

ROSTHWAITE (road) 1

looking south-south-east

continued

ASCENT FROM STONETHWAITE

continued

The upper section of Route A

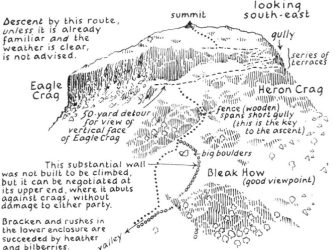

Descent by this route, unless it is already familiar and the weather is clear, is not advised.

summit

looking south-east

gully

series of terraces

Eagle Crag

Heron Crag

50-yard detour for view of vertical face of Eagle Crag

fence (wooden) spans short gully (this is the key to the ascent)

big boulders

Bleak How (good viewpoint)

This substantial wall was not built to be climbed, but it can be negotiated at its upper end, where it abuts against crags, without damage to either party.

Bracken and rushes in the lower enclosure are succeeded by heather and bilberries.

valley

Here, and in other craggy places, sheep should be disturbed as little as possible, even at inconvenience to the walker; otherwise they may become casualties. The walls are not put there for ornament: they serve a vital purpose, and if stones are displaced they should be put back, and firmly.

Eagle Crag is the most distinctive object in the Stonethwaite landscape and its ascent reveals all the beauty of the valley in a pleasant half-day's (or summer evening's) expedition.

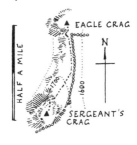

HALF A MILE

▲ EAGLE CRAG

N

1700

1600

▲ SERGEANT'S CRAG

RIDGE ROUTE

TO SERGEANT'S CRAG, 1873'

½ mile : S, then SSW

Minor depressions

250 feet of ascent

Easy, but not safe in mist

A rough little path leads down to the head of a gully at the wall-corner. Do not cross the wall, but accompany it south, finally inclining away from it.

THE SUMMIT

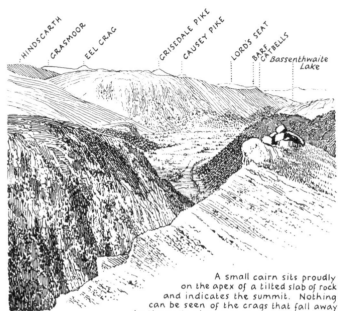

HINDSCARTH — GRASMOOR — EEL CRAG — GRISEDALE PIKE — CAUSEY PIKE — LORD'S SEAT — BARF — CATBELLS — Bassenthwaite Lake

A small cairn sits proudly on the apex of a tilted slab of rock and indicates the summit. Nothing can be seen of the crags that fall away to the valley because of an upper plateau of grass and heather, broken by many outcrops. Eastwards from the cairn there is an acre of flat marshy ground before the slopes descend from sight.

DESCENTS: There must be no thought of a quick romp straight down to the valley immediately below: *it cannot be done.* Unless the route on the Stonethwaite face (Route A) is already known, it should not be sought from above: the crags form an almost continuous barrier here. Palpitations and alarms may be avoided by following the wall down towards Greenup (away from the direction of Stonethwaite) after first crossing it at the corner, and, when rough ground appears ahead, making a wide detour to the right to join the Greenup path down easy bracken slopes. *In bad weather, or if there is deep snow, this is the only route that will ensure the due arrival of the walker at Stonethwaite in one unbroken piece.*

THE VIEW

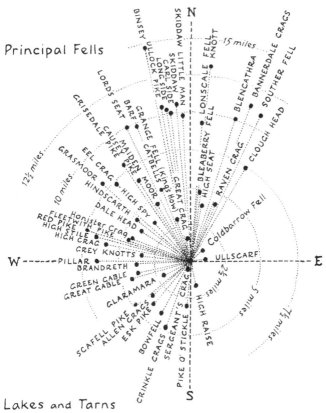

Principal Fells

Lakes and Tarns
NNW : *Bassenthwaite Lake*

 The view of the Stonethwaite valley, which might be expected
to be excellent, is not quite that, the summit being set rather
too far back from the edge of the crags to enable all of it to
be seen; a short and easy descent of the upper slope leads to
better points of vantage. But generally the valley is too short
to be really effective in a view, although the whole picture is
very pleasing to west and north. Eastwards the scene is drab.

8 | Helm Crag

Book Three: The Central Fells

Helm Crag is another fell which wins one of Wainwright's top six summit awards but that won't be a surprise to most Lakeland lovers as it is such a well-known, well-walked fell. For those on the main road from Grasmere to Keswick, it's easily spotted and identified from Dunmail Raise, and easily walked from Grasmere village. Wainwright gives it a positive rave. The route he describes takes two hours, but he wished it could last longer as he enjoyed it so much.

He is well into his writing style by now, having found his own voice. Under Natural Features (Helm Crag 2), he describes the fell as looking 'irascible, like a shaggy terrier in the company of sleek foxhounds'. It's interesting that he should be giving mountains human – or at least animal – virtues, and characteristic. Beatrix Potter did something similar, only she gave animals human feelings. Wainwright, when he was being grumpy, used to say he preferred animals to humans: 'I've never yet met an animal who was deceitful or dishonest but I've met too many humans like that.'

Here he is being far from grumpy. He is happy and exhilarated, knowing that in guiding us to Helm Crag he is passing on a real treasure. In doing so, he becomes at times positively skittish. The remark at the bottom of the first page about his little map – which only has two spots on it, Helm Crag and Grasmere – is one of his little jokes, the sort, no doubt, that municipal accountants will always chuckle at.

On Helm Crag 5, when he reaches the summit, which is dominated by a massive pinnacle of rock, he appears to suggest or let us believe that he has indeed climbed it 'by precarious movements of the body'. But on Helm Crag 8 he comes clean. In the bottom right-hand corner there's a good joke at his own expense, confessing all.

Tourists admiring the view from the summit of Coniston Old Man

The great guidebook writers to the Lake District, starting with Wordsworth, through Otley and Baddeley, never made facetious comments or jokey asides, such as 'a good place to give up and go to sleep', which is how Wainwright describes one ascent. At frequent intervals throughout his guides, he can't resist the odd nice aside, very often at his own expense.

It harks back to his years as a young man in Blackburn, writing his little magazine and drawing cartoons to amuse his fellow office workers. This talent comes through more often as the Guides proceed.

In Book Four, when writing about Coniston Old Man, he includes a drawing of the summit which is, in effect, a cartoon, not an illustration. It mocks tourists whose main interest when they get to the top is in trying to spot Blackpool Tower or Calder Hall Power Station, and then emit 'squeals of joy'. Calder Hall was what Sellafield was named when it opened in 1956. In this case, Wainwright was not just making a joke, but a topical joke.

Helm Crag

1299'

affectionately known as 'The Lion and The Lamb'

HELM CRAG ▲
CRAG

Grasmere ●

MILES
0   1   2

from Grasmere

This is the smallest (and most accurate!) map in the book

NATURAL FEATURES

Helm Crag may well be the best-known of all Lakeland fells, and possibly even the best-known hill in the country. Generations of waggonette and motor-coach tourists have been tutored to recognise its appearance in the Grasmere landscape: it is the one feature of their Lakeland tour they hail at sight, and in unison, but the cry on their lips is not "Helm Crag!" but "The Lion and the Lamb!" — in a variety of dialects. The resemblance of the summit rocks to a lion is so striking that recognition, from several viewpoints, is instant; yet, oddly, the outline most like Leo is not the official 'Lion' at all: in fact there are two lions, each with a lamb, and each guards one end of the summit ridge as though set there by architectural design. The summit is altogether a rather weird and fantastic place, well worth not merely a visit but a detailed and leisurely exploration. Indeed the whole fell, although of small extent, is unusually interesting; its very appearance is challenging; its sides are steep, rough and craggy; its top bristles; it *looks* irascible, like a shaggy terrier in a company of sleek foxhounds, for all around are loftier and smoother fells, circling the pleasant vale of Grasmere out of which Helm Crag rises so abruptly.

The fell is not isolated, nor independent of others, for it is the termination of a long ridge enclosing Far Easedale in a graceful curve on north and east and rising, finally, to the rocky peak of Calf Crag. It drains quickly, is dry underfoot, and has no streams worthy of mention.

The virtues of Helm Crag have not been lauded enough. It gives an exhilarating little climb, a brief essay in real mountaineering, and, in a region where all is beautiful, it makes a notable contribution to the natural charms and attractions of Grasmere.

outline of
STEEL FELL

DUNMAIL
RAISE

THE
GREENBURN
VALLEY

summit
scene

MAP

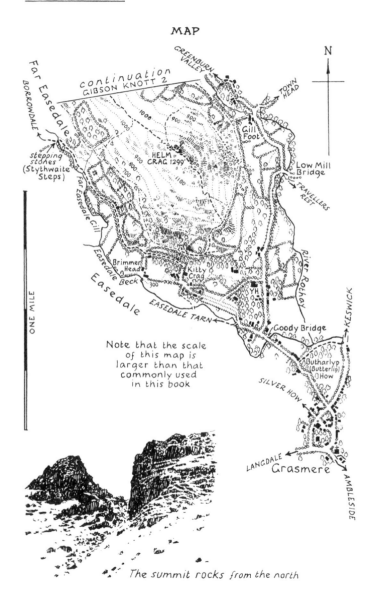

N

Far Easedale

BORROWDALE

continuation
GIBSON KNOTT 2

GREENBURN VALLEY

TOWN HEAD

Gill Foot

HELM CRAG 1299

Low Mill Bridge

TRAVELLERS REST

stepping stones (Stythwaite Steps)

Far Easedale Gill

Easedale Beck

Brimmer Head

Kitty Crag

Easedale

EASEDALE TARN

River Rothay

YH

Goody Bridge

KESWICK

ONE MILE

Note that the scale of this map is larger than that commonly used in this book

Butharlyp (Butterlip) How

SILVER HOW

LANGDALE

Grasmere

AMBLESIDE

The summit rocks from the north

ASCENT FROM GRASMERE
1100 feet of ascent : 1½ miles

HELM CRAG

bracken

When descending (especially in mist) watch for zig zag →

White Crag

bracken

Raven Crag

900

scree

800

700

600

700

seat (perhaps!)

Jackdaw Crag

600

500

Lancrigg Crag

400

Kitty Crag

300

FAR EASEDALE & BORROWDALE (footpath)

Easedale

EASEDALE TARN (footpath)

LOW MILL BRIDGE and GILL FOOT (road)

Goody Bridge

Easedale Beck

Butharlyp (Butterlip) How

studio

LANGDALE

Red Lion Hotel

KESWICK

Grasmere

Church

This is one of the few hills where ascent and descent by the same route is recommended, the popular path depicted being much the best way both up and down. An alternative route (shown on the map but not on this diagram) has nothing in its favour.

If, however, Helm Crag is to be a part only of the day's programme (e.g. the circuit of Far Easedale or the Greenburn valley) it is better reserved for descent, for then the Vale of Grasmere will be directly in view ahead; and this fair scene is at its best when the shadows of evening are lengthening, with the Langdales silhouetted in rugged outline against the sunset. Tarry long over this exquisite picture of serenity and peace, and memorise it for the long winter of exile!

looking north-west

This is a splendid little climb ; if it has a fault it is that it is too short. But for the evening of the day of arrival in Grasmere on a walking holiday it is just the thing : an epitome of Lakeland concentrated in the space of two hours — and an excellent foretaste of happy days to come.

THE SUMMIT

Rocks at the north-west end of the summit ridge, *known by various names:*
(a) The 'Lion Couchant, *or, more popularly,* The Lion and The Lamb. *(as seen from the road below Dunmail Raise)*
(b) The Howitzer *(as seen from Dunmail Raise)*

The highest point of the rocks is the true summit of the fell

In scenic values, the summits of many high mountains are a disappointment after the long toil of ascent, yet here, on the top of little Helm Crag, a midget of a mountain, is a remarkable array of rocks, upstanding and fallen, of singular interest and fascinating appearance, that yield a quality of reward out of all proportion to the short and simple climb. The uppermost inches of Scafell and Helvellyn and Skiddaw can show nothing like Helm Crag's crown of shattered and petrified stone : indeed, its highest point, a pinnacle of rock airily thrust out above a dark abyss, is not to be attained by walking and is brought underfoot only by precarious manœuvres of the body. This is one of the very few summits in Lakeland reached only by climbing rocks, and it is certainly (but not for that reason alone) one of the very best.

continued

THE SUMMIT

continued

The summit ridge is 250 yards in length and is adorned at each end by fangs of rock overtopping the fairly level path. Between these towers there have been others in ages past but all that remains of them now is a chaos of collapsed boulders, choking a strange depression that extends the full length of the summit on the north-east side. The depression is bounded by a secondary ridge, and this in turn descends craggily to an even more strange depression, in appearance resembling a huge ditch cleft straight as a furrow across the breast of the fell for 300 yards; or, more romantically, a deep moat defending the turreted wall of the castle above. This surprising feature, which will not be seen unless searched for, will doubtless be readily explained by geologists (or antiquaries?); to the unlearned beholder it seems likely to be the result of some ancient natural convulsion that caused the side of the fell to slip downwards a few yards before coming to rest. This ditch is also bounded on its far side by a parallel ridge or parapet (narrow, and an interesting walk) beyond which the fellside plunges down almost precipitously to the valley, falling in juniper-clad crags.

Care is necessary when exploring the boulder-strewn depressions on the summit, especially if the rocks are greasy. There are many good natural shelters here, and some dangerous clefts and fissures and holes, so well protected from the weather that summer flowers are to be found in bloom in their recesses as late as mid-winter.

The south-west side of the summit ridge consists mainly of bracken slopes and are of little interest in their upper reaches.

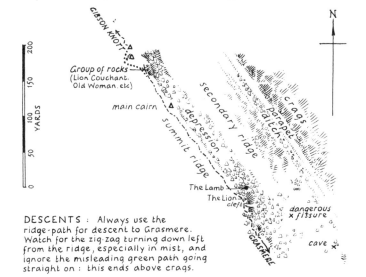

DESCENTS : Always use the ridge-path for descent to Grasmere. Watch for the zig-zag turning down left from the ridge, especially in mist, and ignore the misleading green path going straight on : this ends above crags.

THE SUMMIT

Rocks at the north-west end of the summit-ridge known as The Old Woman Playing the Organ *from their appearance when seen from Tongue Gill and the vicinity of Easedale Tarn*

Rocks at the south-east end of the summit-ridge. *These form the* OFFICIAL *Lion and The Lamb (as seen from the Swan Hotel, Grasmere). The lion's head is the O.S. 'station' (altitude 1299') but is not quite the highest point of the fell*

THE VIEW

This is the view from the cairn on the summit ridge — whether it coincides with the view from the highest point the author will never know for his several attempts to mount to the rocky pate of the Lion Couchant have all been defeated by a lack of resolution; but probably it is the same. In any case, most visitors will be content to study the prospect from the comparative security of the cairn on the ridge.

continued

continued
The Vale of Grasmere is best displayed from the head of the other (official) Lion, which even the author found a simple ascent, (although deeply conscious of precipices all around).

Principal Fells

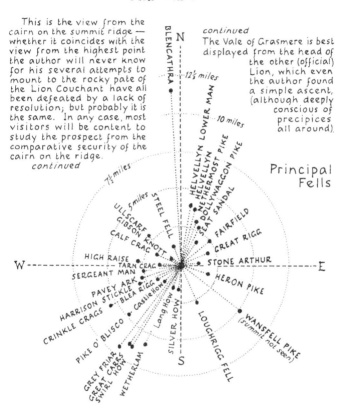

The prominent height south-south-east (to the right of Loughrigg Fell) is Gummer's How, 13 miles distant at the foot of Windermere.

Lakes and Tarns
SE: *Windermere* (upper reach)
SSE: *Grasmere*
SSE: *Esthwaite Water*
WSW: *Easedale Tarn*

This corner was reserved for an announcement that the author had succeeded in surmounting the highest point. Up to the time of going to press, however, such an announcement cannot be made.

Tarn Crag
across Far Easedale
from the slopes of Helm Crag

The north-east face
from Low Mill Bridge

RIDGE ROUTE

To GIBSON KNOTT, 1379'
  1 mile : NW, then W
  Depression at 1050'
  400 feet of ascent
  An interesting ridge climb

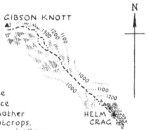

Two big cairns indicate the way off
Helm Crag. A narrow path crosses the
depression and continues up the opposite
slope ; when it starts to traverse the face
leave it and keep to the ridge, where another
track winds charmingly between rock outcrops.
The cairned summit rises across a shallow hollow.

ONE MILE

Helm Crag, from the path to Gibson Knott

9 | Bowfell

Book Four: The Southern Fells

Wainwright worked entirely by hand, and when you come to one of the more important mountains, and his more extensive spreads, you realise the scale of his ambitions and talents and appreciate just how good a graphic artist he was.

Working in black on white in pen might seem rather limiting, and the effect might become monotonous, but over the books, Wainwright developed a huge range of styles of handwriting. Look at the Ascent from Dungeon Ghyll (Bowfell 5), for example, or any of the other four ascents of Bowfell, and on each page you will see up to eight different sizes of handwriting, in either roman or italic. There might be more, but my eyes aren't up to identifying every variation.

He had, for a start, a roman style, with the letters roughly going straight up and down, and an *italic* style, with the letters leaning at a slight angle. On Bowfell 5 you can see this clearly with the letter 'f'. At the top of the page, in the word 'feet', you can see the 'f' sloping. In the second block of text down on the right of the page, and again at the bottom, for example, he is using his roman hand, so that the 'f' stands up straighter.

He also has bold and light forms of handwriting, pressing harder with his pen to make letters stronger, and an even bolder version when he moves into double strokes for fell headings, as with the initial letter of Bowfell on his first page. He writes certain words, such as headings, in capitals, while at other times he sticks to lower case.

As for size, he never gets too big or dramatic, the largest size being used for the title of each section, when he gives the name of the fell. He employs in all about six different sizes, the smallest being the titchy print used on Bowfell 5 in the middle of the copy on the right, where he is making a joke about not ending a sentence with a preposition.

The whole effect is to give his handwriting colour, brightness, variety, light and shade. Technically, it is only ever monotone, being in black ink, but it is never monotonous.

His pen-and-ink drawings are equally remarkable. His view of Bowfell on the first page has the depth and prettiness of a water-colour, good enough to go on any Lake District tourist calendar.

Bowfell also includes a drawing that covers a double page spread – Bowfell 13 and 14 – which is less pretty. Not quite such fun to live with on your wall. But you have to admire the work that has been done, all the hundreds, if not thousands, of miniature marks, individual strokes with his pen, that have gone into his attempt to capture what seems like a fairly boring, featureless slabby stretch of crags. But, as he notes of this slab of Flat Crags, 'Bowfell's unique secrets are locked away amongst its cliffs and crags', and the view from the top is regarded by many as 'the finest in Lakeland'.

On Bowfell 4, there is a reference at the bottom to the county boundary between Cumberland and Westmorland – two counties which no longer exist, alas, as far as our governmental masters are concerned. Since 1974, they were subsumed into one county known as Cumbria. Like Wainwright, I still use the terms Cumberland and Westmorland and in my mind they will always be two distinct places with their own history and character.

Bowfell, so he states here on Bowfell 2, well before he has finished the final book in the series, is going to be one of his best half-dozen Lakeland fells. But then he adds a note saying he will not at this stage reveal the other five until Book Seven. Oh, what a teaser. But as one of his top six, it deserves to be in the Best of Wainwright.

Bowfell

2960'

'Bow Fell' (two words)
on Ordnance Survey maps

from Lingmoor Fell

NATURAL FEATURES

A favourite of all fellwalkers, Bowfell is a mountain that commands attention whenever it appears in a view. And more than attention, respect and admiration, too; for it has the rare characteristic of displaying a graceful outline and a sturdy shapeliness on all sides. The fell occupies a splendid position at the hub of three well-known valleys, Great Langdale, Langstrath and Eskdale, rising as a massive pyramid at the head of each, and it is along these valleys that its waters drain, soon assuming the size of rivers. The higher the slopes rise the rougher they become, finally rearing up steeply as a broken rim of rock around the peaked summit and stony top. These crags are of diverse and unusual form, natural curiosities that add an exceptional interest and help to identify Bowfell in the memory. Under the terraced northern precipices, in a dark hollow, is Angle Tarn.

As much as any other mountain, the noble Bowfell may be regarded as affording an entirely typical Lakeland climb, with easy walking over grass giving place to rough scrambling on scree, and a summit deserving of detailed exploration and rewarding visitors with very beautiful views.

Rank Bowfell among the best half-dozen! ✻

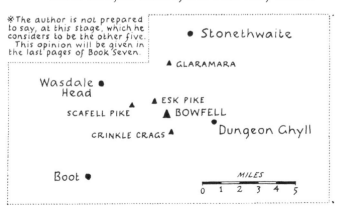

✻ The author is not prepared to say, at this stage, which he considers to be the other five. This opinion will be given in the last pages of Book Seven.

• Stonethwaite

▲ GLARAMARA

Wasdale •
Head

▲ ESK PIKE

▲
SCAFELL PIKE

▲ BOWFELL

•
Dungeon Ghyll

CRINKLE CRAGS ▲

Boot •

MILES

0   1   2   3   4   5

MAP

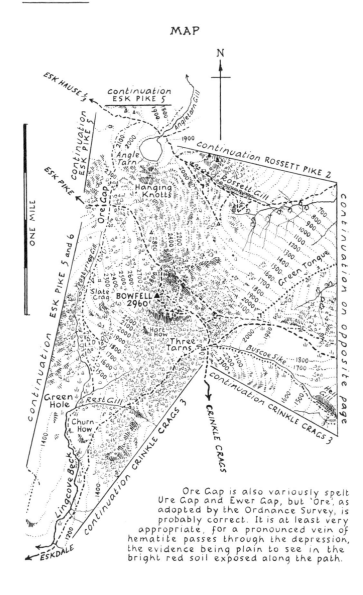

continuation
ESK PIKE 5

continuation ROSSETT PIKE 2

continuation ESK PIKE 5

ESK HAUSE

ESK PIKE

continuation ESK PIKE 5 and 6

continuation on opposite page

N

ONE MILE

Angle Tarn

Angletarn Gill

Hanging Knotts

Ore Gap

Rossett Gill

Foxes Tarn Gill

Green Tongue

Slate Crag

BOWFELL
2960

Hart How

Three Tarns

Buscoe Sike

Hell Gill

continuation CRINKLE CRAGS 3

Green Hole

Rest Gill

Churn How

CRINKLE CRAGS

continuation CRINKLE CRAGS 3

Lingcove Beck

ESKDALE

Ore Gap is also variously spelt
Ure Gap and Ewer Gap, but 'Ore', as
adopted by the Ordnance Survey, is
probably correct. It is at least very
appropriate, for a pronounced vein of
hematite passes through the depression,
the evidence being plain to see in the
bright red soil exposed along the path.

MAP

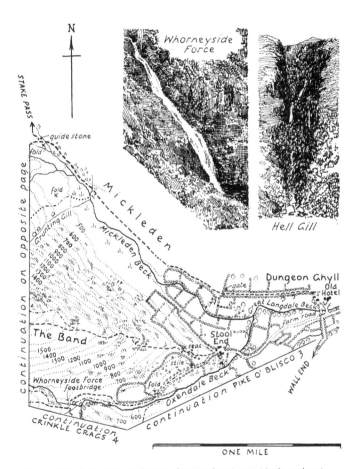

Whorneyside Force

Hell Gill

The county boundary between Cumberland and Westmorland passes over the top of Bowfell, coming up from Wrynose Pass via Crinkle Crags and Three Tarns. From the summit it follows the height of land to Hanging Knotts, where the main ridge is left in favour of the lesser watershed of Rossett Pass, whence it continues the circuit of Mickleden. Thus, Great Langdale and all the waters thereof are wholly within Westmorland.

ASCENT FROM DUNGEON GHYLL
2700 feet of ascent : 3 miles (3¼ via Three Tarns)

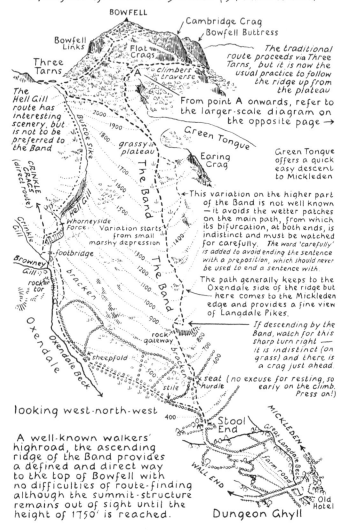

BOWFELL

Cambridge Crag
Bowfell Buttress

Bowfell Links

Flat Crags

Three Tarns

A
climbers traverse

The traditional route proceeds via Three Tarns, but it is now the usual practice to follow the ridge up from the plateau

From point A onwards, refer to the larger-scale diagram on the opposite page →

The Hell Gill route has interesting scenery but is not to be preferred to the Band

2000
1900
1800

Buscoe Sike

grassy plateau

Green Tongue

Earing Crag

Green Tongue offers a quick easy descent to Mickleden

CRINKLE CRAGS (direct route)

1700
1600
1500

Hell Gill

The Band

Crinkle Gill

Whorneyside Force

Variation starts from small marshy depression

footbridge

Browney Gill

rock tor

bracken

1400

This variation on the higher part of the Band is not well known — it avoids the wetter patches on the main path, from which its bifurcation, at both ends, is indistinct and must be watched for carefully. The word 'carefully' is added to avoid ending the sentence with a preposition, which should never be used to end a sentence with.

The path generally keeps to the Oxendale side of the ridge but here comes to the Mickleden edge and provides a fine view of Langdale Pikes.

1300
1200
1100

The Band

Oxendale

Oxendale Beck

900

rock gateway

sheepfold

800

If descending by the Band, watch for this sharp turn right — it is indistinct (on grass) and there is a crag just ahead.

700

600

bracken

500

stile
hurdle

seat (no excuse for resting, so early on the climb. Press on!)

looking west·north·west

400

Stool End

MICKLEDEN

Great Langdale Beck

A well-known walkers' highroad, the ascending ridge of the Band provides a defined and direct way to the top of Bowfell with no difficulties of route-finding although the summit-structure remains out of sight until the height of 1750' is reached.

WALL END

farm road

Dungeon Ghyll

Old Hotel

ASCENT FROM DUNGEON GHYLL

The upper section,
looking west

BB : Bowfell Buttress
CC : Cambridge Crag
FC : Flat Crag

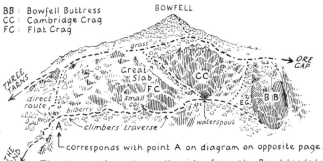

BOWFELL

└ corresponds with point A on diagram on opposite page.

The stony path coming up the ridge from the Band leads to, and is continued as, the climbers' traverse. Ten yards below the point where the horizontal traverse commences the direct route wiggles away up to the left and may be passed unnoticed.

The climbers' traverse is a very enjoyable high-level route leading to excellent rock-scenery. Two recent minor rockfalls have slightly disturbed the path but it is quite distinct and perfectly easy, with a very little mild scrambling, hardly worth mentioning. The traverse is a series of little ups and downs, but generally keeps to a horizontal course. Except at the small col the ground falls away steeply on the valley side of the path.
The best way off the traverse to the summit lies up the fringe of a 'river' of boulders along the south side of Cambridge Crag, or, more tediously, the wide scree gully between Cambridge Crag and Bowfell Buttress may be ascended. (Cambridge Crag is identifiable, beyond all doubt, by the waterspout gushing from the base of the cliff – and nothing better ever came out of a barrel or a bottle).

The climbers' traverse

The striations of Flat Crags are of particular interest, even to non-geologists. Note how the angle of tilt is repeated in the slope of the Great Slab.

ASCENT FROM WASDALE

Although Bowfell is well hidden from Wasdale Head it is not too distant to be climbed from there in comfortable time, but the walk has the disadvantage (for those who object to re-tracing footsteps) that very little variation of route is possible on the return journey to Wasdale Head. Esk Pike stands in the way and must be climbed first (and traversed later).
For a diagram of the ascent of Esk Pike from Wasdale Head see Esk Pike 8

ASCENT FROM MICKLEDEN
2500 feet of ascent : 1¼ miles from the sheepfold

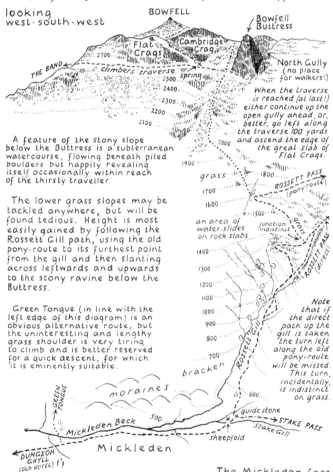

looking west-south-west

BOWFELL

Bowfell Buttress

Flat Crags

Cambridge Crag

THE BAND

climbers traverse — 2700 — 2500 — spring

2400 — 2300 — 2200 — 2100 — 2000 — 1900

North Gully (no place for walkers!)

When the traverse is reached (at last!) either continue up the open gully ahead, or, better, go left along the traverse 100 yards and ascend the edge of the great slab of Flat Crags.

A feature of the stony slope below the Buttress is a subterranean watercourse, flowing beneath piled boulders but happily revealing itself occasionally within reach of the thirsty traveller.

The lower grass slopes may be tackled anywhere, but will be found tedious. Height is most easily gained by following the Rossett Gill path, using the old pony-route to its furthest point from the gill and then slanting across leftwards and upwards to the stony ravine below the Buttress.

Green Tongue (in line with the left edge of this diagram) is an obvious alternative route, but the uninteresting and lengthy grass shoulder is very tiring to climb and is better reserved for a quick descent, for which it is eminently suitable.

grass — 1800 — ROSSETT PASS (pony route)

1700 — 1600 — 1500 — junction indistinct — grass

an area of water-slides on rock slabs

1400 — 1300 — 1200 — 1100 — 1000 — 900 — 800 — 700

ROSSETT PASS (direct)

Rossett Gill

bracken

Note that if the direct path up the gill is taken the turn left along the old pony-route will be missed. This turn, incidentally, is indistinct on grass.

GREEN TONGUE

moraines

500

600

guide stone

Mickleden Beck

sheepfold

STAKE PASS

Stake Gill

Mickleden

DUNGEON GHYLL (OLD HOTEL) 1⅓

The Mickleden face, 2500 feet of continuous ascent, is a route for scramblers rather than walkers. The rock-scenery becomes imposing as height is gained, Bowfell Buttress in particular being an impressive object when seen at close quarters.

ASCENT FROM ESKDALE
2900 feet of ascent : 7½ miles from Boot

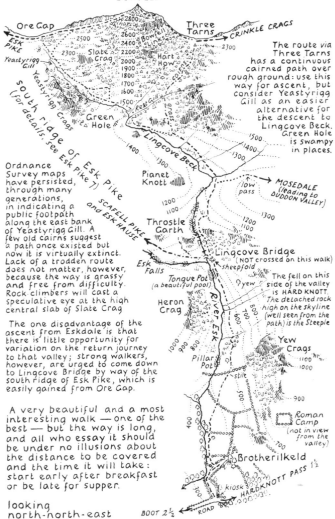

BOWFELL

The route via Three Tarns has a continuous cairned path over rough ground: use this way for ascent, but consider Yeastyrigg Gill as an easier alternative for the descent to Lingcove Beck. Green Hole is swampy in places.

Ordnance Survey maps have persisted, through many generations, in indicating a public footpath along the east bank of Yeastyrigg Gill. A few old cairns suggest a path once existed but now it is virtually extinct. Lack of a trodden route does not matter, however, because the way is grassy and free from difficulty. Rock-climbers will cast a speculative eye at the high central slab of Slate Crag

The one disadvantage of the ascent from Eskdale is that there is little opportunity for variation on the return journey to that valley; strong walkers, however, are urged to come down to Lingcove Bridge by way of the south ridge of Esk Pike, which is easily gained from Ore Gap.

A very beautiful and a most interesting walk — one of the best — but the way is long, and all who essay it should be under no illusions about the distance to be covered and the time it will take: start early after breakfast or be late for supper.

looking north-north-east

MOSEDALE (leading to DUDDON VALLEY)

The fell on this side of the valley is HARD KNOTT. The detached rock high on the skyline (well seen from the path) is the Steeple

Roman Camp (not in view from the valley)

Brotherilkeld

HARDKNOTT PASS 1½

kiosk

BOOT 2½   ROAD

ASCENT FROM STONETHWAITE
2650 feet of ascent : 6½ miles

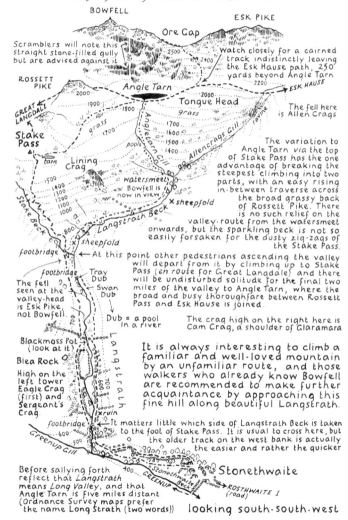

BOWFELL

ESK PIKE

Ore Gap

Scramblers will note this straight stone-filled gully but are advised against it

Watch closely for a cairned track indistinctly leaving the Esk Hause path, 250 yards beyond Angle Tarn

ROSSETT PIKE

Angle Tarn

ESK HAUSE

GREAT LANGDALE

Tongue Head

The fell here is Allen Crags

Stake Pass

Lining Crag

grass

watersmeet

Bowfell is now in view

× sheepfold

The variation to Angle Tarn *via* the top of Stake Pass has the one advantage of breaking the steepest climbing into two parts, with an easy rising in-between traverse across the broad grassy back of Rossett Pike. There is no such relief on the valley-route from the watersmeet onwards, but the sparkling beck is not so easily forsaken for the dusty zig-zags of the Stake Pass.

× sheepfold

footbridge

Langstrath Beck

At this point other pedestrians ascending the valley will depart from it by climbing up to Stake Pass (en route for Great Langdale) and there will be undisturbed solitude for the final two miles of the valley to Angle Tarn, where the broad and busy thoroughfare between Rossett Pass and Esk Hause is joined.

footbridge

Tray Dub

Swan Dub

The fell seen at the valley-head is Esk Pike, not Bowfell.

Dub = a pool in a river

The crag high on the right here is Cam Crag, a shoulder of Glaramara

Blackmoss Pot (look at it)

Blea Rock

High on the left tower Eagle Crag (first) and Sergeant's Crag

It is always interesting to climb a familiar and well-loved mountain by an unfamiliar route, and those walkers who already know Bowfell are recommended to make further acquaintance by approaching this fine hill along beautiful Langstrath.

× ruin

footbridge

Greenup Gill

It matters little which side of Langstrath Beck is taken to the foot of Stake Pass. It is usual to cross here, but the older track on the west bank is actually the easier and rather the quicker

Stonethwaite

ROSTHWAITE 1 (road)

Before sallying forth reflect that *Langstrath* means *Long Valley,* and that Angle Tarn is five miles distant (Ordnance Survey maps prefer the name Long Strath (two words))

GREENUP

looking south-south-west

Cambridge Crag and Bowfell Buttress
from the top of the Great Slab

THE SUMMIT

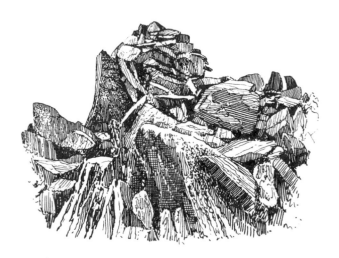

Bowfell's top is a shattered pyramid, a great heap of stones and boulders and naked rock, a giant cairn in itself.

The rugged summit provides poor picking for the Bowfell sheep, who draw the line at mosses and lichens and look elsewhere for their mountain greenery, and reserves its best rewards for the walkers who climb the natural rocky stairway to its upper limit for here, spread before them for their delectation, is a glorious panorama, which, moreover, may be surveyed and appreciated from positions of repose on the comfortable flat seats of stone (comfortable in the sense that everybody arriving here says how nice it is to sit down) with which the summit is liberally equipped. The leisurely contemplation of the scene will not be assailed by doubts as to whether the highest point has in fact been gained for rough slopes tumble away steeply on all sides.

The top pyramid stands on a sloping plinth which, to the east, extends beyond the base of the pyramid and forms a shelf or terrace where stones are less in evidence. It is from this shelf that Bowfell's main crags fall away, and from which, with care, they may be viewed; care is necessary because the boulders to be negotiated in carrying out this inspection are in a state of balance, in places, and liable to heel over and trap a leg.

It is possible, and does happen, that walkers ascend Bowfell and traverse its top quite unaware of the imposing line of crags overlooking Mickleden: from the summit and the shelf-track there is little to indicate the presence of steep cliffs.   But to miss seeing the crags is to miss seeing half the glory of Bowfell.

THE SUMMIT

continued

KEY:

		for ROCK CLIMBERS	for WALKERS
NG :	North Gully	✓	-
BB :	Bowfell Buttress	✓	-
EG :	Easy Gully (scree)	✓	✓
CC :	Cambridge Crag	✓	-
WS :	Waterspout	✓✓	✓✓
RB :	River of Boulders	✓	-
FC :	Flat Crags	✓	-
GS :	do Great Slab	✓	-
CT :	Climbers' Traverse	✓	-
WR :	Walkers' Route to avoid Traverse		✓
BL :	Bowfell Links	✓	-
▲	Summit		✓✓

PLAN OF
THE SUMMIT

YARDS
0   100   200

DESCENTS : The sloping grass shelf, east of the actual summit, carries the only path across the top: it links Ore Gap with Three Tarns. Two well-scratched tracks go down from the cairn and join this path : one, on the south, descends first in line with Three Tarns but is turned leftwards by the uncompromising rim of Bowfell Links ; the other, shorter, goes down north inclining north-east with many simple variations among the boulders. For Langdale the steep lower section of the Three Tarns path may be avoided by using a terrace on the left at a gap in the wall of rocks (WR on the plan above). Direct descents to Eskdale over the steepening boulder slopes are not feasible.

In mist, the only safe objectives are Ore Gap (for Wasdale, Borrowdale or Eskdale) and Three Tarns (for Langdale *via* the Band, or Eskdale) avoiding Bowfell Links on the way thereto.

The Great Slab of Flat Crags

RIDGE ROUTES

To CRINKLE CRAGS, 2816' : 1½ miles
SE, E, SE and then generally S
Main depression (Three Tarns) at 2320'
600 feet of ascent
A rough ridge walk of high quality

A bee-line for Three Tarns runs foul of Bowfell
Links, and the summit notes should be consulted
for getting down to the gap. From there onwards
the gradual climb to Crinkle Crags, with its many
turns and twists and ups and downs is entirely
delightful, *but not in mist*. (See Crinkle Crags 13)

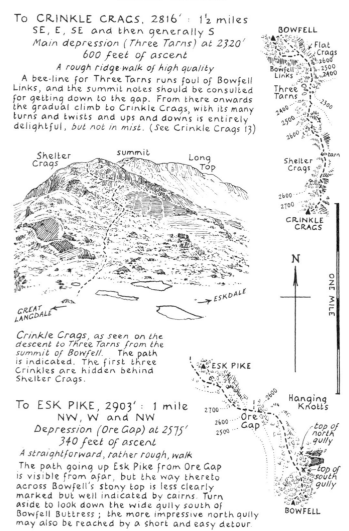

*Crinkle Crags, as seen on the
descent to Three Tarns from the
summit of Bowfell. The path
is indicated. The first three
Crinkles are hidden behind
Shelter Crags.*

To ESK PIKE, 2903' : 1 mile
NW, W and NW
Depression (Ore Gap) at 2575'
340 feet of ascent
A straightforward, rather rough, walk

The path going up Esk Pike from Ore Gap
is visible from afar, but the way thereto
across Bowfell's stony top is less clearly
marked but well indicated by cairns. Turn
aside to look down the wide gully south of
Bowfell Buttress ; the more impressive north gully
may also be reached by a short and easy detour.

*Three views
from the Band*

Right:
Browney Gill and Cold Pike

Bottom Right:
Pike o' Blisco

Below:
Pike o' Stickle

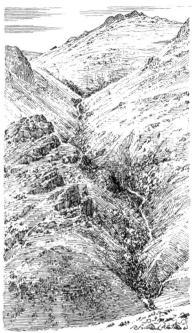

THE VIEW

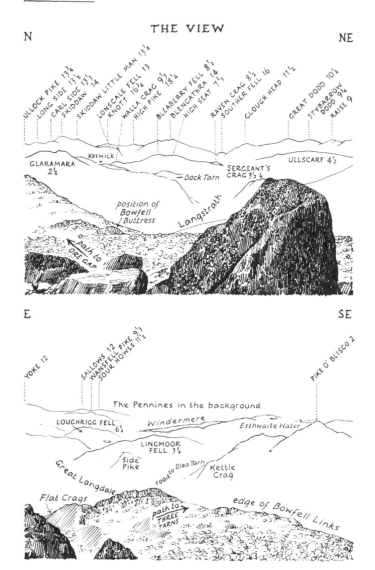

N   NE

ULLOCK PIKE 13¾
LONG SIDE 13¼
CARL SIDE 13½
SKIDDAW 14
SKIDDAW LITTLE MAN 13¼
LONSCALE FELL 13
KNOTT 16¼
WALLA CRAG 9½
HIGH PIKE 18¼
BLEABERRY FELL 8½
BLENCATHRA 14
HIGH SEAT 7½
RAVEN CRAG 8½
SOUTHER FELL 16
CLOUGH HEAD 11½
GREAT DODD 10½
STYBARROW DODD 9¼
RAISE 9

Keswick

GLARAMARA 2½

Dock Tarn

SERGEANT'S CRAG 3½

ULLSCARF 4½

position of Bowfell Buttress

Langstrath

path to ORE GAP

E   SE

YOKE 12
SALLOWS 12
WANSFELL PIKE 9½
SOUR HOWES 11½
PIKE O' BLISCO 2

The Pennines in the background

LOUGHRIGG FELL 6½

Windermere

Esthwaite Water

LINGMOOR FELL 3¾

Side Pike

Great Langdale

road to Blea Tarn

Kettle Crag

Flat Crags

path to THREE TARNS

edge of Bowfell Links

THE VIEW

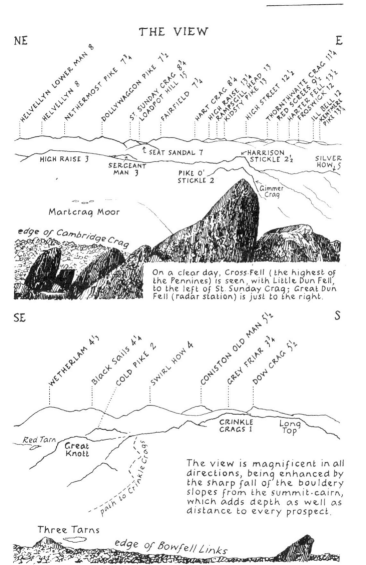

NE

HELVELLYN LOWER MAN 8
HELVELLYN 8
NETHERMOST PIKE 7¾
DOLLYWAGGON PIKE 7½
ST. SUNDAY CRAG 8¾
LOADPOT HILL 15
FAIRFIELD 7¾
HART CRAG 8¼
HIGH RAISE 13¼
RAMPSGILL HEAD 13
KIDSTY PIKE 13
HIGH STREET 12½
THORNTHWAITE CRAG 11¼
RED SCREES 9½
HARTER FELL 13½
FROSWICK 12
ILL BELL 12
KENTMERE PIKE 13¼

E

HIGH RAISE 3
SEAT SANDAL 7
SERGEANT MAN 3
PIKE O' STICKLE 2
HARRISON STICKLE 2½
SILVER HOW 5

Martcrag Moor

Gimmer Crag

edge of Cambridge Crag

On a clear day, Cross-Fell (the highest of the Pennines) is seen, with Little Dun Fell, to the left of St. Sunday Crag; Great Dun Fell (radar station) is just to the right.

SE

WETHERLAM 4½
Black Sails 4¼
COLD PIKE 2
SWIRL HOW 4
CONISTON OLD MAN 5½
GREY FRIAR 3¾
DOW CRAG 5½

S

Red Tarn
Great Knott
CRINKLE CRAGS 1
Long Top

path to Crinkle Crags

The view is magnificent in all directions, being enhanced by the sharp fall of the bouldery slopes from the summit-cairn, which adds depth as well as distance to every prospect.

Three Tarns
edge of Bowfell Links

THE VIEW

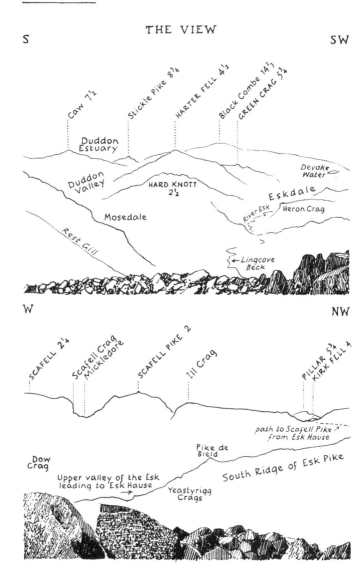

S   SW

Caw 7½
Stickle Pike 8¾
HARTER FELL 4½
Black Combe 14½
GREEN CRAG 5¾

Duddon Estuary

Duddon Valley

HARD KNOTT 2½

Devoke Water

Eskdale

Mosedale

River Esk   Heron Crag

Rest Gill

← Lingcove Beck

W   NW

SCAFELL 2¼
Scafell Crag
Mickledore
SCAFELL PIKE 2
Ill Crag
PILLAR 5¾
KIRK FELL 4

path to Scafell Pike
from Esk Hause →

Dow Crag

Pike de Bield

South Ridge of Esk Pike

Upper valley of the Esk
leading to Esk Hause

Yeastyrigg Crags

THE VIEW

SW

W

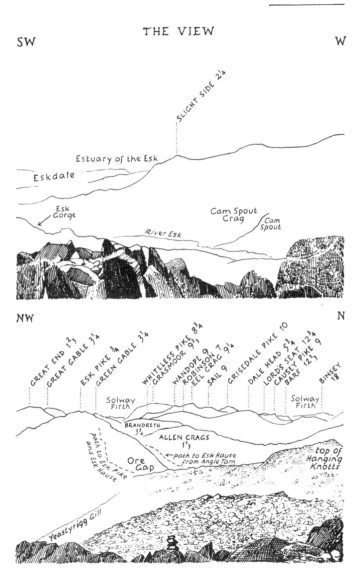

SLIGHT SIDE 24

Estuary of the Esk

Eskdale

Esk Gorge

Cam Spout Crag

Cam Spout

River Esk

NW

N

GREAT END 1²⁄₃
GREAT GABLE 3¼
ESK PIKE 2¾
GREEN GABLE 3¼
WHITELESS PIKE 8¾
GRASMOOR 9²⁄₃
WANDOPE 9
ROBINSON 7
EEL CRAG 9¼
SAIL 9
GRISEDALE PIKE 10
DALE HEAD 5³⁄₄
LORD'S SEAT 12³⁄₄
CAUSEY PIKE 9
BARF 12²⁄₃
BINSEY 18

Solway Firth

Solway Firth

BRANDRETH 3¾

ALLEN CRAGS 1¹⁄₃

path to Esk Pike and Esk Hause

← path to Esk Hause from Angle Tarn

top of Hanging Knotts

Ore Gap

Yeastyrigg Gill

10 | Crinkle Crags

Book Four: The Southern Fells

Wainwright always loved maps. As a boy, he drew them all the time, either copying them from school maps or creating his own, carefully colouring them in. As an adult, they were his favourite reading material. When he couldn't escape out on to the fells in the flesh, either through work or winter, he would sit by the fireside and study his maps, planning routes in his mind, imagining expeditions to come.

Recently, while poking around in a second-hand shop in Keswick, I came across a home-made map-case, about one foot long, like a large pencil case made out of plywood and hardboard, nailed together to make a flat, weatherproof little box. On the cover, the letters etched , using what could have been a red-hot poker, were the words 'A. Wainwright, 19 Castle Grove, Kendal'. The shopkeeper wasn't sure if it could have belonged to *the* Wainwright or another person with the same name. I said yes, that was where he lived in Kendal when he first moved to the Lake District. I sufficiently convinced him of its authenticity that he decided not to sell it after all, but to keep it in his own collection – curses.

I never knew that Wainwright had such a map-case, but I am convinced it was his, made to be taken out on the fells to carry all his various maps. I assume that, fairly battered by then, of no value, it had been left behind when the Wainwrights moved from Castle Grove and then chucked out by some later owner of the house. It is fairly primitive, clearly home-made, but of course in the 1940s and 1950s, you didn't get those fancy plastic map-holders which hang around your neck.

In drawing his own maps, for his Guides, he used the experience and knowledge of all the Lakeland cartographers who had gone before. His panoramas were fairly conventional, using well-established methods for portraying views from the summits, looking towards the horizon, pinpointing other mountains. It was in his ascents that he created his own cartographic systems. They are not strictly plan or elevation views. He deliberately distorted perspectives and scales in order to get in all the information he thought would be valuable for any walker.

Of the six ascents he gives for Crinkle Crags, all begin roughly from the flat, starting from a road or hotel, such as the Old Dungeon Ghyll Hotel, then proceeding right up to the summit. (The simplest ascent, saving a thousand feet of climbing, is from Wrynose Pass.) His routes twist and turn, so you get some idea of the twists and turns along the way. Tarns can lie flat or sideways. Sheepfolds, footbridges, seats, walls and, on some maps, individual trees figure prominently, even though in reality they are totally dwarfed by the mass of the mountain.

His ascent maps are representations, not accurate plans. Down on the road, at the beginning, you are usually looking at a plan, as if viewed from high above it, but the summit is seen as a front

Map case that belonged to 'A. Wainwright'

A sketch of Crinkle Crags from A Second Lakeland Sketchbook

elevation, as if you are looking at it from below or in front of it. He breaks many of the rules of cartography in his attempt to give a three-dimensional feel to a flat map. It does take beginners some time, and a few walks using Wainwright's maps, to pick up and understand his methods. But then it all makes sense. His maps are not just useful but illuminating.

Crinkle Crags is one of Wainwright's six best fells and he rated the traverse of the ridge as 'amongst the grandest mountain walks in Lakeland', one where 'strenuous effort will be recompensed by superlative views'. Other mountains might be climbed and forgotten but 'Crinkle Crags will always be remembered'.

Perhaps this is why he chose to do something unusual with the ridge walks – Crinkle Crags 11 and 13 – calling them here Ridge Plans rather than Ridge Routes, as elsewhere. In this case, he does show it as a plan, as if viewed from a space station above, but he does it twice, so you have the same route shown from opposite directions. Very handy. There is nothing more annoying than having to turn a map upside down, or stand on your head, because the map in your hand doesn't happen to follow the direction you are going.

Looking at the two versions of the same ridge walk, it appears to me as if he drew each separately, even though they contain the same features and much the same words. He was, therefore, giving himself twice the work. Today, a good home computer could have turned the first version round for him. But that would be no fun, no sport, no artistry. I like to think that would have mattered to Wainwright.

Crinkle Crags

2816'

from Pike o' Blisco

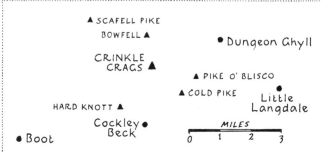

▲ SCAFELL PIKE

BOWFELL ▲

● Dungeon Ghyll

CRINKLE
CRAGS ▲

▲ PIKE O' BLISCO

▲ COLD PIKE

● Little
Langdale

HARD KNOTT ▲

Cockley ●
Beck

● Boot

MILES

0   1   2   3

NATURAL FEATURES

Some mountains are obviously named by reference to their physical characteristics. Crinkle Crags is one of these, and it was probably first so called by the dalesfolk of the valleys to the east and around the head of Windermere, whence its lofty serrated ridge, a succession of knobs and depressions, is aptly described by the name. These undulations, seeming trivial from a distance, are revealed at close range as steep buttresses and gullies above wild declivities, a scene of desolation and rugged grandeur equalled by few others in the district. Nor is the Eskdale flank any gentler, for here too are gaunt shattered crags rising from incredibly rough slopes. The high pass of Three Tarns links the ridge with Bowfell to the north while southwards Wrynose Bottom is the boundary.

Crinkle Crags is much too good to be missed. For the mountaineer who prefers his mountains rough, who likes to see steep craggy slopes towering before him into the sky, who enjoys an up-and-down ridge walk full of interesting nooks and corners, who has an appreciative eye for magnificent views, this is a climb deserving of high priority. But it is not a place to visit in bad weather for the top is confusing, with ins and outs as well as ups and downs and a sketchy path that cannot be relied on. Crinkle Crags merits respect, and should be treated with respect; then it will yield the climber a mountain walk long to be remembered with pleasure.

Is it 'Crinkle Crags IS ...' or 'Crinkle Crags ARE...'?
Is it 'Three Tarns IS ....' or 'Three Tarns ARE...'?
IS sounds right but looks wrong!

The outline of Crinkle Crags from Great Langdale

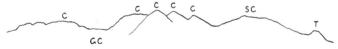

C : The five Crinkles   GC : Great Cove
T : Rock tower near Three Tarns   SC : Shelter Crags

The highest Crinkle (2816') is second from the left on the diagram. When seen from the valley it does not appear to be the highest, as it is set back a little from the line of the others.

MAP

continuation BOWFELL 3

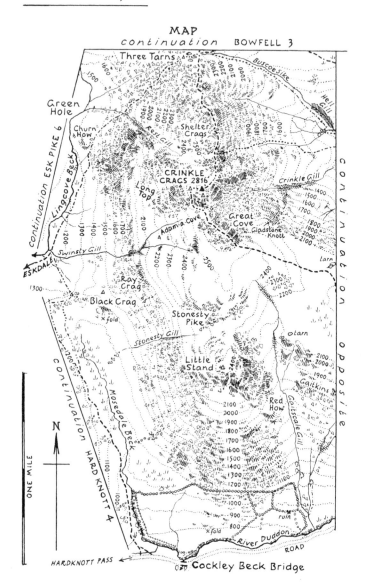

continuation ESK PIKE 6

continuation opposite

continuation HARD KNOTT 4

Three Tarns

Green Hole

Churn How

Shelter Crags

CRINKLE CRAGS 2816

Long Top

Buscoe Sike

Crinkle Gill

Great Cove

Gladstone Knott

Adam-a-Cove

ESKDALE

Swinsty Gill

tarn

Ray Crag

Black Crag

× fold

Stonesty Pike

Stonesty Gill

Little Stand

tarn

Red How

Gaitkins

Mosedale Beck

Gaitscale Gill

ruin

× fold

River Duddon

ROAD

HARDKNOTT PASS ←

Cockley Beck Bridge

ONE MILE

N

 ← 1500

 from Lingcove Beck

2500 Feet Gill

1300

MAP

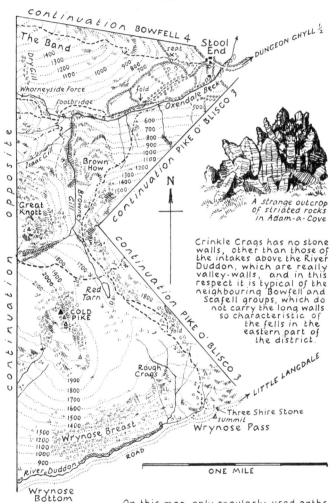

continuation BOWFELL 4

The Band

Dry Gill

1400
1300
1200
1100
1000
900
800

seat

Stool End

DUNGEON GHYLL ½

Whorneyside Force

footbridge

fold

Oxendale Beck

500

600
700
800
900
1000
1100
1200
1300
1400
1500

Isaac Gill

Brown How

Browney Gill

continuation PIKE O' BLISCO 3

N

Great Knott

continuation opposite

1800
1900
2000
2100

Red Tarn

COLD PIKE

1700

1800

continuation PIKE O' BLISCO 3

fold

Rough Crags

LITTLE LANGDALE

Three Shire Stone
summit
Wrynose Pass

1900
1800
1700
1600
1500
1400

Wrynose Breast

1300
1200
1100
1000
900

River Duddon

ROAD

Wrynose Bottom

ONE MILE

A strange outcrop of striated rocks in Adam-a-Cove

Crinkle Crags has no stone walls, other than those of the intakes above the River Duddon, which are really valley-walls, and in this respect it is typical of the neighbouring Bowfell and Scafell groups, which do not carry the long walls so characteristic of the fells in the eastern part of the district.

On this map, only regularly-used paths are shown. Other routes are suggested, with qualifications, on the diagrams of ascents.

ASCENT FROM DUNGEON GHYLL (via RED TARN)
2600 feet of ascent : 4 miles

As far as Red Tarn, the route is that used for the ascent of Pike o' Blisco (the craggy slopes of which tower up on the left throughout) and for the high-level walk to Wrynose Pass.

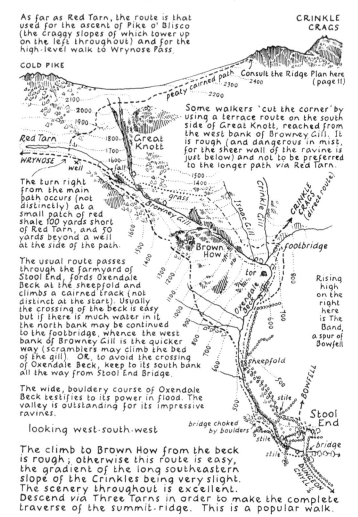

CRINKLE CRAGS

COLD PIKE

peaty cairned path

Consult the Ridge Plan here (page 11)

Some walkers 'cut the corner' by using a terrace route on the south side of Great Knott, reached from the west bank of Browney Gill. It is rough (and dangerous in mist, for the sheer wall of the ravine is just below) and not to be preferred to the longer path via Red Tarn.

Red Tarn

Great Knott

WRYNOSE   well   fall

The turn right from the main path occurs (not distinctly) at a small patch of red shale 100 yards short of Red Tarn, and 50 yards beyond a well at the side of the path.

grass

Browney Gill

Isaac Gill

Crinkle Gill

CRINKLE CRAGS (direct route)

footbridge

Brown How

tor

Oxendale Beck

Rising high on the right here is The Band, a spur of Bowfell

The usual route passes through the farmyard of Stool End, fords Oxendale Beck at the sheepfold and climbs a cairned track (not distinct at the start). Usually the crossing of the beck is easy but if there is much water in it the north bank may be continued to the footbridge, whence the west bank of Browney Gill is the quicker way (scramblers may climb the bed of the gill). OR, to avoid the crossing of Oxendale Beck, keep to its south bank all the way from Stool End Bridge.

sheepfold

BOWFELL

The wide, bouldery course of Oxendale Beck testifies to its power in flood. The valley is outstanding for its impressive ravines.

looking west-south-west

stile

bridge choked by boulders

stile

stile

Stool End

bridge

DUNGEON GHYLL

The climb to Brown How from the beck is rough; otherwise this route is easy, the gradient of the long southeastern slope of the Crinkles being very slight. The scenery throughout is excellent. Descend via Three Tarns in order to make the complete traverse of the summit-ridge. This is a popular walk.

ASCENT FROM DUNGEON GHYLL (via THREE TARNS)
2650 feet of ascent : 4 miles

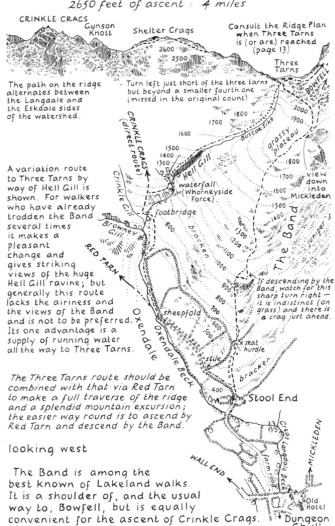

CRINKLE CRAGS
Gunson Knott
Shelter Crags

Consult the Ridge Plan when Three Tarns is (or are) reached (page 13)

Three Tarns

2600
2500

The path on the ridge alternates between the Langdale and the Eskdale sides of the watershed.

Turn left just short of the three tarns but beyond a smaller fourth one (missed in the original count)

BOWFELL

2000
1900
1800

grassy plateau

CRINKLE CRAGS (direct route)

1800
1700
1600

Buscoe Sike

view down into Mickleden

1500
1400
1300

Hell Gill

1700
1600
1500
1400

A variation route to Three Tarns by way of Hell Gill is shown. For walkers who have already trodden the Band several times it makes a pleasant change and gives striking views of the huge Hell Gill ravine; but generally this route lacks the airiness and the views of the Band and is not to be preferred. Its one advantage is a supply of running water all the way to Three Tarns.

Crinkle Gill

waterfall (Whorneyside Force)

footbridge

Browney Gill

800

bracken

1300
1200
1100
1000

juniper

The Band

RED TARN

900

If descending by the Band, watch for this sharp turn right — it is indistinct (on grass) and there is a crag just ahead.

800

700

sheepfold

Oxendale

Oxendale Beck

600
500

seat
hurdle

400

stile

bracken

The Three Tarns route should be combined with that via Red Tarn to make a full traverse of the ridge and a splendid mountain excursion; the easier way round is to ascend by Red Tarn and descend by the Band.

Stool End

looking west

Great Langdale Beck

farm road

MICKLEDEN

The Band is among the best known of Lakeland walks. It is a shoulder of, and the usual way to, Bowfell, but is equally convenient for the ascent of Crinkle Crags.

WALL END

Old Hotel

Dungeon Ghyll

ASCENT FROM DUNGEON GHYLL
(DIRECT CLIMB FROM OXENDALE)
2550 feet of ascent : 3½ miles

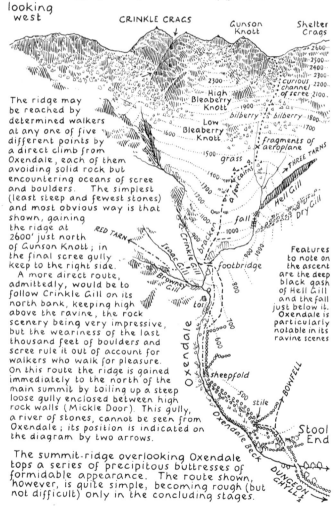

looking west

CRINKLE CRAGS

Gunson Knott

Shelter Crags

2600
2500
2400
2300
2200
2100
curious channel of scree

2300

High Bleaberry Knott — 1900

bilberry   bilberry   1800

Low Bleaberry Knott   1700

1600

fragments of aeroplane

1500   grass

THREE TARNS

1400   a few cairns

1300   Hell Gill

1200   Dry Gill

1100   bracken   fall

1000

RED TARN

900   900   1000

fall

Isaac Gill   Crinkle Gill

Browney Gill

footbridge

tor   800

700

Oxendale   600

500   sheepfold

BOWFELL

stile

Oxendale Beck

Stool End

DUNGEON GHYLL

The ridge may be reached by determined walkers at any one of five different points by a direct climb from Oxendale, each of them avoiding solid rock but encountering oceans of scree and boulders. The simplest (least steep and fewest stones) and most obvious way is that shown, gaining the ridge at 2600' just north of Gunson Knott; in the final scree gully keep to the right side.

A more direct route, admittedly, would be to follow Crinkle Gill on its north bank, keeping high above the ravine, the rock scenery being very impressive, but the weariness of the last thousand feet of boulders and scree rule it out of account for walkers who walk for pleasure. On this route the ridge is gained immediately to the north of the main summit by toiling up a steep loose gully enclosed between high rock walls (Mickle Door). This gully, a river of stones, cannot be seen from Oxendale; its position is indicated on the diagram by two arrows.

Features to note on the ascent are the deep black gash of Hell Gill and the fall just below it. Oxendale is particularly notable in its ravine scenes.

The summit-ridge overlooking Oxendale tops a series of precipitous buttresses of formidable appearance. The route shown, however, is quite simple, becoming rough (but not difficult) only in the concluding stages.

ASCENT FROM ESKDALE
2650 feet of ascent : 7½ miles from Boot
(8 miles via Three Tarns)

CRINKLE CRAGS

Shelter Crags

Three Tarns

BOWFELL CAIRNS

2400
2500
2300

Rest Gill

Long Top

spring

Adam-a-Cove

2500
2400
2300
2200
2100

1900
1800
1700

bristly rocks

grass

2000

Ray Crag

Green Hole

1500
1600
1700

Swinsty Gill

grass

1800

1400

1300

grass

★ In Adam-a-Cove an uncharacteristic outcrop of striated rocks is marked by two cairns.

Rest Gill is identifiable by its very bouldery bed.

Lingcove Beck

1300

low pass

MOSEDALE (for the DUDDON VALLEY)

1300

SCAFELL PIKE and ESK HAUSE

Throstle Garth

Esk Falls

1200

1300

Lingcove Bridge (which is NOT crossed on this walk)

sheepfold

yew

The fell on this side of the valley is HARD KNOTT. The detached rock high on the skyline is the Steeple.

Tongue Pot

Heron Crag

1000

900

River Esk

1100

1200

Yew Crags

Roman Camp

Pillar Pot

900

1000

stile

700

Brotherilkeld

- A study of the map suggests Long Top, the western shoulder of the highest Crinkle, as an obvious approach to the summit from Eskdale, but the wild appearance of its lower crags makes it a less inviting proposition when seen 'in the flesh'. Nevertheless the cliff can be by-passed by a bouldery scramble up the bilberry slope alongside Rest Gill, and a series of stony rises then leads to the top; this is a rough but interesting route, suitable only in fine weather.

- The usual route proceeds to Three Tarns and then follows the ridge, so taking the fullest advantage of paths. The section between Rest Gill and Three Tarns is rough, but most ingeniously and delightfully cairned.

- The easiest route follows Swinsty Gill up into Adam-a-Cove. This is everywhere grassy — a surprising weakness in the armour of the Crinkles — and it is just possible to come within a few feet of the summit cairn without handling rock or treading on stones.

400

300

kiosk
HARDKNOTT PASS 1½

BOOT 2½

ROAD

looking north-east

ASCENT FROM COCKLEY BECK BRIDGE
2350 feet of ascent : 3 miles

CRINKLE CRAGS

Long Top
2700
2500
2700
RED TARN

tarns
grass

If desired, the first Crinkle may be by-passed by skirting its base, but it is better to traverse it by joining the path coming from Red Tarn.

On a hot day, when copious supplies of water are considered essential to survival, there is much to be said, as an alternative to the south ridge, in favour of following Gaitscale Gill to its source. There are no difficulties on either bank and the rock scenery is very good

Stonesty Pike

2400
2300
2200
2100

south ridge

This grassy depression (¼ mile beyond the cairn on Little Stand) is the only place where the ridge can be left, if necessary, without encountering crags.

Little Stand
tarns

1800
1700
1600
1500

Red How

Gaitscale Gill

Strictly, the top of the south ridge (here shown as Little Stand) has no official name. The name 'Red How' is often applied to this part of the fell.

grass shelf
2000

1900
1800
1700
1600
1500
1400
1300
1200
1100
1000
900
800

Mosedale

LINGCOVE BECK

1700
1200
1100

landslip
bracken

sheepfold

big boulder

1000

The approach to the south ridge above the intake wall is very rough and bouldery, but it is just possible to thread a way through the stones, keeping to the grass. This should be done; some of the boulders are unstable

1000
900

Mosedale Beck

WRYNOSE PASS 1½

HARDKNOTT PASS 1

ROAD
R. Duddon
ROAD

Cockley Beck Bridge

700

looking north

DUDDON VALLEY

The scenery of the south ridge is good, with crags and outcrops in abundance, but the approach is fatiguing. This route should not be attempted in bad weather: there is no path to, or on, the ridge, which has escarpments on both flanks.

ASCENT FROM WRYNOSE PASS
1650 feet of ascent : 2¼ miles

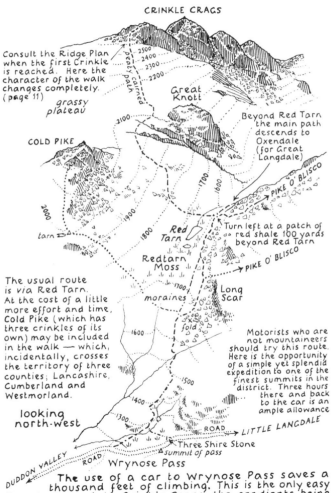

CRINKLE CRAGS

Consult the Ridge Plan when the first Crinkle is reached. Here the character of the walk changes completely. (page 11)

grassy plateau

peaty cairned path

2500
2400
2300
2200

Great Knott

Beyond Red Tarn the main path descends to Oxendale (for Great Langdale)

COLD PIKE

2100

2000

tarn

1900

1800

1700

1600

PIKE O' BLISCO

Turn left at a patch of red shale 100 yards beyond Red Tarn

Red Tarn

Redtarn Moss

PIKE O' BLISCO

Long Scar

The usual route is via Red Tarn. At the cost of a little more effort and time, Cold Pike (which has three crinkles of its own) may be included in the walk — which, incidentally, crosses the territory of three counties; Lancashire, Cumberland and Westmorland.

moraines

1100

fold

Motorists who are not mountaineers should try this route. Here is the opportunity of a simple yet splendid expedition to one of the finest summits in the district. Three hours there and back to the car is an ample allowance

1600

1500

looking north-west

1400

1300

ROAD

LITTLE LANGDALE

Three Shire Stone summit of pass

DUDDON VALLEY

ROAD

Wrynose Pass

The use of a car to Wrynose Pass saves a thousand feet of climbing. This is the only easy line of approach to Crinkle Crags, the gradients being gentle and the walking pleasant throughout.

RIDGE PLAN
for use when traversing the ridge from SOUTH to NORTH

- Read upwards from the bottom

All heights ending in 0 are approximate and unofficial

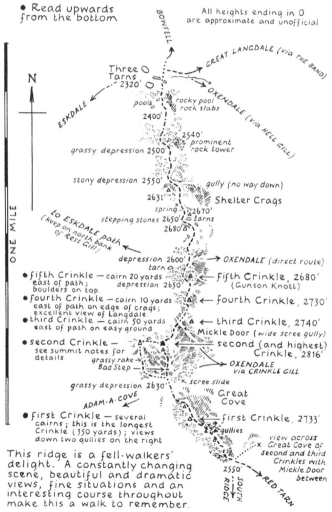

BOWFELL

Three Tarns 2320'

GREAT LANGDALE (VIA THE BAND)

N

ESKDALE

pools

rocky pool rock slabs

OXENDALE (VIA HELL GILL)

2400'

2540' prominent rock tower

grassy depression 2500'

stony depression 2550'

gully (no way down)

Shelter Crags

2631'

spring 2670'

stepping stones 2650' tarns

ONE MILE

to ESKDALE path (keep on north bank of Rest Gill)

2680'

depression 2600' tarn

OXENDALE (direct route)

- fifth Crinkle — cairn 20 yards east of path; boulders on top.

depression 2650'

fifth Crinkle, 2680' (Gunson Knott)

- fourth Crinkle — cairn 10 yards east of path on edge of crags; excellent view of Langdale.

fourth Crinkle, 2730'

- third Crinkle — cairn 50 yards east of path on easy ground.

third Crinkle, 2740' Mickle Door (wide scree gully)

- second Crinkle — see summit notes for details

second (and highest) Crinkle, 2816'

grassy rake Bad Step

OXENDALE via CRINKLE GILL

grassy depression 2630'

scree slide

Great Cove

ADAM·A·COVE

- first Crinkle — several cairns; this is the longest Crinkle (350 yards); views down two gullies on the right

first Crinkle, 2733'

gullies

view across Great Cove of second and third Crinkles with Mickle Door between

2550' SOUTH RIDGE

RED TARN

This ridge is a fell-walkers' delight. A constantly changing scene, beautiful and dramatic views, fine situations and an interesting course throughout make this a walk to remember.

Looking NORTH along the ridge ....

The second (and highest)
Crinkle, Mickle Door,
and the third Crinkle,
seen across Great Cove

The fourth and fifth
Crinkles (Shelter Crags
and Bowfell behind), seen
from the third Crinkle

RIDGE PLAN
for use when traversing the ridge from NORTH to SOUTH

● **Read upwards from the bottom**

This is, of course, the same plan as that already given for the south-to-north traverse but reversed for easier reference. Reading upwards, left and right on the plan will agree with left and right as they appear to the walker.

All heights ending in 0 are approximate and unofficial.

RED TARN

SOUTH RIDGE

2550'

viewpoint x (fourth and third Crinkles, with Mickle Door between)

gullies

Great Cove

← **fifth Crinkle, 2733'** — the longest Crinkle; several cairns along its top

grassy depression 2630' → ADAM-A-COVE

Bad Step   grassy rake

OXENDALE via CRINKLE GILL

← **fourth Crinkle** — see summit notes for details

fourth (and highest) Crinkle
Mickle Door (wide scree gully)   2816'

third Crinkle, 2740' →   ● **third Crinkle** — cairn 50 yards east of path on easy ground

second Crinkle, 2730' →   ● **second Crinkle** — cairn on edge of crags 10 yards east of path; excellent view of Langdale

2650'

first Crinkle, 2680' (Gunson Knott)   tarn   ● **first Crinkle** — cairn 20 yards east of path; boulders (shelter) on top

OXENDALE (direct route) ←   2600'   easy route to ESKDALE path (keep on north bank of Rest Gill)

first four Crinkles came into sight   2680'

tarns   stepping stones
2670'   2650'
spring

Shelter Crags   △ 2631'
gully   2550' stony depression

2500' grassy depression

prominent rock tower 2540'   2400'

Some writers have greatly exaggerated the dangers of the ridge. Nowhere is it anything but a pleasantly rough walk — except for the Bad Step, which can be avoided. (Bowfell and Scafell Pike are rougher)

rock slabs
rocky pools   pools

ESKDALE

OXENDALE (via HELL GILL)   **Three Tarns 2320'**

GREAT LANGDALE (via THE BAND)   BOWFELL

Note that the arrow is upside-down, too.

HALF A MILE

N

Introducing Lakeland's best ridge-mile!

Looking SOUTH along the ridge ....

Four Crinkles come suddenly into view from the path as it rounds a corner of Shelter Crags

The fifth Crinkle as seen from the main Crinkle on the descent to the Bad Step

THE SUMMIT

← BOWFELL

There are five Crinkles (not counting Shelter Crags) and therefore five summits, each with its own summit-cairn. The highest is, however, so obviously the highest that the true top of the fell is not in doubt in clear visibility, and this is the Crinkle (the fourth from the north and second from the south) with which these notes are concerned. It is not the stoniest of the five, nor the greatest in girth, but, unlike the others, it extends a considerable distance as a lateral ridge (Long Top) descending westwards. On the actual summit are two principal cairns separated by 40 yards of easy ground; that to the north, standing on a rock platform, is slightly the more elevated. The eastern face descends in precipices from the easy grass terraces above it; there are crags running down steeply from the south cairn also, but in other directions the top terrain is not difficult although everywhere rough.

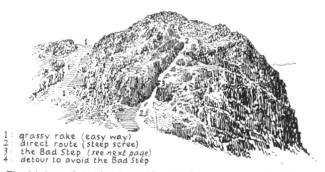

1 : grassy rake (easy way)
2 : direct route (steep scree)
3 : the Bad Step (see next page)
4 : detour to avoid the Bad Step

The highest Crinkle, from the south

continued

THE SUMMIT

continued

DESCENTS

to **GREAT LANGDALE** : The orthodox routes are (1) *via* Red Tarn and Brown How, and (2) *via* Three Tarns and the Band, both excellent walks, and in normal circumstances no other ways should be considered. If time is very short, however, or if it is necessary to escape quickly from stormy conditions on the ridge, quick and sheltered routes are provided by (3) the scree gully of Mickle Door or (4) the Gunson Knott gully, which is easier : both are very rough initially but lead to open slopes above Oxendale.

to **ESKDALE** : Much the easiest way, and much the quickest, is to descend from Adam-a-Cove (no path), keeping *left* of Swinsty Gill where it enters a ravine. Long Top is a temptation to be resisted, for it leads only to trouble.

to **COCKLEY BECK BRIDGE** : The south ridge is interesting (no path and not safe in mist), but tired limbs had better take advantage of the easy way down from Adam-a-Cove, inclining left below Ray Crag into Mosedale.

to **WRYNOSE PASS** : Reverse the route of ascent. Cold Pike may be traversed with little extra cost in energy.

In mist, take good care to keep to the ridge-path, which, in many places, is no more than nail-scratches on rocks and boulders but is generally simple to follow. Go nowhere unless there is evidence that many others have passed that way before. (The exception to this golden rule is Adam-a-Cove, which is perfectly safe *if it is remembered to keep to the left bank of the stream*).

The Bad Step

Caution is needed on the descent southwards from the summit. A walker crossing the top from the north will naturally gravitate to the south cairn and start his descent here. A steep path goes down rock ledges to a slope of loose scree, which spills over the lip of a chockstone (two, really) bridging and blocking a little gully. Anyone descending at speed here is asking for a nasty fall. The impasse is usually avoided and the gully regained below the chockstone by an awkward descent of the rock wall to the left, which deserves the name 'The Bad Step', for it is 10 feet high and as near vertical as makes no difference.   This is the sort of place that everybody would get down in a flash if a £5 note was waiting to be picked up on the scree below, but, without such an inducement, there is much wavering on the brink. Chicken-hearted walkers, muttering something about discretion being the better part of valour, will sneak away and circumvent the difficulty by following the author's footsteps around the left flank of the buttress forming the retaining wall of the gully, where grassy ledges enable the foot of the gully to be reached without trouble; here they may sit and watch, with ill-concealed grins, the discomfiture of other tourists who may come along.

The Bad Step is the most difficult obstacle met on any of the regular walkers' paths in Lakeland.

*The Bad Step
from below*

continued

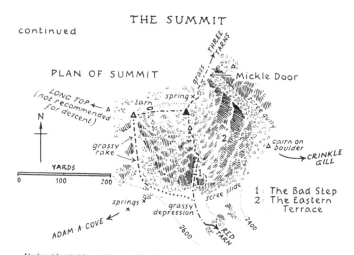

continued

THE SUMMIT

PLAN OF SUMMIT

LONG TOP → (not recommended for descent)

N

YARDS
0   100   200

THREE TARNS

Mickle Door

SCREE GULLY

2

cairn on boulder

CRINKLE GILL

1: The Bad Step
2: The Eastern Terrace

scree slide

grassy depression

springs ×

ADAM·A·COVE

2600

RED TARN

2400

Note that the steep direct descent from the south cairn may be by-passed altogether (it was formerly customary to do so) by proceeding west from the main cairn for 140 yards to another on grass in a slight depression, whence a grassy rake on the left goes down, skirting completely the rocks of the Crinkle, to join the direct route at its base.

The welcome spring on the summit (usually reliable after recent rain) is remarkable for its proximity to the top cairn (30 yards north-east, in the bend of the path); it is only 20 feet lower than the cairn, and has a very limited gathering-ground. Find it by listening for it — it emerges as a tiny waterfall from beneath a boulder. This is not the highest spring in the district but it is the nearest to a high summit.

The Eastern Terrace

A conspicuous grass terrace slants at an angle of 30° across the eastern cliffs of the main Crinkle, rising from the screes of the Mickle Door gully to the direct ridge-route just above the Bad Step. It is not seen from the ridge but appears in views of the east face clearly, being the middle of three such terraces and most prominent. It is of little use to walkers, except those who (in defiance of advice already given) are approaching the summit from Crinkle Gill: for them it offers

1: the Bad Step
2: the Eastern Terrace
3: Mickle Door
4: scree slide

cairn on boulder

The Eastern Face

a way of escape from the final screes. The terrace (identified by a little wall at the side of the gully) is wide and without difficulties but is no place for loitering, being subject to bombardments of stones by bloody fools, if any, on the summit above. It is well to remember, too, that the terrace is bounded by a precipice. At the upper end the terrace becomes more broken near the Bad Step and is not quite easy to locate when approached from this direction.

RIDGE ROUTES

To BOWFELL, 2960' : 1½ miles : Generally N, then WNW
Five depressions; final one (Three Tarns) at 2320': 850 feet of ascent
    Positively one of the finest ridge-walks in Lakeland.

The rough stony ground makes progress slow, but this walk is, in any case, deserving of a leisurely appreciation; it is much too good to be done in a hurry. Every turn of the fairly distinct track is interesting, and in places even exciting, although no difficulty is met except for an occasional awkward stride on rock.   In mist, the walker will probably have to descend to Three Tarns anyway, but should give Bowfell a miss, especially if the route is unfamiliar.

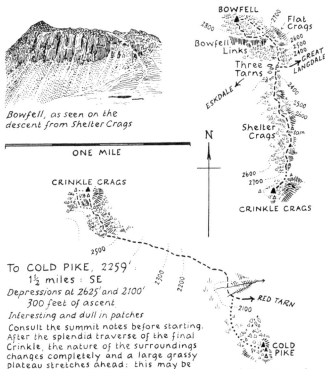

Bowfell, as seen on the descent from Shelter Crags

ONE MILE

N

To COLD PIKE, 2259':
    1½ miles : SE
Depressions at 2625' and 2100'
    300 feet of ascent
Interesting and dull in patches

Consult the summit notes before starting. After the splendid traverse of the final Crinkle, the nature of the surroundings changes completely and a large grassy plateau stretches ahead: this may be crossed in a beeline, but it is preferable, especially after rain, to keep to the Red Tarn path until a gentle slope, becoming craggy, leads easily to the attractive triple summit of Cold Pike.

THE VIEW

The view is not quite as comprehensive as might be expected, the western and north-western fells (with the exception of Eel Crag) being out of sight behind the bulky Scafell group and Bowfell, but is excellent nevertheless. Of special distinction is the supremely beautiful view of the valleys of the Duddon and the Esk winding down to the sea: from no other summit are they so well seen. There is a more dramatic but less attractive picture of Great Langdale, best seen from the edge of the eastern cliffs.

Intruding in the fine array of mountains and lakes and valleys and sea is a comparatively new feature — the cooling towers of the Calder Hall atomic power station, neatly framed in the dip of the skyline between Whin Rigg and Illgill Head, the two heights above Wastwater Screes. The summit of Crinkle Crags is ageless, the cooling towers are symbols of one particular age. Here, on this rugged mountain-top, is an everlasting permanence, something simple, and we can understand; but *there*, on the horizon, is something that is temporary, and complicated beyond our comprehension. Those modern structures, out of place in a landscape that is constant and unchanging, will vanish from the scene with the passing years. The mountains, nature's symbols of power and strength, will remain.

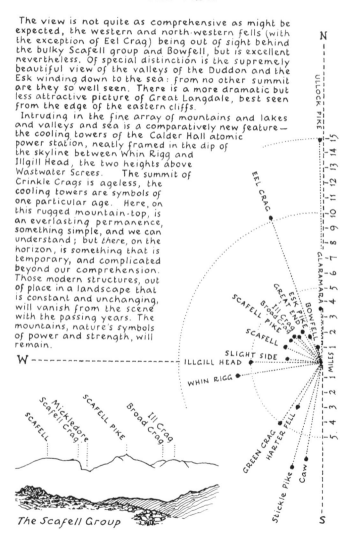

The Scafell Group

THE VIEW

Principal Fells

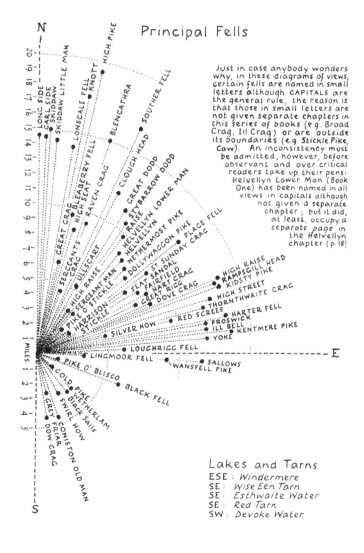

Just in case anybody wonders why, in these diagrams of views, certain fells are named in small letters although CAPITALS are the general rule, the reason is that those in small letters are not given separate chapters in this series of books (e.g. Broad Crag, Ill Crag) or are outside its boundaries (e.g. Stickle Pike, Caw). An inconsistency must be admitted, however, before observant and over-critical readers take up their pens: Helvellyn Lower Man (Book One) has been named in all views in capitals although not given a separate chapter; but it did, at least, occupy a separate page in the Helvellyn chapter (p. 18)

Lakes and Tarns

ESE : *Windermere*
SE : *Wise Een Tarn*
SE : *Esthwaite Water*
SE : *Red Tarn*
SW : *Devoke Water*

11 | Scafell Pike

Book Four: The Southern Fells

In 1802, Samuel Taylor Coleridge, a keen Lakeland walker, climbed Scafell, on his own, without a guide, which was normal at the time. He took with him a portable ink horn and paper and on the top he wrote a letter to Sarah Hutchinson – a woman not his wife but Wordsworth's sister-in-law, whom he fancied. In it, he boasted, 'surely the first letter written from the top of Scafell'. Then he came straight down, scrambling over ridges, ignoring all the easy ways.

This is seen as the first-ever recorded climb of Scafell Pike (although he simply called it Scafell). In earlier years, it must have been climbed many times, but it is unlikely that any shepherds ever got round to committing their climb to paper.

People do boast about having climbed Scafell Pike. After all, it is England's highest mountain and one of Wainwright's top six. Climbing it is a full-day expedition: from Boot, in Eskdale, the best line of approach in Wainwright's view, he recommends allowing $4^1/_2$ hours up and $3^1/_2$ down. I took all my children up it when they were young, plus a nephew and niece, and I still get out the photographs and go, 'Ahh, remember that day?' It was a foolhardy climb, one Easter, since halfway up we ran into snow and got lost, even though we were carrying the Blessed Wainwright's detailed instructions. Despite the bad weather, there was a queue to get to the summit cairn. On the way down, the sun came out and we all swam in our underclothes in the marble waters at Stockley Bridge. Ahh, what a day.

Wainwright does a bit of joking in the thirty pages devoted to the Pike. On Scafell Pike 16, at the bottom, he says walkers may have some trouble with the route at this point, if not equipped with his book. Then he laughs off his boast by adding ADVT in brackets.

On Scafell Pike 11, he mentions the joys of camping out overnight in a bivouac, making it pretty clear that he personally has done it: 'Watch the rising sun flush Scafell Crag and change a black silhouette into a rosy-pink castle! (This doesn't always happen. Sometimes it never stops raining.)'

In 1955, at the time of Book One's publication, Wainwright wrote a question-and-answer article for the little magazine *Cumbria*, but it never got posted so it was never published at the time. However, it was found after he died and I used it in my biography. In the article, he describes bivouacking:

I would say that the most intense experiences have occurred during nights spent on the fells. Occasionally (not often, and only in Summer) I have bivouacked alone in high places; these occasions remain vivid in my memory! Nobody who has not done it can imagine the splendours of sunset and sunrise from the summits, the eerie stillness of the hours of darkness, the joy of being on the tops at dawn when the larks are rising. I recommend this to everyone who loves the fells, but I recommend company to all but guide-book writers.

Towards the end of his Scafell Pike pages, on Scafell Pike 24, he allows himself an unusual pause in his preoccupations with getting us up and down the mountain in order to sit back and reflect. He calls his 28 lines a Soliloquy. The actual handwriting is not quite as neat as usual, and appears a bit cramped towards the end, so perhaps it was a very late afterthought, but the sentiments are worth reading and nicely done. Except for one phrase which some modern editors might not allow. This is when he is writing about the other things a man could do instead of climbing mountains and mentions 'looking at girls in bikinis'.

Scafell Pike

3210'

the highest mountain in England

formerly 'The Pikes' or 'The Pikes of Scawfell';
'Scafell Pikes' on Ordnance Survey maps.

from Great Moss,
Upper Eskdale

Scafell Pike

Ill Crag

*from the gorge
of the Esk*

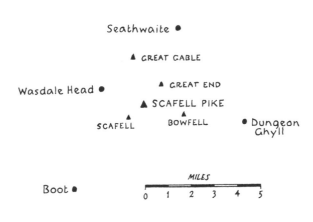

Seathwaite ●

▲ GREAT GABLE

▲ GREAT END

Wasdale Head ●

▲ SCAFELL PIKE

▲   ▲   ● Dungeon
SCAFELL   BOWFELL   Ghyll

MILES

0   1   2   3   4   5

Boot ●

Scafell Pike 3

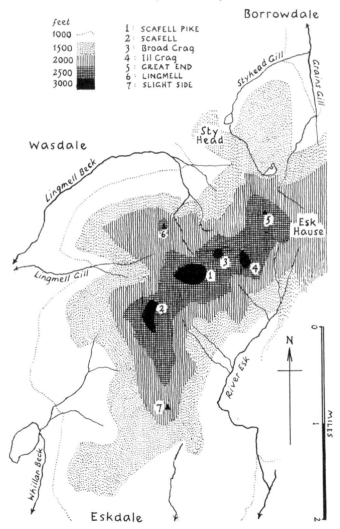

The Scafell Range

feet	
1000	
1500	
2000	
2500	
3000	

1 : SCAFELL PIKE
2 : SCAFELL
3 : Broad Crag
4 : Ill Crag
5 : GREAT END
6 : LINGMELL
7 : SLIGHT SIDE

Borrowdale

Wasdale

Sty Head

Styhead Gill

Grains Gill

Lingmell Beck

Lingmell Gill

Esk Hause

5

6

3

1

4

2

River Esk

7

N

Whillan Beck

Eskdale

0

1

2

MILES

Scafell Pike's grandest crag:
Dow Crag

Known to climbers as Esk Buttress, this 400-foot near-vertical crag rises from the fellside low down on the mountain's east flank, overlooking the River Esk.

Scafell Pike's best-known crag:
Pulpit Rock

This fine pinnacle (seen here from Mickledore) is the best feature of Pikes Crag, above Hollow Stones. Its top (easily reached from the summit-to-Mickledore path) is the best of all viewpoints for Scafell Crag.

NATURAL FEATURES

The difference between a hill and a mountain depends on *appearance*, not on *altitude* (whatever learned authorities may say to the contrary) and is thus arbitrary and a matter of personal opinion. Grass predominates on a hill, rock on a mountain. A hill is smooth, a mountain rough.   In the case of Scafell Pike, opinions must agree that here is a mountain without doubt, and a mountain that is, moreover, every inch a mountain.   Roughness and ruggedness are the necessary attributes, and the Pike has these in greater measure than other high ground in the country —— which is just as it should be, for there is no higher ground than this.

Strictly, the name 'Scafell Pike' should be in the plural, there being three principal summits above 3000 feet, the two lesser having the distinguishing titles of Broad Crag and Ill Crag. The main Pike is, however, pre-eminent, towering over the others seemingly to a greater extent than the mere 160 feet or so by which it has superiority in altitude, and in general being a bulkier mass altogether.

The three summits rise from the main spine of an elevated ridge which keeps above 2800 feet to its abrupt termination in the cliffs of Great End, facing north to Borrowdale; lower spurs then run down to that valley.   In the opposite direction, southwest, across the deep gulf of Mickledore, is the tremendous rock wall of the neighbouring and separate mountain of Scafell, which also exceeds 3000 feet: this is the parent mountain in the one sense that its name has been passed on to the Pikes. Scafell's summit-ridge runs south and broadens into foothills, descending ultimately to mid-Eskdale.

continued

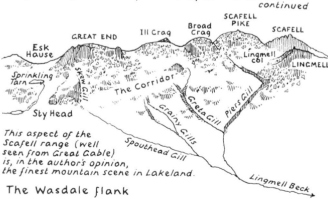

This aspect of the Scafell range (well seen from Great Gable) is, in the author's opinion, the finest mountain scene in Lakeland.

The Wasdale flank

NATURAL FEATURES

The flanks of the range are bounded on the west by Wasdale, and by the upper reaches of Eskdale, east. All the waters from the Pikes (and from Scafell) flow into one or other of these two valleys, ultimately to merge in the Ravenglass estuary. Thus it will be seen that Scafell Pike, despite a commanding presence, has not the same importance, geographically, as many other fells in the district. It does not stand at the head of any valley, but between valleys: it is not the hub of a wheel from which watercourses radiate; it is one of the spokes. It is inferior, in this respect, to Great Gable or Bowfell nearby, or even its own Great End.

Another interesting feature of Scafell Pike is that although it towers so mightily above Wasdale it can claim no footing in that valley, its territory tapering quickly to Brown Tongue, at the base of which it is nipped off by the widening lower slopes of Lingmell and Scafell.

Tarns are noticeably absent on the arid, stony surface of the mountain, but there is one sheet of water below the summit to the south, Broadcrag Tarn, which is small and unattractive but, at 2725 feet, can at least boast the highest standing water in Lakeland.

Crags are in evidence on all sides, and big areas of the upper slopes lie devastated by a covering of piled-up boulders, a result not of disintegration but of the volcanic upheavals that laid waste to the mountain during its formation. The landscape is harsh, even savage, and has attracted to itself nothing of romance or historical legend. There is no sentiment about Scafell Pike.

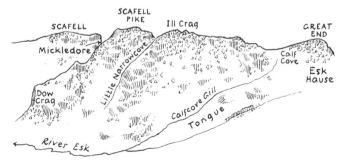

This view is as seen from the south ridge of Esk Pike

The Eskdale flank

MAP

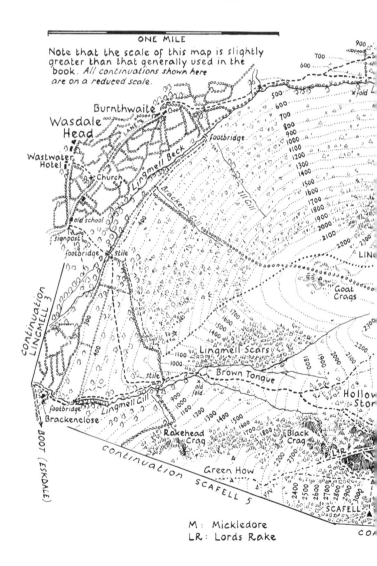

ONE MILE

Note that the scale of this map is slightly greater than that generally used in the book. All continuations shown here are on a reduced scale.

M : Mickledore
LR : Lords Rake

MAP

A: to BORROWDALE
B: to GREAT LANGDALE
C: to ESKDALE (via CAM SPOUT)

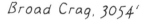

Broad Crag, 3054'

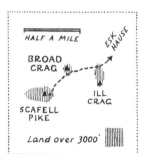

Broad Crag is the second of the Scafell Pikes, and a worthy mountain in itself — but it has little fame, is not commonly regarded as a separate fell, and its summit is rarely visited. This latter circumstance appears strange, because the blazed highway between Esk Hause and the main Pike not only climbs over the shoulder of Broad Crag but actually passes within a hundred yards of its summit, which is not greatly elevated above the path. Yet not one person in a thousand passing along here (and thousands do!) turns aside to visit the cairn. The reason for this neglect is more obvious when on the site than it is from a mere study of the map, for the whole of the top is littered deep with piled boulders across which it is quite impossible to walk with any semblance of dignity, the detour involving a desperate and inelegant scramble and the risk of breaking a leg at every stride. Most walkers using the path encounter enough trouble underfoot without seeking more in the virgin jungle of tumbled rock all around. Broad Crag is, in fact, the roughest summit in Lakeland.

The eastern slope descends into Little Narrowcove, and is of small consequence, but the western flank is imposing. On this side the top breaks away in a semi-circle of crags, below which is a shelf traversed by the Corridor Route and bounded lower down a steepening declivity by the great gash of Piers Gill.

Only the proximity of the main Scafell Pike, overtopping the scene, robs Broad Crag of its rightful place as one of the finest of fells.

Broad Crag, and Broad Crag col (right)
from the Corridor Route

Ill Crag, 3040'

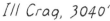

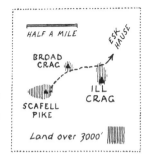

HALF A MILE

ESK HAUSE

BROAD CRAC

ILL CRAG

SCAFELL PIKE

Land over 3000'

Ill Crag is the third of the Scafell Pikes, and the most shapely, appearing as a graceful peak when viewed from upper Eskdale, which it dominates. Like Broad Crag, the summit lies off the path from Esk Hause to the main Pike but is more distant, although in this case too the shoulder of the fell is crossed at a height exceeding 3000', so that the summit is raised but little above it. The detour to the top is simple, only the final short rise being really rougher than the boulder-crossings on the path itself. Ill Crag is prominently seen from the vicinity of Esk Hause, and many wishful (and subsequently disappointed) walkers hereabouts, engaged on their first ascent of Scafell Pike will wrongly assume it to be their objective.

The western slope goes down uneventfully between Broad Crag and Great End to the Corridor Route, and the glory of the fell is its excessively steep and rough fall directly from the cairn eastwards into the wilderness of upper Eskdale: a chaotic and desolate scene set at a precipitous gradient, a frozen avalanche of crags and stones, much of it unexplored and uncharted, wild in the extreme, and offering a safe refuge for escaped convicts or an ideal depository for murdered corpses. Someday, when the regular paths become overcrowded, it may be feasible to track out an exciting and alternative route of ascent for scramblers here, but the author prefers to leave the job to someone with more energy and a lesser love of life.

Ill Crag, from the path above Esk Hause

Pikes Crag · Pulpit Rock · Mickledore Buttress · Mickledore · Scafell Craig

from Hollow Stones

Once in a while every keen fellwalker should have a *pre-arranged* night out amongst the mountains. Time drags and the hours of darkness can be bitterly cold, but to be on the tops at dawn is a wonderful experience and much more than recompense for the temporary discomfort.

Hollow Stones is an excellent place for a bivouac, with a wide choice of overhanging boulders for shelter, many of which have been walled-up and made draught-proof by previous occupants. Watch the rising sun flush Scafell Crag and change a black silhouette into a rosy-pink castle! (This doesn't always happen. Sometimes it never stops raining).

Not many readers, not even those who are frequent visitors to Scafell Pike, could give a caption to this picture. It is, in fact, a scene in the unfrequented hollow of Little Narrowcove, looking up towards the summit of the Pike (the top cairn is out of sight). The crags, unsuspected on the usual routes, are a great surprise. Little Narrowcove (reached from Broad Crag col) is a grassy basin sheltered or encircled by cliffs: a good site for a mountain camp.

ASCENTS

The ascent of Scafell Pike is the toughest proposition the 'collector' of summits is called upon to attempt, and it is the one above all others that, as a patriot, he cannot omit. The difficulties are due more to roughness of the ground than to altitude, and to the remoteness of the summit from frequented valleys. From all bases except Wasdale Head the climb is long and arduous, and progress is slow: this is a full-day expedition, and the appropriate preparations should be made. Paths are good, but only in the sense that they are distinct; they are abominably stony, even bouldery — which is no great impediment when ascending but mitigates against quick descent. Ample time should be allowed for getting off the mountain.

In winter especially, when conditions can be Arctic, it is important to select a fine clear day, to start early, and keep moving; reserve three hours of daylight for the return journey. If under deep snow the mountain is better left alone altogether, for progress would then be laborious, and even dangerous across the concealed boulders, with a greater chance of death from exposure than of early rescue if an accident were to occur.

Scafell Pike may be ascended most easily from Wasdale Head, less conveniently from Borrowdale or Great Langdale or Eskdale. But all routes are alike in grandeur of scenery.

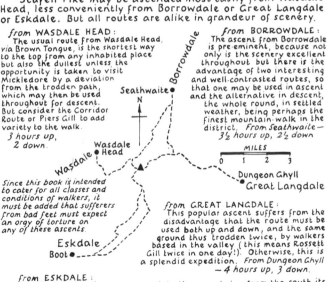

from WASDALE HEAD:
The usual route from Wasdale Head, via Brown Tongue, is the shortest way to the top from any inhabited place but also the dullest unless the opportunity is taken to visit Mickledore by a deviation from the trodden path, which may then be used throughout for descent. But consider the Corridor Route or Piers Gill to add variety to the walk.
3 hours up, 2 down.

from BORROWDALE:
The ascent from Borrowdale is pre-eminent, because not only is the scenery excellent throughout but there is the advantage of two interesting and well-contrasted routes, so that one may be used in ascent and the alternative in descent, the whole round, in settled weather, being perhaps the finest mountain-walk in the district. *From Seathwaite —* 3½ hours up, 2½ down

Since this book is intended to cater for all classes and conditions of walkers, it must be added that sufferers from bad feet must expect an orgy of torture on any of these ascents.

from GREAT LANGDALE:
This popular ascent suffers from the disadvantage that the route must be used both up and down, and the same ground thus trodden twice, by walkers based in the valley (this means Rossett Gill twice in one day!). Otherwise, this is a splendid expedition. *From Dungeon Ghyll* — 4 hours up, 3 down.

from ESKDALE:
This is the best line of approach to the mountain: from the south its grandest and most rugged aspect is seen. Variations of route may be adopted, but time is a great enemy: the walk is lengthy (a feature most noticed when returning). *From Boot* — 4½ hours up, 3½ down.

ASCENT FROM WASDALE HEAD
via BROWN TONGUE

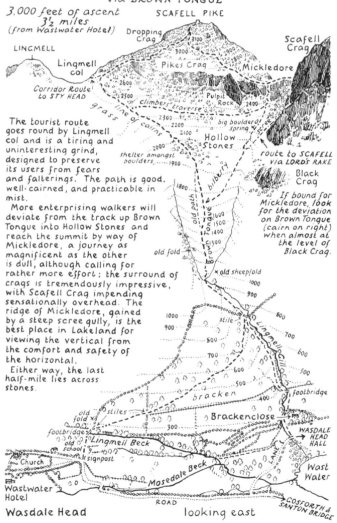

3,000 feet of ascent
3½ miles
(from Wastwater Hotel)

SCAFELL PIKE

LINGMELL

Dropping Crag

Scafell Crag

Lingmell col

Pikes Crag

Mickledore

Corridor Route to STY HEAD

Climbers traverse

Pulpit Rock

line of cairns

big boulder & spring

Hollow Stones

route to SCAFELL via LORD'S RAKE

shelter amongst boulders

Black Crag

old path

bilberry

Lingmell Gill

old fold

old sheepfold

stile

If bound for Mickledore, look for the deviation on Brown Tongue (cairn on right) when almost at the level of Black Crag.

bracken

footbridge

old fold x6

stiles

Brackenclose

WASDALE HEAD HALL

footbridge

old school

Lingmell Beck

signpost

Church

Mosedale Beck

LANE

Wast Water

Wastwater Hotel

ROAD

GOSFORTH & SANTON BRIDGE

Wasdale Head

looking east

The tourist route goes round by Lingmell col and is a tiring and uninteresting grind, designed to preserve its users from fears and falterings. The path is good, well-cairned, and practicable in mist.

More enterprising walkers will deviate from the track up Brown Tongue into Hollow Stones and reach the summit by way of Mickledore, a journey as magnificent as the other is dull, although calling for rather more effort: the surround of crags is tremendously impressive, with Scafell Crag impending sensationally overhead. The ridge of Mickledore, gained by a steep scree gully, is the best place in Lakeland for viewing the vertical from the comfort and safety of the horizontal.

Either way, the last half-mile lies across stones.

ASCENT FROM WASDALE HEAD
via PIERS GILL

3,000 feet of ascent
3¾ miles
(from Wastwater Hotel)

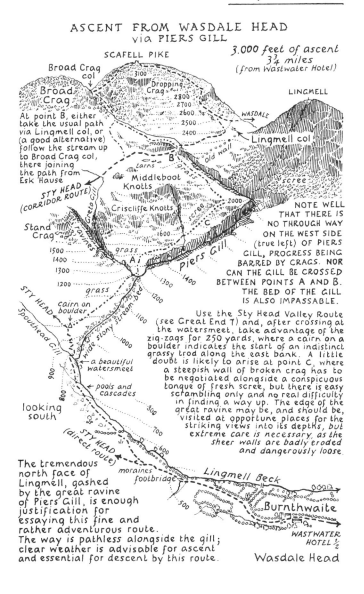

SCAFELL PIKE

Broad Crag col

Broad Crag

Dropping Crag

3100
2800
2700
2600
2500
2400

LINGMELL

WASDALE

Lingmell col

Lingmell

At point B, either take the usual path via Lingmell col, or (a good alternative) follow the stream up to Broad Crag col, there joining the path from Esk Hause

tarns

old wall

rough grass

scree

STY HEAD
(CORRIDOR ROUTE)

Greta Gill

Middleboot Knotts

Criscliffe Knotts

2000

scree

B

C

scree

Stand Crag

ravine

1500
1400
1300
1200

grass

A

grass

Piers Gill

1300

1400

NOTE WELL THAT THERE IS NO THROUGH WAY ON THE WEST SIDE (true left) OF PIERS GILL, PROGRESS BEING BARRED BY CRAGS. NOR CAN THE GILL BE CROSSED BETWEEN POINTS A AND B. THE BED OF THE GILL IS ALSO IMPASSABLE.

STY HEAD

cairn on boulder

Spouthead Gill

1200
1100
1000

wide stony stream-bed

a beautiful watersmeet

pools and cascades

900
800

looking south

STY HEAD
(direct route)

300
200

700
600

Use the Sty Head Valley Route (see Great End 7) and, after crossing at the watersmeet, take advantage of the zig-zags for 250 yards, where a cairn on a boulder indicates the start of an indistinct grassy trod along the east bank. A little doubt is likely to arise at point C, where a steepish wall of broken crag has to be negotiated alongside a conspicuous tongue of fresh scree, but there is easy scrambling only and no real difficulty in finding a way up. The edge of the great ravine may be, and should be, visited at opportune places for the striking views into its depths, but extreme care is necessary, as the sheer walls are badly eroded and dangerously loose.

moraines
footbridge

Lingmell Beck

500

Burnthwaite

WASTWATER HOTEL ½

The tremendous north face of Lingmell, gashed by the great ravine of Piers Gill, is enough justification for essaying this fine and rather adventurous route. The way is pathless alongside the gill; clear weather is advisable for ascent and essential for descent by this route.

Wasdale Head

ASCENT FROM BORROWDALE
via STY HEAD

3,000 feet of ascent
6 miles from Seatoller

Sty Head

Having duly arrived at Styhead Tarn (so proving the reliability of the diagram thus far) refer now (with confidence) to the foot of the next page for the continuation of the route.

Styhead Tarn

boulder

Patterson's Fold (sheepfold)

The footbridge was originally sited 150 yards downstream, where the buttresses of the former bridge can still be seen.

By keeping to the left of the many variations, a section of the original grooved and paved path will be found, and how superior it is to the modern 'short-cuts'!

Don't panic if unable to ford the stream here (normally easy); keep on along the west bank

cascades

ESK HAUSE

Taylorgill Force

The steep fell here is BASE BROWN

Stockley Bridge

old folds

Styhead Gill

River Derwent

GREAT GABLE via GREEN GABLE

The crag high on the left is Hind Crag

gates

Seathwaite Slabs

Sourmilk Gill

Seathwaite

one of the friendliest of farms. No need to fear the dogs or other animals here: visitors merely bore them.
The lane to the footbridge here passes under the arch of the farm buildings

sheepfold

disused plumbago mines

The Borrowdale Yews ('the fraternal four')

LANE

ROAD

River Derwent

Seathwaite Bridge

gate

Few readers will need to refer to this page, as the walk to Sty Head is amongst the best-known in the district, this being evidenced by the severe wear and tear of the path.

It is remarkable that the splendid variation route passing up through the gorge of Taylorgill Force has never found popular favour and is ignored by map-makers although it has been used by discerning walkers for many decades. This, compared with the usual Stockley Bridge path, is often rather wet in the lower intakes, a small disadvantage to set against its merits of quietness, quickness, sustained interest and waterfall and ravine scenery of high quality. A certain amount of delectable clambering on rocky sections of the path is likely to prohibit its use generally by all and sundry (including the many Sunday afternoon picnic parties), which is a good thing for the genuine fellwalker.

Taylorgill Force

ROSTHWAITE 1¼

bus terminus

Seatoller

HONISTER PASS

looking south-south-west

ASCENT FROM BORROWDALE
via STY HEAD

continued

SCAFELL PIKE

looking south

Broad Crag col

Broad Crag

ESK HAUSE

3100

Dropping Crag

2700
2600
2500
2400
2300

LINGMELL

Lingmell col

old wall

striking view down Piers Gill

This new and recently-cairned variation (joining the path from Esk Hause at the Broad Crag col) is well worth trying. When *descending* from the Pike, it is preferable to the usual route *via* the Lingmell col, especially in mist, and certainly quicker.

2200

tarns

Piers Gill

Round How

2100

easy access to GREAT END (see page Great End 8)

2000

1900

The point of bifurcation of the lower path is not apparent when descending the Corridor (fortunately, because the loose slope above the ravine can be dangerous in descent)

falls

grass

Stand Crag

1800

awkward exit

1700

Skew Gill

upper (direct) path

1600

lower path

NOTE

1500

Greta Gill

The one redeeming feature of the lower path (which was, incidentally, the *original* route) is its superb view of the Greta Gill ravine; this is not seen effectively from the upper path

Piers Gill

1400

slight descent

Many good men have gone wrong here. TWO paths leave the far bank of the gill: the direct route slants upwards across the wide and stony bed and climbs a short red gully, while the other goes straight across the gill, after which it maintains a horizontal course until forced upwards by the magnificent Greta Gill ravine, a loose and unpleasant scramble being then necessary to join the direct path.

ESK HAUSE

short cut

Sty Head

GREAT GABLE

not clear

path goes on to Wasdale Head

The Corridor starts from the path to Esk Hause and crosses the ruins of a wall below a crag. The short cut leads to it exactly.

Styhead Tarn

BORROWDALE

Carry on here from top of page opposite

The Corridor Route (formerly known as the Guides Route) links grassy shelves on the very rough western slope of Great End and Broad Crag and is, in fact, the one and only easy passage possible along this flank, which is deeply cut by ravines. It provides an excellent way to the Lingmell col (for Scafell Pike or Scafell) from Sty Head, interesting throughout and is the easiest of all routes to the Pike. In recent years the Corridor has become very popular and is now a well-blazoned track, but its start, at the Sty Head end, is indistinct and a newcomer here, not equipped with Book 4, may have trouble in locating it. (ADVT)

ASCENT FROM BORROWDALE
via ESK HAUSE
3,200 feet of ascent : 5½ miles from Seatoller

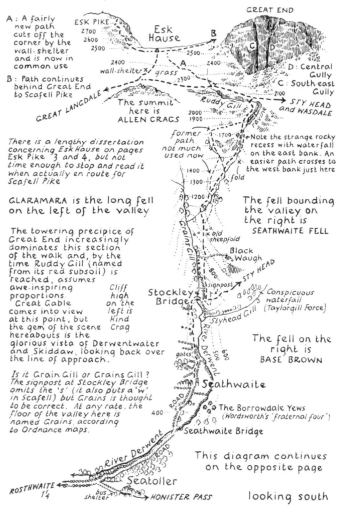

A : A fairly new path cuts off the corner by the wall-shelter and is now in common use

B : Path continues behind Great End to Scafell Pike

ESK PIKE
2700
2600
2500

Esk Hause

2400
wall-shelter   grass

2300

A

2500

2400

GREAT END

C   D

D : Central Gully
C : South-east Gully

STY HEAD and WASDALE

2100

GREAT LANGDALE

The summit here is ALLEN CRAGS

2000
1900

Ruddy Gill

There is a lengthy dissertation concerning Esk Hause on pages Esk Pike 3 and 4, but not time enough to stop and read it when actually en route for Scafell Pike

former path not much used now

1700

Note the strange rocky recess with waterfall on the east bank. An easier path crosses to the west bank just here

GLARAMARA is the long fell on the left of the valley

1400

1300

fold

The fell bounding the valley on the right is SEATHWAITE FELL

The towering precipice of Great End increasingly dominates this section of the walk and, by the time Ruddy Gill (named from its red subsoil) is reached, assumes awe-inspiring proportions. Great Gable comes into view at this point, but the gem of the scene hereabouts is the glorious vista of Derwentwater and Skiddaw, looking back over the line of approach.

1200

Grains Gill

x old sheepfold

Black Waugh

Cliff high on the left is Hind Crag

signpost   STY HEAD

Stockley Bridge

Conspicuous waterfall (Taylorgill Force)

Styhead Gill

River Derwent

The fell on the right is BASE BROWN

Is it Grain Gill or Grains Gill? The signpost at Stockley Bridge omits the 's' (it also puts a 'w' in Scafell) but Grains is thought to be correct. At any rate, the floor of the valley here is named Grains, according to Ordnance maps.

600

500

gates

Seathwaite

400

ROAD

The Borrowdale Yews (Wordsworth's 'fraternal four')

Seathwaite Bridge

River Derwent

ROAD

This diagram continues on the opposite page

ROSTHWAITE 1¼

Seatoller

bus shelter   HONISTER PASS

looking south

ASCENT FROM BORROWDALE
via ESK HAUSE

continued

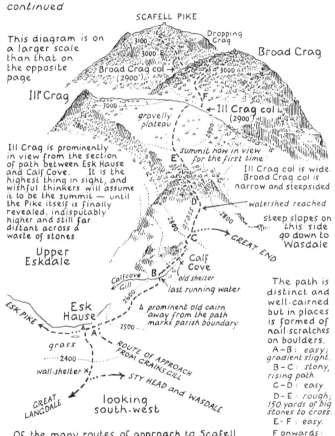

This diagram is on a larger scale than that on the opposite page.

SCAFELL PIKE

Dropping Crag

3100
3000

Broad Crag

Broad Crag col (2900')

Ill Crag

3000

3000

gravelly plateau

Ill Crag col (2900')

Ill Crag is prominently in view from the section of path between Esk Hause and Calf Cove. It is the highest thing in sight, and wishful thinkers will assume it to be the summit — until the Pike itself is finally revealed, indisputably higher and still far distant across a waste of stones.

summit now in view for the first time

2800

2800

Ill Crag col is wide. Broad Crag col is narrow and steepsided

watershed reached

GREAT END

steep slopes on this side go down to Wasdale

Upper Eskdale

grass

2800

Calf Cove

old shelter

last running water

Calfcove Gill

2600

ESK PIKE

Esk Hause

△ prominent old cairn away from the path marks parish boundary

2500

ROUTE OF APPROACH FROM GRAINS GILL

grass

2400

wall-shelter ✕

STY HEAD and WASDALE

GREAT LANGDALE

looking south-west

The path is distinct and well-cairned but in places is formed of nail-scratches on boulders.

A–B: easy; gradient slight.
B–C: stony, rising path.
C–D: easy.
D–E: rough; 150 yards of big stones to cross.
E–F: easy.
F onwards: excessively rough — inescapable boulders, stones and scree.

Of the many routes of approach to Scafell Pike, this, from Borrowdale via Esk Hause, is the finest. The transition from the quiet beauty of the valley pastures and woods to the rugged wildness of the mountain-top is complete, but comes gradually as height is gained and after passing through varied scenery, both nearby and distant, that sustains interest throughout the long march.

ASCENT FROM GREAT LANGDALE
3,400 feet of ascent : 5½ miles (from Dungeon Ghyll, Old Hotel)

From Esk Hause onwards the route coincides with that from Borrowdale. Please see the previous page for a description

The walk falls into four distinct and well-contrasted sections:

1: to Mickleden sheepfold — easy, level walking. Gimmer Crag and Pike o' Stickle high on the right and the Band rising on the left.

2: Rossett Gill — gradual climbing, becoming steep and very stony; zig-zags preferable. Bowfell's crags well seen on left, Rossett Pike on right.

3: Rossett Pass to Esk Hause — undulating grass shelf with two descents where streams flow to Langstrath, right. Esk Pike is on the left, Great End ahead and Allen Crags right.

4: Esk Hause to the summit — easy gradients, but becoming very rough across a lofty plateau; two more descents before the final steep, stony rise. Great End, right, Broad Crag, right, and Ill Crag, left, are by-passed.

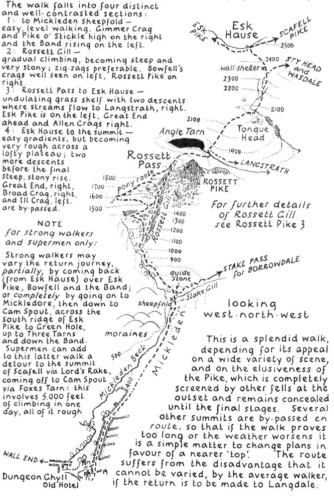

NOTE
for strong walkers and supermen only:

Strong walkers may vary the return journey, partially, by coming back (from Esk Hause) over Esk Pike, Bowfell and the Band; or completely by going on to Mickledore, then down to Cam Spout, across the south ridge of Esk Pike to Green Hole, up to Three Tarns and down the Band. Supermen can add to this latter walk a detour to the summit of Scafell via Lord's Rake, coming off to Cam Spout via Foxes Tarn: this involves 5,000 feet of climbing in one day, all of it rough

For further details of Rossett Gill see Rossett Pike 3

looking
west·north·west

This is a splendid walk, depending for its appeal on a wide variety of scene, and on the elusiveness of the Pike, which is completely screened by other fells at the outset and remains concealed until the final stages. Several other summits are by-passed en route, so that if the walk proves too long or the weather worsens it is a simple matter to change plans in favour of a nearer 'top'. The route suffers from the disadvantage that it cannot be varied, by the average walker, if the return is to be made to Langdale.

Two views on the walk from Esk Hause to the summit

Many hearts have sunk into many boots as this scene unfolds. Here, on the shoulder of Ill Crag, the summit comes into sight, at last; not almost within reach as confidently expected by walkers who feel they have already done quite enough to deserve success, but still a rough half-mile distant, with two considerable descents (Ill Crag col and Broad Crag col) and much climbing yet to be faced before the goal is reached.

Bowfell   Crinkle Crags

Looking down into Little Narrowcove and Eskdale, with Ill Crag on the left, from Broad Crag col

ASCENT FROM ESKDALE
3100 feet of ascent : 7½ miles from Boot

continued on following page

Is there time enough to go on from Cam Spout? 3 hours is not too much to allow for the rest of the climb and return to this point.

Wet and bedraggled pedestrians can rejoice at the prospect of shelter upon reaching Sampson's Stones (huge boulders) but should not go further if bad weather persists.

Do not follow the sketchy path along the west bank of the Esk (except for the purpose of photographing Esk Falls): it enters a gorge below Green Crag from which escape is difficult.

✻ At the crossing of the small stream (which unexpectedly flows to the left) the path becomes indistinct on wet ground; aim for a cairn, half-right, to rejoin it. Ignore the track going straight on: this has been formed by walkers who lost the main path here, and involves 300 feet of unnecessary ascent and descent. (This confusion will not arise if returning by this route, because the main path leaves the Cam Spout sheepfold quite distinctly, but the variation does not).

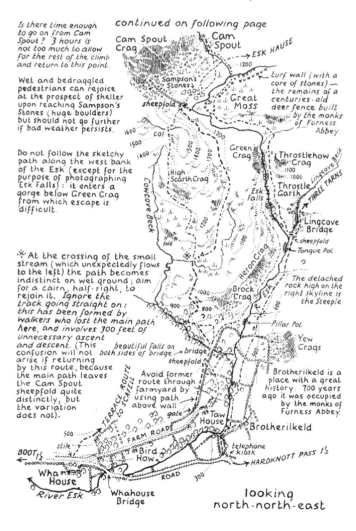

turf wall (with a core of stones) — the remains of a centuries-old deer fence built by the monks of Furness Abbey.

The detached rock high on the right skyline is the Steeple

Brotherikeld is a place with a great history. 700 years ago it was occupied by the monks of Furness Abbey.

beautiful falls on both sides of bridge

Avoid former route through farmyard by using path above wall

looking north-north-east

ASCENT FROM ESKDALE

continued

SCAFELL — SCAFELL PIKE — Broad Crag col — Broad Crag — Ill Crag — East Buttress — Mickledore — Broad Craggs — Rough Crag — Foxes Tarn — Pen — grass — Dow Crag — Little Narrowcove — Cam Spout — recent landslide — ESK HAUSE — Sampsons Stones — How Beck — River Esk

looking north-west

TO CAM SPOUT:

There is no time for dawdling when bound for Scafell Pike, and the fine high-level approach by way of Taw House and the Cowcove zigzags (avoiding the new variation via High Scarth Crag) is recommended as the quickest route to Cam Spout. The path from Brotherilkeld via Lingcove Bridge has too many distractions and temptations to halt and provides a final problem in crossing Great Moss dryshod.

FROM CAM SPOUT ONWARDS:

The usual route from Cam Spout goes up steeply by the waterfalls and proceeds thereafter on a good path, becoming a river of stones, to the ridge of Mickledore, where a well-blazed track climbs across boulders to the summit. The rock-scenery on the last stages of the struggle to Mickledore is good, Scafell East Buttress being extremely impressive, but conditions underfoot are abominable. The variation just below Mickledore that cuts off a corner and gains the ridge at its lowest point is rather easier. This route can be done in mist.

A secluded but circuitous and no less rough alternative is offered by Little Narrowcove, reached by passing below the imposing buttress of Dow Crag and completely dominated by the tremendous cliff of Ill Crag. Note the dotted line on the diagram indicating a shorter way that skirts the left edge of Dow Crag, crosses a col near the rocky peak of Pen and enters Little Narrowcove at mid-height; by careful observation it is possible, on this variation, to keep to grass all the way across the breast of the Pike. Clear weather is needed here.

It seems remarkable that England's highest mountain has no direct path to its summit on this, its finest side. It is not merely steepness that has kept walkers away from it, but rather the unavoidable, inescapable shawl of boulders covering the final 500 feet, where progress is not only painfully slow but carries a risk of displacing stones that have never before been trodden and may be balanced precariously and easily disturbed. There is no fun in pioneering routes over such rough terrain, which is safest left in virgin state.

THE SUMMIT

This is it: the Mecca of all weary pilgrims in Lakeland; the place of many ceremonies and celebrations, of bonfires and birthday parties; the ultimate; the supreme; the one objective above all others; the highest ground in England; the top of Scafell Pike.

It is a magnet, not because of its beauty for this is not a place of beauty, not because of the exhilaration of the climb for there is no exhilaration in toiling upwards over endless stones, not because of its view for although this is good there are others better. It is a magnet simply because it is the highest ground in England.

There is a huge cairn that from afar looks like a hotel: a well-built circular edifice now crumbling on its east side, with steps leading up to its flat top. Set into the vertical nine-foot north wall of the cairn is a tablet commemorating the gift of the summit to the nation. A few yards distant, west, is a triangulation column of the Ordnance Survey; a visitor in doubt and seeking confirmation of his whereabouts should consult the number on the front plate of the column: if it is anything other than S.1537 he has good cause for doubt — heaven knows where his erring steps have led him, but it is certainly not to the summit of Scafell Pike.

The surrounding area is barren, a tumbled wilderness of stones of all shapes and sizes, but it is not true, as has oft been written and may be thought, that the top is entirely devoid of vegetation: there is, indeed, a patch of grass on the south side of the cairn sufficient to provide a couch for a few hundredweights of exhausted flesh.

Yet this rough and desolate summit is, after all, just as it should be, and none of us would really want it different. A smooth green promenade here would be wrong. This is the summit of England, and it is fitting that it should be sturdy and rugged and strong.

THE SUMMIT

DESCENTS: It is an exaggeration to describe walkers' routes across the top of Scafell Pike as *paths*, because they make an uneasy pavement of angular boulders that are too unyielding ever to be trodden into subjection; nevertheless the routes are quite distinct, the particular boulders selected for their feet by the pioneers having, in the past century or so, become so extensively scratched by bootnails that they now appear as white ribbons across the grey waste of stones. Thus there is no difficulty in following them, even in mist.

The only place in descent where a walker might go astray is in going down by the Wasdale Head path to join the Corridor Route for Sty Head, the bifurcation above Lingmell col being surprisingly vague: in mist a walker might find himself well down Brown Tongue before discovering his error. It is actually safer for a stranger seeking the Corridor Route, particularly in mist, to use the Esk Hause path as far as the first col, at this point turning off *left* down into a hollow; a stream rises here and is a certain guide to the Corridor, which is reached exactly and unmistakably at the head of Piers Gill.

PLAN OF SUMMIT

Soliloquy.........

In summertime the cairn often becomes over-run with tourists, and a seeker after solitary contemplation may then be recommended to go across to the south peak, where, after enjoying the splendid view of Eskdale, he can observe the visitors to the summit from this distance. He may find himself wondering what impulse had driven these good folk to leave the comforts of the valley and make the weary ascent to this inhospitable place.

Why *does* a man climb mountains? Why has he forced his tired and sweating body up here when he might instead have been sitting at his ease in a deckchair at the seaside, looking at girls in bikinis, or fast asleep, or sucking ice-cream, according to his fancy. On the face of it the thing doesn't make sense.

Yet more and more people are turning to the hills; they find something in these wild places that can be found nowhere else. It may be solace for some, satisfaction for others: the joy of exercising muscles that modern ways of living have cramped, perhaps; or a balm for jangled nerves in the solitude and silence of the peaks; or escape from the clamour and tumult of everyday existence. It may have something to do with a man's subconscious search for beauty, growing keener as so much in the world grows uglier. It may be a need to re-adjust his sights, to get out of his own narrow groove and climb above it to see wider horizons and truer perspectives. In a few cases, it may even be a curiosity inspired by ~~awainwright's~~ Pictorial Guides. Or it may be, and for most walkers it *will* be, quite simply, a deep love of the hills, a love that has grown over the years, whatever motive first took them there: a feeling that these hills are friends, tried and trusted friends, always there when needed.

It is a question every man must answer for himself.

THE VIEW

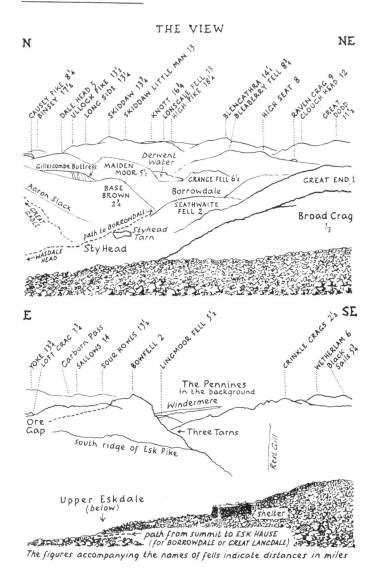

N   NE

CAUSEY PIKE 8¼
BINSEY 17½
DALE HEAD 5
ULLOCK PIKE 13½
LONG SIDE 13¾
SKIDDAW 13¾
SKIDDAW LITTLE MAN 13
KNOTT 16¾
LONSCALE FELL 13
HIGH PIKE 18¾
BLENCATHRA 14½
BLEABERRY FELL 8¾
HIGH SEAT 8
RAVEN CRAG 9
CLOUCH HEAD 12
GREAT DODD 11½

Derwent
Water

Gillercombe Buttress   MAIDEN MOOR 5½
BASE BROWN 2¼
GRANGE FELL 6¼
GREAT END 1

Aaron Slack
GREAT GABLE
Borrowdale
SEATHWAITE FELL 2
Broad Crag ⅓

path to BORROWDALE
Styhead Tarn
← WASDALE HEAD
Sty Head

E   SE

YOKE 13¾
LOFT CRAG 3¾
Garburn Pass
SALLOWS 14
SOUR HOWES 13½
BOWFELL 2
LINGMOOR FELL 5½
CRINKLE CRAGS 2½
WETHERLAM 6
Black 5¾
Sails 5¾

The Pennines
in the background

Windermere

Ore Gap
← Three Tarns

south ridge of Esk Pike

Rest Gill

Upper Eskdale
(below)
↓

shelter

← path from summit to ESK HAUSE
(for BORROWDALE or GREAT LANGDALE) →

The figures accompanying the names of fells indicate distances in miles

THE VIEW

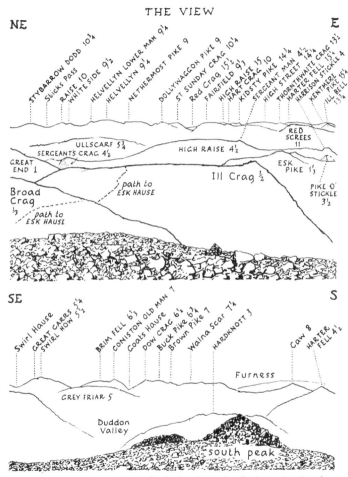

NE

STYBARROW DODD 10¾
Sticks Pass
RAISE 10
WHITE SIDE 9½
HELVELLYN LOWER MAN 9¼
HELVELLYN 9¼
NETHERMOST PIKE 9
DOLLYWAGGON PIKE 9
St SUNDAY CRAG 10¼
Red Crag 15½
FAIRFIELD 9½
HART CRAG 15
KIDSTY PIKE 14¾
SERGEANT MAN 4½
HIGH STREET 14½
THORNTHWAITE CRAG 13½
HARTER FELL 15½
HARRISON STICKLE 4
KENTMERE PIKE 15¾
ILL BELL 13¾

E

ULLSCARF 5¾
SERGEANTS CRAG 4½
GREAT END 1
HIGH RAISE 4½
RED SCREES 11
ESK PIKE 1⅓
Ill Crag ½
PIKE O' STICKLE 3½

Broad Crag ⅓
path to ESK HAUSE
path to ESK HAUSE

SE

Swirl Hause
GREAT CARRS 5¼
SWIRL HOW 5½
BRIM FELL 6½
CONISTON OLD MAN 7
Goats Hause
Dow Crag 6½
Buck Pike 6¾
Brown Pike 7
Walna Scar 7¼
HARDKNOTT 3
Caw 8
HARTER FELL 4½

S

Furness

GREY FRIAR 5

Duddon Valley

south peak

This being the highest ground in England the view is the most extensive, although not appreciably more so than those seen from many nearby fells. There is much interesting detail in every direction, and no denying the superiority of altitude, for all else is below eye-level, with old favourites like Great Gable and Bowfell seeming, if not humbled, less proud than they usually do (Scafell, across Mickledore, often *looks* of equal or greater height). Despite the wide variety of landscape, however, this is not the most pleasing of summit views, none of the valleys or lakes in view being seen really well.

THE VIEW

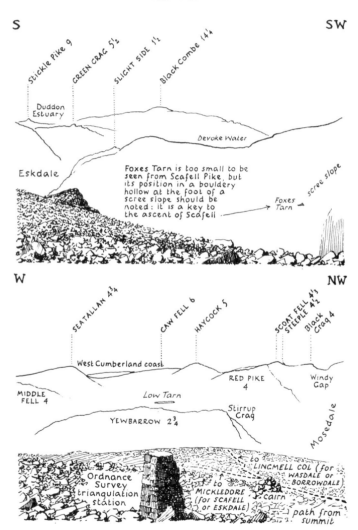

S

SW

Stickle Pike 9

GREEN CRAG 5½

SLIGHT SIDE 1½

Black Combe 14¼

Duddon Estuary

Devoke Water

Eskdale

Foxes Tarn is too small to be seen from Scafell Pike, but its position in a bouldery hollow at the foot of a scree slope should be noted: it is a key to the ascent of Scafell

Foxes Tarn

scree slope

W

NW

SEA TALLAN 4¾

CAW FELL 6

HAYCOCK 5

SCOAT FELL 4½
STEEPLE 4½

Black Crag 4

West Cumberland coast

RED PIKE 4

Windy Gap

MIDDLE FELL 4

Low Tarn

Stirrup Crag

YEWBARROW 2¾

Mosedale

Ordnance Survey triangulation station

to LINGMELL COL (for WASDALE or BORROWDALE)

to MICKLEDORE (for SCAFELL or ESKDALE)

cairn

path from summit

THE VIEW

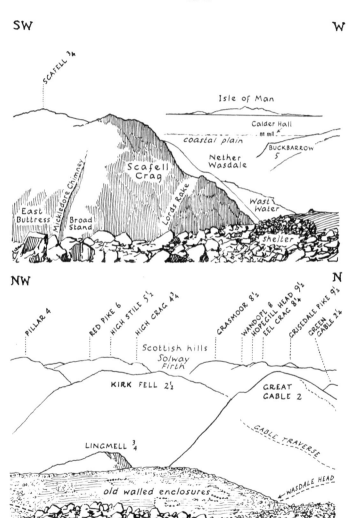

RIDGE ROUTES

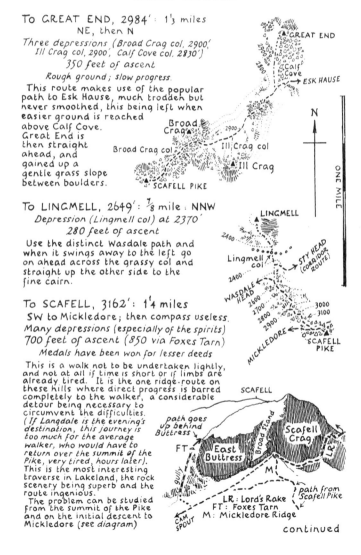

To GREAT END, 2984': 1⅓ miles
NE, then N

Three depressions (Broad Crag col, 2900',
Ill Crag col, 2900', Calf Cove col, 2830')
350 feet of ascent
Rough ground; slow progress.

This route makes use of the popular
path to Esk Hause, much trodden but
never smoothed, this being left when
easier ground is reached
above Calf Cove.
Great End is
then straight
ahead, and
gained up a
gentle grass slope
between boulders.

To LINGMELL, 2649': ⅞ mile : NNW
Depression (Lingmell col) at 2370'
280 feet of ascent

Use the distinct Wasdale path and
when it swings away to the left go
on ahead across the grassy col and
straight up the other side to the
fine cairn.

To SCAFELL, 3162': 1¼ miles
SW to Mickledore; then compass useless.
Many depressions (especially of the spirits)
700 feet of ascent (850 via Foxes Tarn)
Medals have been won for lesser deeds

This is a walk not to be undertaken lightly,
and not at all if time is short or if limbs are
already tired. It is the one ridge-route on
these hills where direct progress is barred
completely to the walker, a considerable
detour being necessary to circumvent the difficulties.
(If Langdale is the evening's
destination, this journey is
too much for the average
walker, who would have to
return over the summit of the
Pike, very tired, hours later).
This is the most interesting
traverse in Lakeland, the rock
scenery being superb and the
route ingenious.
   The problem can be studied
from the summit of the Pike
and on the initial descent to
Mickledore (see diagram)

LR : Lord's Rake
FT : Foxes Tarn
M : Mickledore Ridge

continued

RIDGE ROUTES

To SCAFELL (continued)

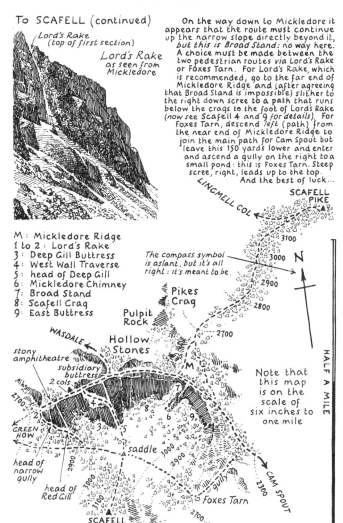

Lord's Rake
(top of first section)

Lord's Rake
as seen from
Mickledore

On the way down to Mickledore it appears that the route must continue up the narrow slope directly beyond it, *but this is Broad Stand: no way here.* A choice must be made between the two pedestrian routes via Lord's Rake or Foxes Tarn. For Lord's Rake, which is recommended, go to the far end of Mickledore Ridge and (after agreeing that Broad Stand is impossible) slither to the right down scree to a path that runs below the crags to the foot of Lord's Rake (*now see Scafell 4 and 9 for details*). For Foxes Tarn, descend *left* (path) from the near end of Mickledore Ridge to join the main path for Cam Spout but leave this 150 yards lower and enter and ascend a gully on the right to a small pond: this is Foxes Tarn. Steep scree, right, leads up to the top.
And the best of luck...

M : Mickledore Ridge
1 to 2 : Lord's Rake
3 : Deep Gill Buttress
4 : West Wall Traverse
5 : head of Deep Gill
6 : Mickledore Chimney
7 : Broad Stand
8 : Scafell Crag
9 : East Buttress

The compass symbol is aslant, but it's all right: it's meant to be.

Note that this map is on the scale of six inches to one mile

SCAFELL PIKE
LINGMELL COL
3100
3000
2900
2800
2700
N
Pikes Crag
Pulpit Rock
WASDALE
Hollow Stones
stony amphitheatre
subsidiary buttress
2 cols
GREEN HOW
2700
head of narrow gully
head of Red Gill
saddle
3000
2900
2900
3000
3100
SCAFELL
2700
Foxes Tarn
CAM SPOUT
2300
HALF A MILE

12 | Blencathra

Book Five: The Northern Fells

When we first discovered Wainwright in the 1970s, using Book Five for explorations of the Northern Fells, my wife and I raved about his maps, his artwork, his words, his accuracy. Fifty years on, fellwalkers are still using his books. But can you rely on him? Is he out of date?

It is true that Wainwright was a bit cavalier about rights of way, leading people on routes that were not quite public, and some farmers became upset by hordes of walkers trailing through their farmyard or disturbing their stock. They didn't say much in public, because by then Wainwright had become an icon, loved by all Lakeland walkers, but when he died, a few protested to the then publishers, demanding changes. Now that the right to roam on open land is becoming more strongly established in law, the situation is changing. As new laws come into effect, we will all have more rights than in Wainwright's day.

Some details in the books have inevitably dated. Look at Blencathra 7 and at the bottom of the map you'll see 'Railway'. This was the much-loved, but alas eventually little-used Cockermouth, Keswick and Penrith Railway, opened in 1865. It closed in 1972, ten years after Book Five appeared. You can still see the line of the track – and walk bits of it – so its existence on the map won't cause much confusion. Further up on that map, Blencathra Hospital, once a sanatorium, has also gone. Drawing this map today you would have to include the Threlkeld Mining Museum, opened just a few years ago, an excellent, mainly open-air museum of which I am sure Wainwright would have approved.

On the opposite page, Blencathra 8, Wainwright has a real rant against the road-widening schemes being discussed at the time Book Five was being written. Today the A66, thundering along the foothills of Blencathra, is indeed horrendous. I dread going on it, but it cuts my journey from Penrith to my house in Loweswater almost in half. The 'main road' on his map no longer goes through Threlkeld village. The schemes Wainwright deplored – 'cutting off corners, easing gradients' – have been a godsend for local people, diverting lorries on to a bigger, straighter road.

Wainwright goes on to say that 'barriers should be put up' to keep out what he thinks are the wrong sort of visitors. This is an old cry. Wordsworth said much the same in 1820, fearing that the Lake District would be swamped by the unwashed from Lancashire arriving by railway. The barrier cry very often comes from people like Wainwright, off-comers, who have got in, love the place to death, and would like it kept as it is for ever, keeping the wrong sort out.

The truth is, in my opinion, the Lake District has not been ruined. It is better conserved and cared for than ever before. Annual tourist figures have not, in fact, increased in the last thirty years, despite roads like the M6 and A66 making it so much easier for people to come from further afield. The Lake District belongs to us all. And all should be welcome, as long as they don't frighten the sheep.

Artistically, Wainwright's work has not dated at all. If you look at other publications from the 1950s and 1960s, the writing, layout, drawings, even the photographs seem somehow old fashioned. Because Wainwright did his books his way, not following any current fashion, they look as original and fresh as when they first appeared.

Wainwright hasn't dated either in the spiritual sense. He is clearly passionate about Blencathra and his enthusiasm and joy jump out from the pages. He devotes 36 pages to it, the most to any single mountain. Does that suggest it was his top, top fell? Maybe, maybe not. In his final six, he didn't indicate in what order they were listed. Very wise.

Blencathra

2847'

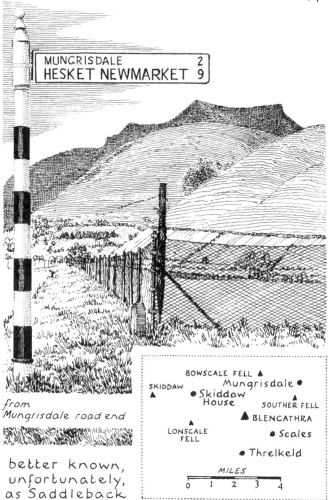

MUNGRISDALE 2
HESKET NEWMARKET 9

from
Mungrisdale road end

better known,
unfortunately,
as Saddleback

BOWSCALE FELL ▲
Mungrisdale ●
SKIDDAW
▲   ● Skiddaw
House   SOUTHER FELL
▲ BLENCATHRA
▲   ● Scales
LONSCALE
FELL   ● Threlkeld

MILES
0 1 2 3 4

NATURAL FEATURES

Blencathra is one of the grandest objects in Lakeland. And one of the best known. Seen from the south-west, the popular aspect, the mountain rises steeply and in isolation above the broad green fields of Threlkeld, a feature being the great sweeping curve leaping out of the depths to a lofty summit-ridge, where the skyline then proceeds in a succession of waves to a sharp peak before descending, again in a graceful curve, to the valley pastures far to the east.

This is a mountain that compels attention, even from those dull people whose eyes are not habitually lifted to the hills. To artists and photographers it is an obvious subject for their craft; to sightseers passing along the road or railway at its base, between Keswick and Penrith, its influence is magnetic; to the dalesfolk it is the eternal background to their lives, there at birth, there at death. But most of all it is a mountaineers' mountain.

continued

from Castlerigg Stone Circle

NATURAL FEATURES

continued

The supreme feature of Blencathra, the one that invests the mountain with special grandeur, is the imposing southern front, a remarkable example of the effect of elemental natural forces. It forms a tremendous facade above the valley, and makes a dark, towering backcloth to a stage of farmsteads and cottages, of emerald pastures and meadows and woodlands along its base. There is nothing inviting in these shattered cliffs and petrified rivers of stone that seem to hold a perpetual threat over the little community below : the scene arrests attention, but intimidates and repels. Few who gaze upon these desolate walls are likely to feel any inclination and inspiration to scramble up through their arid, stony wildernesses to the contorted skyline so high above. Consequently the area has remained a no-man's-land for walkers, even though closely within sight of road and railway travellers. Blencathra is ascended thousands of times a year but rarely by ways up the southern front. This is a pity. Here is the greatness of the mountain. Its detail is a fascinating study.

west   east

THE SOUTHERN FRONT
3¼ miles

The outer slopes, rising on the west and east flanks from valley level to the uppermost escarpment below the summit ridge, are smoothly curved, massive and yet so symmetrical that they might well have been designed by a master architect to supply a perfect balance to the structure. These two outlyers are Blease Fell and Scales Fell.

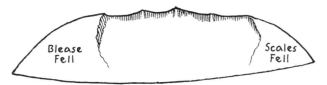

Blease
Fell   Scales
Fell

continued

NATURAL FEATURES

continued

From their extremities the slopes of Blease Fell and Scales Fell extend uneventfully towards each other across the front until, suddenly and dramatically, they are halted at the edge of a scene of devastation, the wreckage of what appears to have been, in ages past, a tremendous convulsion that tore the heart out of the mountain and left the ruins seemingly in a state of tottering collapse. The picture is chaotic: a great upheaval of ridges and pinnacles rising out of dead wastes of scree and penetrated by choked gullies and ravines, the whole crazily tilted through 2000' of altitude. Even in this area of confusion and disorder, however, Nature has sculptured a distinct pattern.

Four watercourses emerge from surrounding debris to escape to the valley:

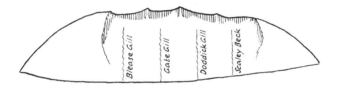

Between the four ravines, three lofty spurs, alike in main characteristics, thrust far out; narrow and frail where they leave the solid mass of the mountain, they widen into substantial buttresses as they descend to the valley. It is as though a giant hand had clawed at the mountain, each finger scooping out a deep hollow, with narrow strips of ground left undisturbed between.

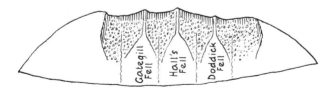

There are thus five buttresses on the southern front, each named as a separate fell. The two outer are grassy, with flat tops; the three in the middle are heathery and rise to distinct peaks, the central one being Blencathra's summit. Such is the pattern of the southern front.

continued

NATURAL FEATURES

continued

The other flanks of the mountain are mainly smooth and rounded, although on the east side Scales Fell breaks its curve to form the hollow of Mousthwaite Combe. But, from the summit, high ground continues north across a slight depression (the Saddle) to the prominent top of Foule Crag, this being the outline from which the alternative name, Saddleback, derives. A distinct ridge curves away to the Glenderamackin col from Foule Crag, while a rocky spur goes off to the east, this latter being the well-known Sharp Edge, second in fame to Striding Edge on Helvellyn as a test for walkers. Deepset in the hollow between Sharp Edge and the main ridge is one of the most characteristic mountain tarns in the district, Scales Tarn.

It is interesting to note that although Blencathra lies well to the east of the axis of Lakeland, approximately 99% of its drainage joins the Derwent in the west, only a few drops being gathered by the Eden catchment.

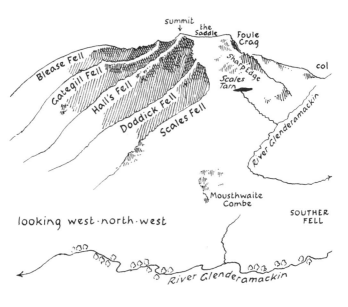

Blencathra joins Bowfell in the author's best half-dozen.

The summit escarpment

looking west

from Scales Fell to the summit

from the summit to Gategill Fell Top

from Gategill Fell Top to Blease Fell

Blencathra 7

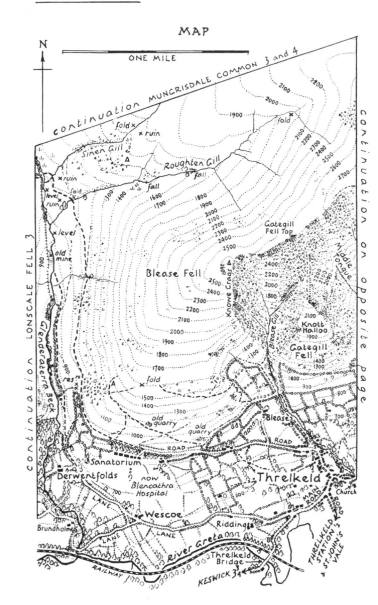

MAP

ONE MILE

N

continuation MUNGRISDALE COMMON 3 and 4

continuation on opposite page

continuation LONSCALE FELL 3

fold ✗
✗ ruin
Sinen Gill
△
Roughten Gill
fall
fall
1300 1400
1600
1700
1800
1900
2000
2200
2300
2500

fold ✗
1900
2000
fold ✗
2100
2200
2300
2500
2600
2700

✗ ruin
✗ fold
level
ruin
✗ level
old mine

Gategill
Fell Top

Middle Tongue

Blease Fell
△ Knowe Crags
2500
2400
2300
2200
2100
2000
1900
1800
1700
1600
1500
1400
1300
1100
1000

2400
2200
2000
1800

Blease Gill

2100
Knott
Halloo

Gategill
Fell
1400
1300

res'r
Glenderaterra Beck
continuation

900
900

A
fold
old
quarry
old
quarry

1300
1600
900
800
700

Blease

ROAD

Sanatorium
now
Blencathra
Hospital
Derwentfolds

ROAD

Threlkeld

MAIN ROAD
Church

Wescoe
LANE
LANE
LANE

Riddings

River Greta

Brundholme

RAILWAY

Threlkeld
Bridge

KESWICK 3¾

THRELKELD
STATION 2
& ST JOHN'S
VALE

ROAD
ST JOHN'S
VALE

MAP

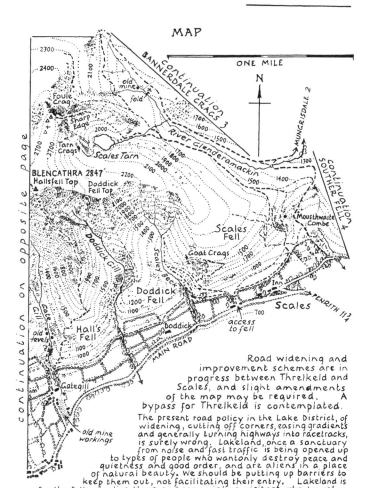

ONE MILE

N

continuation on opposite page

continuation BANNERDALE CRAGS 3

MUNGRISDALE 2

continuation SOUTHER FELL 4

2300
2400
2100
old mine
fold
Foule Crag
Sharp Edge
2000
Tarn Crags
2700
Scales Tarn
2200
2100
2000
1900
1800
1700
1600
1500
River Glenderamackin
1400
1300
BLENCATHRA 2847
Hallsfell Top
Doddick Fell Top
Mousthwaite Combe
Doddick Gill
Scales Fell
Goat Crags
Scaley Beck
Gate Gill
old levels
Doddick Fell
Hall's Fell
Doddick
access to fell
Scales
Inn
PENRITH 11 3
MAIN ROAD
Gategill
old mine workings

Road widening and improvement schemes are in progress between Threlkeld and Scales, and slight amendments of the map may be required. A bypass for Threlkeld is contemplated.

The present road policy in the Lake District, of widening, cutting off corners, easing gradients and generally turning highways into racetracks, is surely wrong. Lakeland, once a sanctuary from noise and fast traffic is being opened up to types of people who wantonly destroy peace and quietness and good order, and are aliens in a place of natural beauty. We should be putting up barriers to keep them out, not facilitating their entry. Lakeland is for the folk who live there and appreciative visitors who travel on foot or leisurely on wheels to enjoy the scenery, and the roads should be no better than are needed for local traffic. The fragrant lanes and narrow winding highways add greatly to the charm of the valleys; it is an offence against good taste to sacrifice their character to satisfy speeding motorists and roadside picnickers. Lakeland is unique: it cannot conform to national patterns and modern trends under the guise of improvement (mark the word!) without losing its very soul.

Let's leave it as we found it, as a haven of refuge and rest in a world going mad, as a precious museum piece.

Where are the men of vision in authority?

ASCENT FROM THRELKELD
via ROUGHTEN GILL
2400 feet of ascent : 5 miles

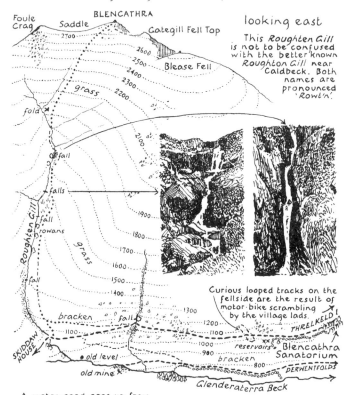

looking east

This *Roughten Gill* is not to be confused with the better known *Roughton Gill* near Caldbeck. Both names are pronounced 'Rowt'n'.

Curious looped tracks on the fellside are the result of motor·bike scrambling by the village lads.

A motor·road goes up from Threlkeld to the Sanatorium and ends there. Its direction is continued by a wide grass path (gate in fence) along the side of the Sanatorium wall. Use this.

For walkers who panic at the proximity of precipices and cannot face steep slopes, the roundabout route by Roughten Gill, which holds no terrors at all, is a good way to the top, but most people will find it unexciting and dreary. The best thing about it is delayed until the very end : the sudden thrilling view of Lakeland, which has been hidden during the climb.

ASCENT FROM THRELKELD
via BLEASE FELL
2450 feet of ascent : 2½ miles

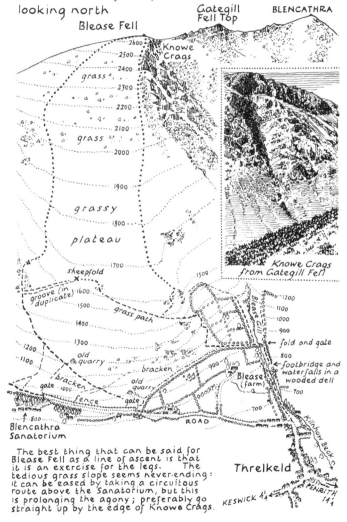

looking north
Blease Fell

Gategill
Fell Top

BLENCATHRA

2600
2500
2400
grass
2300
2200
2100
grass
2000

1900

grassy

1800

plateau

1700

Knowe
Crags

sheepfold
×
groove (in
duplicate)
1600
1500
grass path
1400
1300
old
quarry
1200
1100
bracken
gate 1000
fence
800
Blencathra
Sanatorium

bracken
old
quarry
gate

Knowe Crags
from Gategill Fell

1500

1200
1100
1000
900

fold and gate

800
footbridge and
waterfalls in a
wooded dell

Blease
(farm)
900
700

700
ROAD

Blease Gill

Kilnhow Beck

Threlkeld

KESWICK 4¼
PENRITH 14¼

The best thing that can be said for
Blease Fell as a line of ascent is that
it is an exercise for the legs.   The
tedious grass slope seems never-ending:
it can be eased by taking a circuitous
route above the Sanatorium, but this
is prolonging the agony; preferably go
straight up by the edge of Knowe Crags.

Blease Gill

ASCENT FROM THRELKELD
via BLEASE GILL
2400 feet of ascent : 2 miles

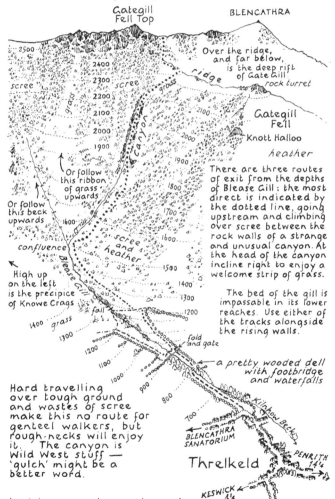

Gategill
Fell Top

BLENCATHRA

2500

2400
2300
2200
2100
2000
1900

scree

scree

grass

grass

canyon

ridge

Over the ridge,
and far below,
is the deep rift
of Gate Gill

rock turret

Gategill
Fell

Knott Halloo

heather

2100

2000

1900

Or follow
this ribbon
of grass
upwards

1800

There are three routes
of exit from the depths
of Blease Gill: the most
direct is indicated by
the dotted line, going
upstream and climbing
over scree between the
rock walls of a strange
and unusual canyon. At
the head of the canyon
incline right to enjoy a
welcome strip of grass.

Or follow
this beck
upwards

1700

scree
and
heather

1600

1600

1500

confluence

High up
on the left
is the precipice
of Knowe Crags

Blease Gill

1400

1300

fall

1400

grass

1300

1200

1100

1000

900

800

700

The bed of the gill is
impassable in its lower
reaches. Use either of
the tracks alongside
the rising walls.

fold
and gate

a pretty wooded dell
with footbridge
and waterfalls

Kinhow Beck

BLENCATHRA
SANATORIUM

Threlkeld

PENRITH
14¼

Hard travelling
over tough ground
and wastes of scree
make this no route for
genteel walkers, but
rough-necks will enjoy
it. The canyon is
Wild West stuff —
'gulch' might be a
better word.

KESWICK
4¼

looking north-north-east

ASCENT FROM THRELKELD
via GATEGILL FELL
2450 feet of ascent : 2 miles

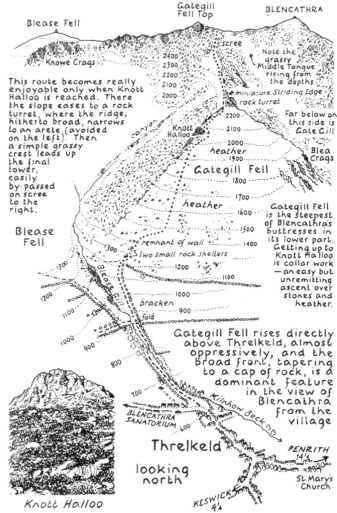

Blease Fell

Gategill Fell Top

BLENCATHRA

Knowe Crags

scree

Note the grassy Middle Tongue rising from the depths

2400
2300
2200
2100
2000

miniature Striding Edge
rock turret

This route becomes really enjoyable only when Knott Halloo is reached. There the slope eases to a rock turret, where the ridge, hitherto broad, narrows to an arete (avoided on the left). Then a simple grassy crest leads up the final tower, easily by-passed on scree to the right.

canyon

Knott Halloo

2200
2100
2000

Far below on this side is Gate Gill

heather
1900

Blea Crags

Gategill Fell
1800

Blease Fell

1700

heather
1600
1500

remnant of wall
two small rock shelters

1400

1300

1200
1100

Gategill Fell is the steepest of Blencathra's buttresses in its lower part. Getting up to Knott Halloo is collar-work — an easy but unremitting ascent over stones and heather.

Blease Gill

1300
1200

1000

900

fold

bracken

Gategill Fell rises directly above Threlkeld, almost oppressively, and the broad front, tapering to a cap of rock, is a dominant feature in the view of Blencathra from the village

1100
1000

800

700

Kilnhow Beck

BLENCATHRA SANATORIUM

600

PENRITH
14¼

Threlkeld

looking north

St. Mary's Church

KESWICK
4¼

Knott Halloo

looking up to Gategill Fell Top
from just above Knott Halloo,
with the rock turret
on the right

Gategill Fell

looking up the
ridge from the
rock turret

looking down the ridge
from Gategill Fell Top

The rock turret is at the far end of
the shadow; to the right is Knott
Halloo, the furthest point in view.

Gate Gill

Blencathra's summit is directly ahead. Gategill Fell rises on the left, and Hall's Fell on the right.

ASCENT FROM THRELKELD
via MIDDLE TONGUE
2400 feet of ascent : 2 miles

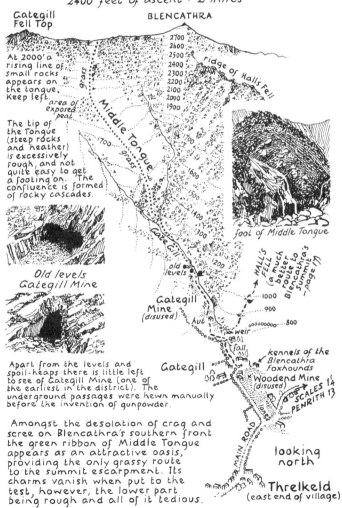

Gategill Fell Top

BLENCATHRA

2700
2600
2500
2400
2300
2200
2100
2000
1900

ridge of Hall's Fell

At 2000' a rising line of small rocks appears on the tongue. Keep left.

grass

Middle Tongue

area of exposed peat

The tip of the Tongue (steep rocks and heather) is excessively rough, and not quite easy to get a footing on. The confluence is formed of rocky cascades.

1700

grass

1700

1600

1500

1400

1300

1200

foot of Middle Tongue

Old levels Gategill Mine

Gate Gill

old levels

HALL'S FELL (a much better route to Blencathra's summit — page 11)

1000

900

800

Gategill Mine (disused)

hut

weir

fall

Gategill

kennels of the Blencathra Foxhounds

Woodend Mine (disused)

SCALES 1¼
PENRITH 13

Apart from the levels and spoil-heaps there is little left to see of Gategill Mine (one of the earliest in the district). The underground passages were hewn manually before the invention of gunpowder.

Amongst the desolation of crag and scree on Blencathra's southern front the green ribbon of Middle Tongue appears as an attractive oasis, providing the only grassy route to the summit escarpment. Its charms vanish when put to the test, however, the lower part being rough and all of it tedious.

MAIN ROAD

looking north

Threlkeld (east end of village)

ASCENT FROM THRELKELD
via HALL'S FELL
2400 feet of ascent : 2 miles

Gategill Fell Top

BLENCATHRA (Hallsfell Top)

Doddick Fell Top

2700
2600
2500
2400
2300
2200
2100
2000
1900
1800
1700
1500
1400
1300
1200
1100
1000
900
800
700
600

arete
pinnacle
tower

The last half mile of the ridge, from 2000, is entirely delightful. This section, known as Narrow Edge with good reason, is a succession of low crags, with steps and gateways and towers of rock. A distinct track on grass is available for walkers — at first this keeps mostly on the Doddick side and later prefers the other, occasionally being forced along the crest. Care is needed in places but there are no difficulties. Scramblers will enjoy following the crest throughout.

Under ice and snow the ridge is for experts only

care needed in traversing rockface by horizontal crack

From the ridge there are tremendous views down to Doddick and Gate Gills

heather

Doddick Gill

Middle Tongue

Gategill Fell

Doddick Fell and Scales Fell come into view

Hall's Fell

heather

Doddick Fell

Gate Gill

level

Gategill Mine (disused)

hut

bracken

weir

fold

fall

Gategill

kennels (the home of the Blencathra Foxhounds)

Woodend Mine (disused)

spoil heaps

SCALES 1¼
PENRITH 13

An enchanting track climbs the broad base of the fell. Unseen from below, this track reveals itself in the heather a few yards at a time, beckoning irresistibly upwards to the exciting ridge above.

For active walkers and scramblers, this route is *positively* the finest way to any mountain-top in the district. It is direct, exhilarating, has glorious views, and (especially satisfying) scores a bull's-eye by leading unerringly to the summit-cairn.

MAIN ROAD

THRELKELD HALL (from which Hall's Fell is named)

looking north

Threlkeld (east end of village)

looking down the ridge from the summit

Hall's Fell

the middle section

the curve in the ridge

looking up the ridge to the summit

Doddick Gill

from 1350' on Doddick Fell. On the left is Hall's Fell, rising to Hall's Fell Top (the summit of Blencathra).

ASCENT FROM THRELKELD
via DODDICK GILL
2150 feet of ascent : 2¾ miles

BLENCATHRA

2700
2600
arête
pinnacle
2400
rock tower
chimney
2300
scree gully
ravine
ridge of Hall's Fell

2300
2200
2100
rock finger
2000
grass
1900
heather
confluence

Doddick Fell Top

From the confluence there is a simple escape to the ridge of Doddick Fell by contouring the slope on the right. This is the only easy exit from the gill

On the map Doddick Gill appears to be an obvious and direct route — hence its inclusion in this book — but the truth is different. This is the roughest way of all. There is no comfort in it. Almost every step has to be planned.

In the easy lower section, some dodging from one side to the other is necessary; around the big bend the east bank is followed, using heather as handholds, until a crag stops this tortuous progress, whereupon continue along the slabby bed of the stream. At the confluence an intimidating 1000-foot façade of chaotic crags and scree appears ahead. Go up the ravine to the left but get out of it before the walls narrow. Climb the bilberry slope alongside, returning to the gully in its grassy upper section. A little chimney leads up to the ridge of Hall's Fell exactly at the pinnacle. Thence the route goes up the arête to the summit.

1700 ridge of Doddick Fell
enter stream bed
1600
slow progress in steep heather
1500
1700
1600
heather
1500
1400
1300
heather
1200
1100
1000
900
Doddick Fell

SCALES 1
stile
900
SCALES ¾
PENRITH 13½

Hall's Fell
bracken
800
Gategill
fall
700
Gategill
THRELKELD 1   MAIN   ROAD
looking north
lane THRELKELD 2

- Hard scrambling throughout.
- For tough guys only.
- Not for solitary walkers.
- Not to be used for descent
- A route to commend heartily to one's worst enemy.

ASCENT FROM SCALES
via DODDICK FELL
2150 feet of ascent : 1¼ miles

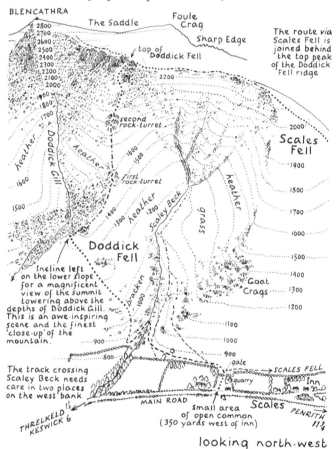

BLENCATHRA

2800
2700
2600
2500
2400
2300
2200
2100
2000
1900
1800
1700

The Saddle

Foule Crag

Sharp Edge

top of Doddick Fell

2200

The route via Scales Fell is joined behind the top peak of the Doddick Fell ridge

second rock-turret

2000

Scales Fell

1900

1800

1700

1600

1500

heather

Doddick Gill

heather

1600
1500

first rock-turret

1400

1300

heather

Scaley Beck

1200

grass

heather

1600

1500

1400

1300

1200

Doddick Fell

Incline left on the lower slope for a magnificent view of the summit towering above the depths of Doddick Gill. This is an awe-inspiring scene and the finest 'close-up' of the mountain.

bracken

1100

1000

900

Goat Crags

The track crossing Scaley Beck needs care in two places on the west bank

900

800

gate

SCALES FELL

quarry

Inn

Scales

MAIN ROAD

small area of open common (350 yards west of inn)

THRELKELD 1½
KESWICK 6

PENRITH 11¾

looking north-west

It is usual, from Scales, to ascend by way of Scales Fell, a very popular route, but better by far is the more direct ridge of Doddick Fell, a grand climb, quite easy, with striking views of the objective.
This is a splendid way to the top of Blencathra.

looking up to Doddick Fell Top from 1450'

Doddick Fell

looking down the ridge from Doddick Fell Top

Scaley Beck

Doddick Fell is on the left, rising to the peak of Doddick Fell Top. Blencathra's summit is seen in the top left corner.

ASCENT FROM SCALES
via SCALEY BECK
2150 feet of ascent : 2 miles

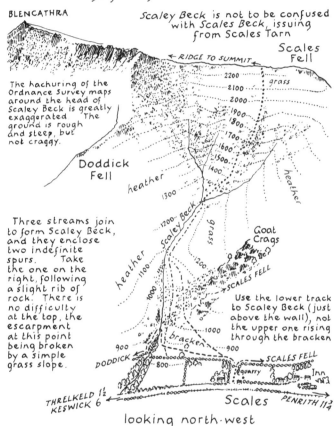

BLENCATHRA

Scaley Beck is not to be confused with Scales Beck, issuing from Scales Tarn

Scales Fell

← RIDGE TO SUMMIT →

2200
2100
2000
1900
1800
1700
1600
1500
1400

grass

The hachuring of the Ordnance Survey maps around the head of Scaley Beck is greatly exaggerated. The ground is rough and steep, but not craggy.

Doddick Fell

heather

1300

heather

Three streams join to form Scaley Beck, and they enclose two indefinite spurs.   Take the one on the right, following a slight rib of rock.   There is no difficulty at the top, the escarpment at this point being broken by a simple grass slope.

1200
Scaley Beck
1100
1000

heather

grass

Goat Crags

1200

SCALES FELL

Use the lower track to Scaley Beck (just above the wall), not the upper one rising through the bracken

1000

bracken

900

900

DODDICK

800

SCALES FELL →

quarry

Inn

THRELKELD 1½
KESWICK 6

Scales

SCALES FELL →

PENRITH 11¾

looking north-west

Of the various watercourses on the south front Scaley Beck is the most practicable as a route of ascent, being nowhere too rough to stop progress; the exit, too, is easy.   There is little of interest, however, and the route falls far short of that via the adjacent ridge of Doddick Fell.

ASCENT FROM SCALES
via SHARP EDGE
2250 feet of ascent : 2¾ miles

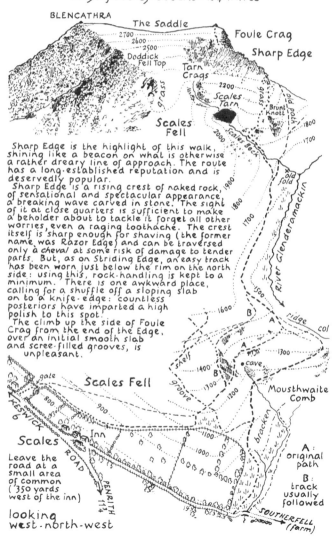

BLENCATHRA
The Saddle
2700
2600
2500
Doddick
Fell Top
Foule Crag
Sharp Edge
Tarn
Crags
2200
Scales
Tarn
Scales
Fell
grass
grass
Brunt
Knott
1800
1700
Scales Beck
2000
1900
old
fold
1800
1700
River Glenderamackin
1600
1500
B
A
ridge
col
A
1300
shelf
1400
B
cave
Mousthwaite
Comb
groove
1300
1200
gate
Scales Fell
800
900
KESWICK 6
Scales
Inn
1100
1000
bracken
A:
original
path
B:
track
usually
followed
PENRITH 11¼
SOUTHERFELL
(farm)

Sharp Edge is the highlight of this walk,
shining like a beacon on what is otherwise
a rather dreary line of approach. The route
has a long-established reputation and is
deservedly popular.
Sharp Edge is a rising crest of naked rock,
of sensational and spectacular appearance,
a breaking wave carved in stone. The sight
of it at close quarters is sufficient to make
a beholder about to tackle it forget all other
worries, even a raging toothache. The crest
itself is sharp enough for shaving (the former
name was Razor Edge) and can be traversed
only à cheval at some risk of damage to tender
parts. But, as on Striding Edge, an easy track
has been worn just below the rim on the north
side: using this, rock-handling is kept to a
minimum. There is one awkward place,
calling for a shuffle off a sloping slab
on to a knife-edge: countless
posteriors have imparted a high
polish to this spot.
The climb up the side of Foule
Crag from the end of the Edge,
over an initial smooth slab
and scree-filled grooves, is
unpleasant.

Leave the
road at a
small area
of common
(350 yards
west of the inn)

looking
west-north-west

looking down from
Foule Crag

looking east
along the Edge
(the 'awkward
place' in the
foreground)

Sharp Edge

the approach from
Scales Tarn

from Scales Tarn

Foule Crag
Sharp Edge
Brunt
Knott

the path from Scales

ASCENT FROM SCALES
via SCALES FELL
2150 feet of ascent : 2¼ miles

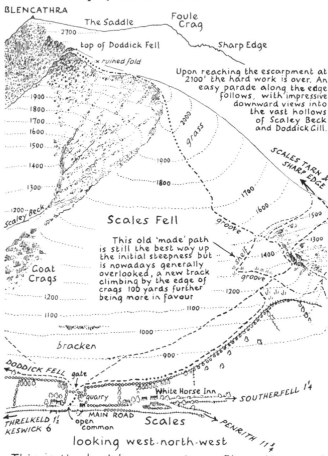

BLENCATHRA

The Saddle

Foule Crag

2700

top of Doddick Fell

Sharp Edge

× ruined fold

Upon reaching the escarpment at 2100' the hard work is over. An easy parade along the edge follows, with impressive downward views into the vast hollows of Scaley Beck and Doddick Gill.

1900
1800
1700
1600
1500
1400
1300
1200 Beck
Scaley Beck

2000 grass

SCALES TARN & SHARP EDGE

1900

1800

1700

1600

1500

groove

Scales Fell

1400

1300

shelf

This old 'made' path is still the best way up the initial steepness but is nowadays generally overlooked, a new track climbing by the edge of crags 100 yards further being more in favour

groove

Coat Crags

1200

1200

1100

1100

1000

bracken

900

DODDICK FELL gate

SOUTHERFELL 1¼

quarry

White Horse Inn

THRELKELD 1½
KESWICK 6

MAIN ROAD open common

Scales

PENRITH 11¾

looking west·north·west

This is the best-known route up Blencathra, and has been in common use for over a century. Even so, the tough grass of Scales Fell has resisted the formation of a continuous track. The climb, tedious up to 2000', becomes excellent in its later stages.

ASCENT FROM MUNGRISDALE
2250 feet of ascent : 4 miles

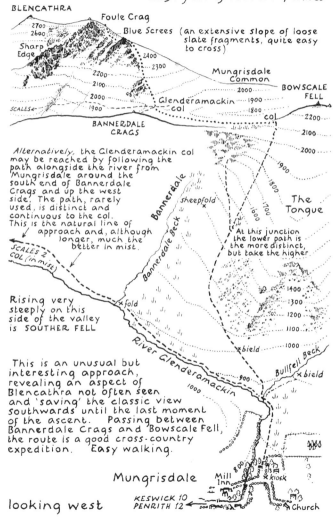

BLENCATHRA

Foule Crag

Blue Screes (an extensive slope of loose slate fragments, quite easy to cross)

2700
2600

Sharp Edge

2400
2300

2200
2100
2000
1900

SCALES

Mungrisdale Common

2000
1900
1800

BOWSCALE FELL

col

2200
2100
2000

Glenderamackin col

BANNERDALE CRAGS

Alternatively, the Glenderamackin col may be reached by following the path alongside the river from Mungrisdale around the south end of Bannerdale Crags and up the west side. The path, rarely used, is distinct and continuous to the col. This is the natural line of approach and, although longer, much the better in mist.

Bannerdale

sheepfold

Bannerdale Beck

1900
1800
1700
1600

The Tongue

At this junction the lower path is the more distinct, but take the higher.

SCALES 2 COL (in mist)

Rising very steeply on this side of the valley is SOUTHER FELL

×fold

1400
1300
1200
1100

This is an unusual but interesting approach, revealing an aspect of Blencathra not often seen and 'saving' the classic view southwards until the last moment of the ascent. Passing between Bannerdale Crags and Bowscale Fell, the route is a good cross-country expedition. Easy walking.

River Glenderamackin

1000

×bield

Bullfell Beck

×bield

900

1000

Mungrisdale

Mill Inn

×kiosk

Church

looking west

KESWICK 10
PENRITH 12

THE VIEW

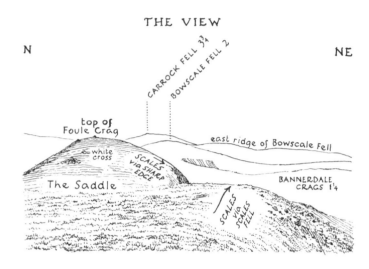

N   NE

CARROCK FELL 3¾
BOWSCALE FELL 2

top of
Foule Crag

east ridge of Bowscale Fell

white
cross

SCALES VIA SHARP EDGE

The Saddle

BANNERDALE
CRAGS 1¼

SCALES VIA SCALES FELL

THE SUMMIT

The summit is effectively poised above the abyss, precisely at the point where the ridge of Hall's Fell comes up out of the depths to a jutting headland. The summit is, in fact, known as Hallsfell Top. Much slaty stone is lying exposed here, but it is small stuff unsuitable for building imposing cairns, and nothing marks the highest point but a poor untidy heap of rubble; on occasion attempts are made to give the thing some shape and dignity but until somebody carries up a few decent-sized blocks the cairn will continue to disappoint by its insignificance.

The summit is windswept and shelterless and lacks a natural seat, but a few yards down Hall's Fell on the left the lee-side of a small outcrop usually cuts off the prevailing wind.

The excellent turf along the top deserves special mention.

continued

THE VIEW

NE   E

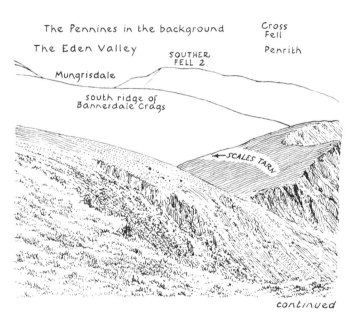

The Pennines in the background

Cross Fell

The Eden Valley

Penrith

SOUTHER FELL 2

Mungrisdale

south ridge of
Bannerdale Crags

← SCALES TARN

continued

Descents:

The best *ascents* are by the narrow ridges —— Hall's Fell,
Sharp Edge, Doddick Fell and Gategill Fell, *in that order* ——
but the best routes of *descent* are those tedious in ascent:
Blease Fell, Scales Fell, Glenderamackin col and Roughten
Gill, *in that order*. The latter two are roundabout and not
suitable in mist, but Blease Fell and Scales Fell, lying at
opposite ends of the well-defined summit escarpment, are
simple ways off in any weather. The narrow ridges will be
found bumpy going down, although Hall's Fell and Doddick
Fell are quite practicable and enjoyable, but all may become
dangerous under ice and snow.   The gills and ravines on
the southern front are much too rough to be considered for
descent no matter how good the weather.

THE VIEW

continued

E

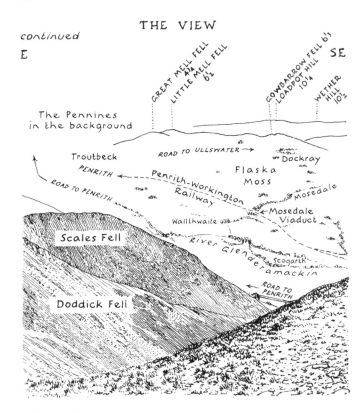

SE

Great Mell Fell 474
Little Mell Fell 612

Gowbarrow Fell 6's
Loadpot Hill 104
Wether Hill 102

The Pennines in the background

ROAD TO ULLSWATER →

Troutbeck

PENRITH ←

ROAD TO PENRITH

Penrith-Workington Railway

Dockray

Flaska Moss

Mosedale

Mosedale Viaduct

Wallthwaite

River Glenderamackin

Scogarth

ROAD TO PENRITH

Scales Fell

Doddick Fell

Mosedale....

The Mosedale appearing in the view above is not the Mosedale mentioned elsewhere in this book and situated at the foot of Carrock Fell. There are, in fact, six valleys of this name (signifying *desolation, dreariness*) in Lakeland and a pastime that might be adopted to fill in a few minutes while waiting for the rain to stop is to find them all on the 1" Ordnance Survey map of the district (one of them is spelt *Moasdale*). If, having done this, it still looks like raining for ever, make a list of all the different names on the map in which "thwaite" (a *clearing*) appears; this occupation will fill in the rest of the day until bedtime. On the 1" Tourist Map there are 81 *different*, many of them recurring. Enthusiastic thwaite-spotters will find several others on larger-scale maps.

THE VIEW

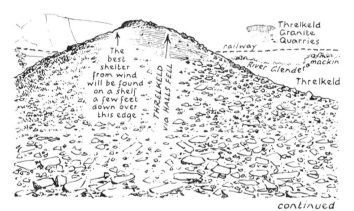

SE

HIGH RAISE 11¾
RAMPSGILL HEAD 11¾
PLACE FELL 8½
HIGH STREET 12½
THORNTHWAITE CRAG 12¾
FROSWICK 13¼
ILL BELL 14¼
CAUDALE MOOR 12½
HART SIDE 5½
RED SCREES 12½
ST SUNDAY CRAG 9½
GREAT DODD 4½
CATSTYCAM 7½
HELVELLYN 8
HELVELLYN LOWER MAN 7½

S

Wolf Crags
White Pike
CLOUGH HEAD 3¼

Threlkeld Common

The best shelter from wind will be found on a shelf a few feet down over this edge

THRELKELD VIA HALLS FELL

Threlkeld Granite Quarries
railway
River Glenderamackin
Threlkeld

continued

at Threlkeld....

• Look over both parapets of Threlkeld Bridge. Two streams, the River Glenderamackin and St. John's Beck, at this point unite, passing under the bridge individually but emerging as one: the River Greta. The bridge is built over the confluence.

• Walk up the lane signposted Wescoe for 200 yards to the entrance to Riddings, where excellent effigies of a fox and a hound surmount the gateposts. The Blencathra pack was formerly kennelled at Riddings, but is now at Gategill.

• Visit the little glen of Kilnhow Beck. A pleasant path starts near the Horse and Farrier and proceeds upstream to the open fell at Blease Gill with the help of footbridges. This sylvan dell is not publicised and is a charming surprise.

THE VIEW

continued

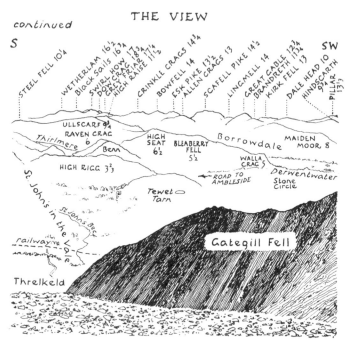

S · STEEL FELL 10¼ · WETHERLAM 16½ · BLACK SAILS 16¾ · SWIRL HOW 17½ · DOW CRAG 18¾ · GREY FRIAR 17¼ · HIGH RAISE 11½ · CRINKLE CRAGS 14¾ · BOWFELL 14 · ESK PIKE 13½ · ALLEN CRAGS 13 · SCAFELL PIKE 14½ · LINGMELL 14 · GREAT GABLE 12¾ · BRANDRETH 11¾ · KIRK FELL 13 · DALE HEAD 10 · HINDSCARTH 9¾ · PILLAR 13½ · SW

ULLSCARF 9½ · RAVEN CRAG · HIGH SEAT 6½ · BLEABERRY FELL 5½ · Borrowdale · MAIDEN MOOR 8

Thirlmere 6 · Bem · HIGH RIGG 3⅔ · WALLA CRAG 5 · Derwentwater

ROAD TO AMBLESIDE · Stone Circle

St. Johns in the · St Johns Beck · Tewet Tarn

railway · Threlkeld

Gategill Fell

The White Cross

In view from the summit is a landmark that has aroused the curiosity of visitors for a great many years: a collection of white crystallised stones of high quartz content, laid on the grass in the form of a cross on the easy rise to the top of Foule Crag, north of the Saddle.

This cross owes its existence to the industry of Harold Robinson of Threlkeld. Formerly there was a very small cross of stones here (locally ascribed as a memorial to a walker who lost his life on a rough slope adjacent) and Mr. Robinson, an enthusiastic lone hill-wanderer who has climbed his favourite Blencathra hundreds of times, collected more stones (veins of quartzite occur in the native slate nearby) and extended the cross to its present size of 16' by 10' during a succession of visits from 1945 onwards.

A much smaller but similar white cross on the southern slope of the Saddle is more recent, and the work of persons unknown.

THE VIEW

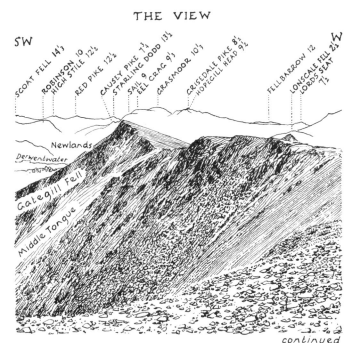

SW

Scoat Fell 14¾
Robinson 10
High Stile 12½
Red Pike 12½
Causey Pike 7¾
Starling Dodd 13½
Sail 9
Eel Crag 9¼
Grasmoor 10¼
Grisedale Pike 8½
Hopegill Head 9½
Fellbarrow 12
Lonscale Fell 21¼
Lords Seat 7½
W

Newlands
Derwentwater
Gategill Fell
Middle Tongue

continued

Blencathra's old mines

Blencathra has been mined fairly extensively and a variety of ores extracted from workings in the valleys of the Glenderaterra and Glenderamackin and from the adjacent and interlinked Gategill and Woodend mines, the debris of which is still very conspicuous in the Threlkeld landscape. All the mines are now closed, but within living memory were in production and prospering, and finding work for a labour force of 100.

Illustrated is an old level (a little beauty) at the northern workings of the Glenderaterra Mine, leading to a copper vein. The warning must be repeated that disused mine levels are unsafe because of flooding and collapse and often open into vertical pits.

THE VIEW

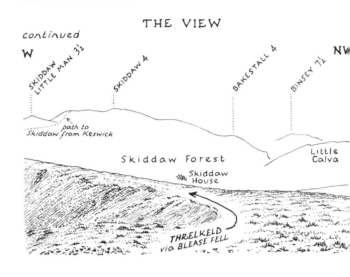

continued

W → NW

SKIDDAW LITTLE MAN 3½
SKIDDAW 4
BAKESTALL 4
BINSEY 7½
Little Calva

Skiddaw Forest

Skiddaw House

path to Skiddaw from Keswick

THRELKELD via BLEASE FELL

RIDGE ROUTE

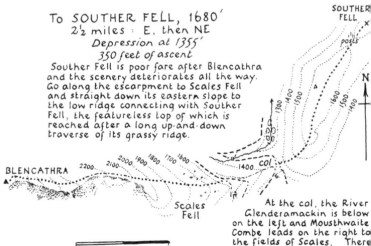

To SOUTHER FELL, 1680'
2½ miles : E, then NE
Depression at 1355'
350 feet of ascent

Souther Fell is poor fare after Blencathra and the scenery deteriorates all the way. Go along the escarpment to Scales Fell and straight down its eastern slope to the low ridge connecting with Souther Fell, the featureless top of which is reached after a long up-and-down traverse of its grassy ridge.

SOUTHER FELL
posts

N

BLENCATHRA
2200 2100 2000 1900 1800 1700 1600
1400
col
1300 1400 1500 1600 1500 1400

Scales Fell

HALF A MILE

At the col, the River Glenderamackin is below on the left and Mousthwaite Combe leads on the right to the fields of Scales. There are many tracks hereabouts.

THE VIEW

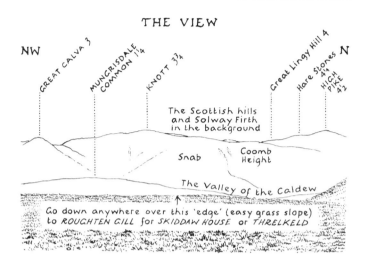

NW

GREAT CALVA 3
MUNGRISDALE COMMON 1¼
KNOTT 3¼
Great Lingy Hill 4
Hare Stones 4½
HIGH PIKE 4½

N

The Scottish hills and Solway Firth in the background

Snab
Coomb Height

The Valley of the Caldew

Go down anywhere over this 'edge' (easy grass slope) to ROUGHTEN GILL for SKIDDAW HOUSE or THRELKELD

RIDGE ROUTE

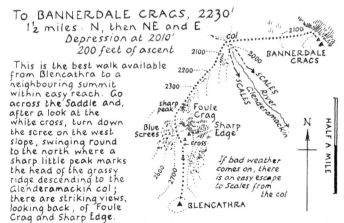

To BANNERDALE CRAGS, 2230'
1½ miles : N, then NE and E
Depression at 2010'
200 feet of ascent

This is the best walk available from Blencathra to a neighbouring summit within easy reach. Go across the Saddle and, after a look at the white cross, turn down the scree on the west slope, swinging round to the north where a sharp little peak marks the head of the grassy ridge descending to the Glenderamackin col; there are striking views, looking back, of Foule Crag and Sharp Edge.
 Cross the col, heading eastwards over a grassy expanse until halted by the edge of Bannerdale Crags, then turn to the right to reach the summit.

col
2100
BANNERDALE CRAGS
2100
2000
2200
SCALES
2300
SCALES River
Glenderamackin
sharp peak
Foule Crag
Blue Screes
Sharp Edge
SCALES
cross
2600
2700
N
HALF A MILE

If bad weather comes on, there is an easy escape to Scales from the col

▲ BLENCATHRA

13 | Skiddaw

Book Five: The Northern Fells

People can be a bit snobby about Skiddaw. Real climbers consider it too bland, too easy, nowt more than a stroll, nothing dangerous to fall off. It's easy to get to, with excellent access, unlike Scafell Pike. You can start climbing as soon as you park the car and be up and down in three hours, with all the kids, the family dog as well. Nae bother.

In 1815, Wordsworth and Southey took their respective families for a bonfire party and feast on top of Skiddaw to celebrate victory at Waterloo. The servants did the actual carrying up of the roast beef and plum pudding, but it's an indication of how easy the fell can be.

Wainwright doesn't fall into the trap of being dismissive, but it's noticeable that he devotes only 28 pages to Skiddaw, eight fewer than he does to Blencathra next door, which is a lower mountain (albeit with more ascents). But he loves Skiddaw nonetheless and does all walkers a great service by giving details of seven other ascents, apart from the one from Keswick. That's the one most people take, and usually cheat by driving up to Gale Road and parking there. Wainwright didn't give parking possibilities, since, of course, he didn't have a car. That could have been a hostage to fortune, as we know parking places and regulations change all the time.

Now and again, he mentions bus routes and numbers, as on Skiddaw 17 where he lists routes 35 and 71. He knew Lakeland bus routes by heart, depended totally upon them, and perhaps assumed they would last, if not for always then long enough to see him out. Today, he could wait for ever for a bus and wouldn't even recognize the names of the bus companies if any did come along.

Ribble has gone from Cumbria. It was part of Cumbrian life and my life at one time. As a student, I worked as a Ribble conductor in the university long vacations and was properly trained, going to Preston for a residential weekend, which included an exam and a passing-out parade. I wonder if Wainwright ever got on my bus? Probably not. In 1958, when I was a Ribble clippie, he was still working on *The Southern Fells*.

When compiling *The Northern Fells*, he was still able to manage a lot of the main fells by taking the bus on the road from Kendal up to Keswick and then immediately starting to walk up Skiddaw, or the Back o' Skidda', as locals call the mountains behind.

On Skiddaw 6, there is a nice drawing of Skiddaw House, a remarkable feature of Skiddaw, since it is unusual to have a proper building halfway up a mountain. On Skiddaw 8, he described it as a 'row of cottages in partial occupation by shepherds'. He even named the present resident shepherd who stayed there five nights a week. By using the word 'present', he made it clear he realised that that particular shepherd would not always be there. He probably presumed, however, that the building itself would last for ever, a haven for other shepherds.

So is Skiddaw House still there? It certainly is. And it looks pretty much like his drawing. Time and the economy might have caught up with him on buses and railways, but not Skiddaw House, which is in good condition and since 1991 has been used as a Youth Hostel. As we all know, Youth Hostels no longer just take youths, but are open to any age, and you don't even have to do chores like cleaning floors any more.

If Wainwright is watching us from up there, I'm sure he'll be pleased to know that if he were compiling Skiddaw again, he should be able to stay in Skiddaw House overnight, as long as it remains a hostel. No need to bivouac on the mountainside.

Skiddaw

3053'

from Burntod Gill

NATURAL FEATURES

Make no mistake about Skiddaw.

Heed not the disparaging criticisms that have been written from time to time, often by learned men who ought to have known better, about this grand old mountain. It is an easy climb, yes; its slopes are smooth and grassy, yes; it has no frightful precipices, no rugged outcrops, agreed; it offers nothing of interest or entertainment to rock-gymnasts, agreed. If these are failings, they must be conceded. But are they not quite minor failings? Are they failings at all?

Skiddaw is the fourth highest peak in Lakeland and but little lower than the highest, Scafell Pike. It is the oldest mountain in the district, according to the evidence of its rocks, definitely not the most impressive in appearance but certainly one of the noblest. The summit is buttressed magnificently by a circle of lesser heights, all of them members of the proud Skiddaw family, the whole forming a splendid and complete example of the structure of mountains, especially well seen from all directions because of its isolation. Its lines are smooth, its curves graceful; but because the slopes are steep everywhere, the quick build-up of the *massif* from valley levels to central summit is appreciated at a glance — and it should be an appreciative glance, for such massive strength and such beauty of outline rarely go together....... Here, on Skiddaw, they do.

● Orthwaite

Bassenthwaite
●

● Dash

▲ BAKESTALL

High ● Side

SKIDDAW
▲

ULLOCK PIKE ▲   ● Skiddaw
LONG SIDE ▲   House
CARL SIDE ▲   ▲ SKIDDAW LITTLE MAN
Little ● Crosthwaite   ▲ LONSCALE
      ▲ DODD   FELL

● Millbeck
● Applethwaite
                              ●
LATRIGG ▲ Threlkeld

MILES

0   1   2   3   ● Keswick

continued

NATURAL FEATURES
continued

Geographically, too, the mountain is of great importance, its main ridge forming the watershed between the Derwent and the Eden. This feature emphasises Skiddaw's supremacy over the rest of the northern fells, for, although situated in the south-west corner of the group, the waters from its eastern slopes cut through the middle of this outlying barrier to augment the drainage from the Pennines — and not even the neighbouring Blencathra, much more handily placed to the east, has been able to accomplish this feat. Engineers have noted this enterprise on the part of Skiddaw and are planning to impound its eastern flow in a reservoir at Caldew Head.

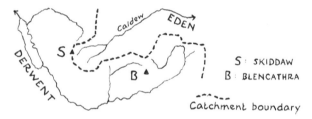

S : SKIDDAW
B : BLENCATHRA

Catchment boundary

Skiddaw has special interests for geologists. It is apparent, even to unobservant walkers, that the stones covering the summit and exposed in eroded gullies and valleys are very different in character from those seen in the central parts of the district: the latter are of volcanic origin, those on Skiddaw are marine deposits and consist in the main of soft shale or slate which splits readily into thin wafers and soon decays and crumbles when exposed to the atmosphere; hence it has no commercial value. Skiddaw was formed long before the volcanos of central Lakeland became active; later it overlooked a vast glacier system, a world of ice. Some volcanic boulders are found along the lower southern slopes of the Skiddaw group: these rocks have been identified with those of the cliffs enclosing St.John's-in-the-Vale, having been carried along and deposited here when the glaciers retreated and scoured the flanks of Skiddaw on their passage to the frozen sea.

continued

NATURAL FEATURES

continued

Skiddaw displays a quite different appearance to each of the four points of the compass. The southern aspect is a very familiar sight to visitors, being in unrestricted view from Derwentwater, the Borrowdale fells and most of the higher summits of Lakeland. There is a classical quality about this view from the south. Skiddaw and its outliers rise magnificently across the wide Vale of Keswick in a beautifully-symmetrical arrangement, as if posed for a family photograph. The old man himself is the central figure at the back of the group, with his five older children in a line before him (the favourite son, Little Man, being placed nearest) and the two younger children at the front. (Finicky readers who dispute this analogy because no mother to the brood is included in the picture (this is admitted, all the characters being masculine except sweet little Latrigg) are proferred the explanation that Skiddaw is a widower, the old lady having perished in the Ice Age — she couldn't stand the cold).

from the south

SKIDDAW

ULLOCK PIKE   LONG SIDE   CARL SIDE   LITTLE MAN   Jenkin Hill   LONSCALE FELL

DODD   Underskiddaw   LATRIGG

The western aspect is best known to Bassenthwaite folk, who enjoy a secret delight few others have discovered — the glorious sunset colourings of the mountain, winter and summer alike : a beauty that brings people to their doors in rapt admiration. There is little beauty of outline, though, Skiddaw here appearing at its most massive, a great arc high in the sky, and the only shapeliness in the scene from the west is provided by the graceful cone of Ullock Pike and the curving ridge beyond. Two deep valleys, long shadowy recesses in the mountain, are conspicuous features.

from the west

SKIDDAW

Broad End   CARL SIDE   LITTLE MAN

BAKESTALL

LONG SIDE

Cockup   ULLOCK PIKE   LATRIGG

DODD

Bassenthwaite

continued

NATURAL FEATURES

continued

Skiddaw, northwards, faces the unfrequented Uldale Fells, and not many regular visitors to Lakeland would recognise it in an uncaptioned photograph taken from this side. The northern aspect is truly impressive nonetheless; not quite so overpowering as when viewed from Bassenthwaite to the west but having now a greater majesty and dignity. The summit-ridge is seen end-on and appears as a neat pyramid overtopping the sprawling mass of Broad End, below which is the remarkable combe of Dead Crags. All waters coming down this side of Skiddaw, as those on the south and west, in due course reach the Derwent.

from the north

The east slopes of the mountain, collectively known as Skiddaw Forest, dominate the vast upland basin of Caldew Head, a scene more suggestive of a Scottish glen than of Lakeland, a place incredibly wild and desolate and bare, its loneliness accentuated by the solitary dwellings of Skiddaw House, yet strongly appealing and, in certain lights, often strangely beautiful. In this great hollow the waters unite to form the River Caldew, an important feeder of the Eden. Skiddaw is least impressive from the east because there is much less fall on this side. The scene is in view, although not intimately, from Blencathra.

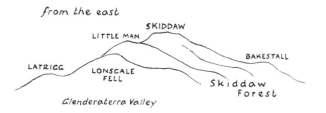

from the east

continued

NATURAL FEATURES

continued

This, then, is Skiddaw, a giant in stature. But an affable and friendly giant.

And a benevolent one. Keswick people have an inborn affection for Skiddaw, and it is well earned. The mountain makes a great contribution to the scenic beauty of this most attractively-situated town, shelters it from northerly gales, supplies it with pure water, feeds its sheep, and provides a recreation ground for its visitors. Throughout the centuries Skiddaw's beacon has warned of the town's troubles and alarms — "the red glare on Skiddaw roused the burghers of Carlisle" — and today shares in its rejoicings.

Skiddaw's critics have passed on, or will soon pass on. Their span of life is short. Skiddaw has stood there in supreme majesty, the sole witness to the creation of Lakeland, for millions of years and will be there to the end of time, continuing to give service and pleasure to insignificant and unimportant mortals.

Let us at least be grateful.

At the back o' beyond.....   *Skiddaw House*

MAP

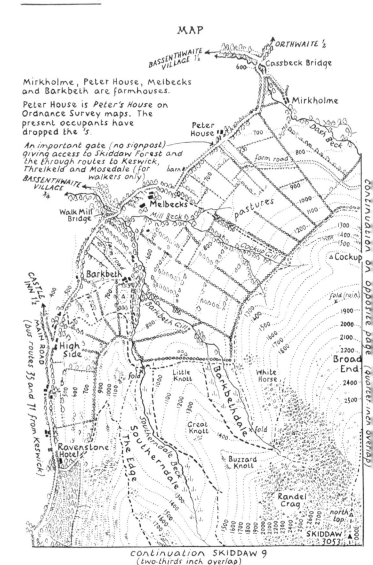

ORTHWAITE ½

BASSENTHWAITE
VILLAGE 1½

Cassbeck Bridge

600

Mirkholme

Mirkholme, Peter House, Melbecks
and Barkbeth are farmhouses.

Peter House is *Peter's House* on
Ordnance Survey maps. The
present occupants have
dropped the 's.

Peter
House

700

Dash Beck

800

An important gate (no signpost)
giving access to Skiddaw Forest and
the through routes to Keswick,
Threlkeld and Mosedale (for
walkers only)

farm road

barn

900

BASSENTHWAITE
VILLAGE ¾

pastures

1000

1100

Walk Mill
Bridge

Melbecks

Mill Beck

700

800

1300

1400

1500

Cockup Gill

Cockup

Barkbeth

400

fold (ruin)

1900

CASTLE
INN 1½

400

Barkbeth Gill

1500

2000

2100

2200

Broad
End

MAIN ROAD
(bus routes 35 and 71 from Keswick)

High
Side

fold

900

Little
Knott

White
Horse

2400

2300

Barkbethdale

Ravenstone
Hotel

Southerndale Beck

The Edge

Southerndale

Great
Knott

1400

fold

Buzzard
Knott

1400

1500

Randel
Crag

north
top

1700

SKIDDAW
3053

continuation SKIDDAW 9
(two-thirds inch overlap)

continuation on opposite page (quarter inch overlap)

MAP

For ease of reference, the map of Skiddaw on this and the accompanying pages includes the whole *massif*, although the outlying summits (shown in CAPITALS) have separate chapters in the book.

The supply road to Skiddaw House is narrow and unenclosed, with a loose and gravelly surface. It is not good enough for cars (cheers) but is a very convenient means of access to the great wilderness of Skiddaw Forest for travellers on foot.

Skiddaw Forest is the general name of the vast heathery amphitheatre at the base of the eastern slopes of Skiddaw. It is a forest entirely without trees (except for a planted windbreak at Skiddaw House).

Skiddaw House is not a single residence, but a row of cottages in partial occupation by shepherds. The present shepherd in residence here (five days a week, with only his dogs for company) is Pearson Dalton of Fell Side.

The shelter indicated on this page is a substantial open-fronted, well-roofed structure, furnished with seats. (Weary novices should note that it's no use waiting here for a bus.) The presence of butts in the vicinity suggests that it was provided originally for shooting parties.

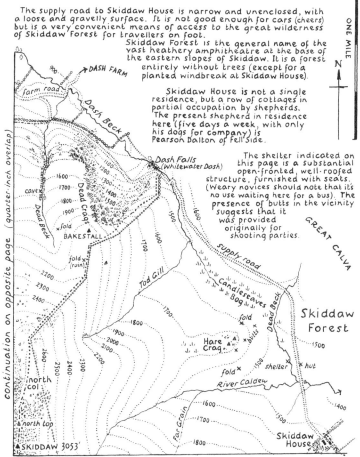

continuation on opposite page (quarter-inch overlap)

continuation SKIDDAW 10
(two-thirds inch overlap)

MAP
continuation SKIDDAW 7

Keswick's water supplies
are drawn from
  Mill Beck (main source)
  Applethwaite Gill
  Burr Gill and
  Whit Beck

ONE MILE

MAP

continuation SKIDDAW 8

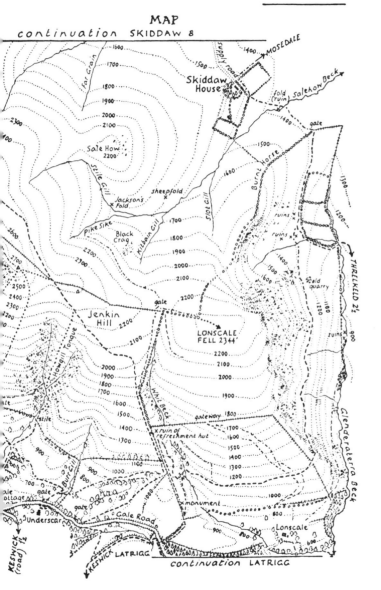

ASCENT FROM KESWICK
2850 feet of ascent : 5½ miles

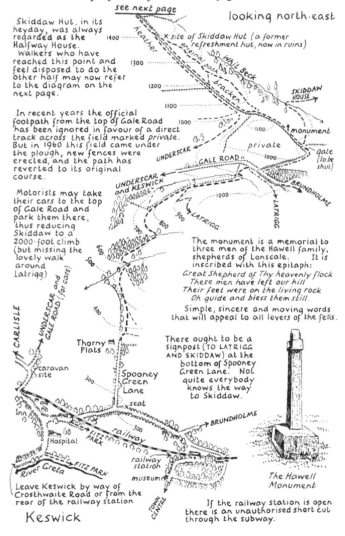

see next page

looking north-east

× site of Skiddaw Hut (a former refreshment hut, now in ruins)

1400

1300

1200

1100

heather

original path

Whit Beck

bracken

1000

SKIDDAW HOUSE

1100

monument

private

gate (to be shut)

UNDERSCAR

GALE ROAD

1000

UNDERSCAR and KESWICK

BRUNDHOLME

LATRIGG

1000

LATRIGG

900

800

700

600

500

400

UNDERSCAR and GALE ROAD (for cars)

CARLISLE

Thorny Plats

Spooney Green Lane

300

seat

Inn

Hospital

FITZ PARK

railway

300

BRUNDHOLME

caravan site

FITZ PARK

River Greta

railway station

museum

TOWN CENTRE

Keswick

Skiddaw Hut, in its heyday, was always regarded as the Halfway House.
Walkers who have reached this point and feel disposed to do the other half may now refer to the diagram on the next page.

In recent years the official footpath from the top of Gale Road has been ignored in favour of a direct track across the field marked *private*. But in 1960 this field came under the plough, new fences were erected, and the path has reverted to its original course.

Motorists may take their cars to the top of Gale Road and park them there, thus reducing Skiddaw to a 2000-foot climb (but missing the lovely walk around Latrigg).

The monument is a memorial to three men of the Hawell family, shepherds of Lonscale. It is inscribed with this epitaph:
*Great Shepherd of Thy heavenly flock
These men have left our hill
Their feet were on the living rock
Oh guide and bless them still.*

Simple, sincere and moving words that will appeal to all lovers of the fells.

There ought to be a signpost (TO LATRIGG AND SKIDDAW) at the bottom of Spooney Green Lane. Not quite everybody knows the way to Skiddaw.

The Hawell Monument

Leave Keswick by way of Crosthwaite Road or from the rear of the railway station

If the railway station is open there is an unauthorised short cut through the subway.

ASCENT FROM KESWICK

continued

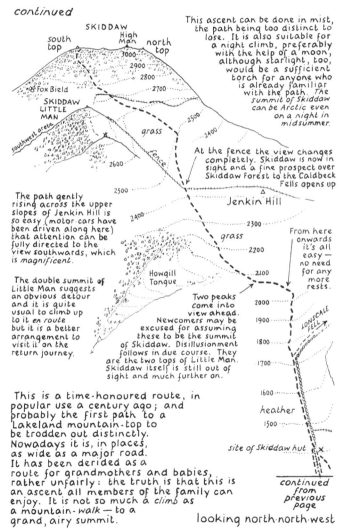

SKIDDAW
High
Man

south
top

3000

north
top

2900

2800

2700

Fox Bield

SKIDDAW
LITTLE
MAN

2500

southwest arête

grass

2400

2600

fence

2500

This ascent can be done in mist, the path being too distinct to lose. It is also suitable for a night climb, preferably with the help of a moon, although starlight, too, would be a sufficient torch for anyone who is already familiar with the path. *The summit of Skiddaw can be Arctic even on a night in midsummer.*

At the fence the view changes completely. Skiddaw is now in sight and a fine prospect over Skiddaw Forest to the Caldbeck Fells opens up

Jenkin Hill

The path gently rising across the upper slopes of Jenkin Hill is so easy (motor-cars have been driven along here) that attention can be fully directed to the view southwards, which is *magnificent*.

2400

grass

2300

2200

Howgill
Tongue

2100

From here onwards it's all easy — no need for any more rests.

The double summit of Little Man suggests an obvious detour and it is quite usual to climb up to it *en route* but it is a better arrangement to visit it on the return journey.

Two peaks come into view ahead. Newcomers may be excused for assuming these to be the summit of Skiddaw. Disillusionment follows in due course. They are the two tops of Little Man. Skiddaw itself is still out of sight and much further on.

2000

1900

1800

1700

LONSCALE FELL

This is a time-honoured route, in popular use a century ago; and probably the first path to a Lakeland mountain-top to be trodden out distinctly. Nowadays it is, in places, as wide as a major road. It has been derided as a route for grandmothers and babies, rather unfairly: the truth is that this is an ascent all members of the family can enjoy. It is not so much a *climb* as a mountain-*walk* — to a grand, airy summit.

1600

heather

1500

site of Skiddaw hut

continued from previous page

looking north-north-west

ASCENT FROM MILLBECK
2750 feet of ascent : 2¾ miles

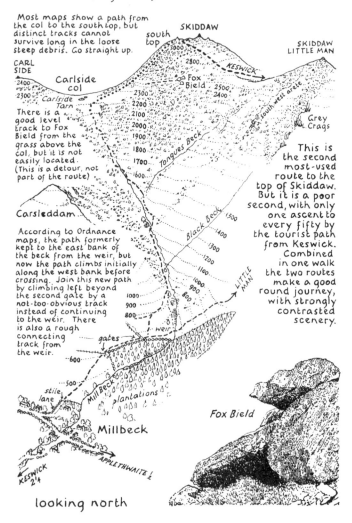

Most maps show a path from the col to the south top, but distinct tracks cannot survive long in the loose steep debris. Go straight up.

CARL SIDE

Carlside col

Carlside Tarn

2400
2300

SKIDDAW

south top

3000

2800

Fox Bield

2300
2200
2100
2000
1900
1800
1700
1600

KESWICK

2500
2400

SKIDDAW LITTLE MAN

south west arête

Grey Crags

There is a good level track to Fox Bield from the grass above the col, but it is not easily located. (This is a detour, not part of the route)

Tongues Beck

Carsleddam

According to Ordnance maps, the path formerly kept to the east bank of the beck from the weir, but now the path climbs initially along the west bank before crossing. Join this new path by climbing left beyond the second gate by a not-too-obvious track instead of continuing to the weir. There is also a rough connecting track from the weir.

Black Beck

1500
1400
1300
1200
1100
1000
900
800

LITTLE MAN

1000
900
800

weir

gates

600

500

stile lane

Mill Beck

plantations

Millbeck

APPLETHWAITE ½

KESWICK 2¼

This is the second most-used route to the top of Skiddaw. But it is a poor second, with only one ascent to every fifty by the tourist path from Keswick. Combined in one walk the two routes make a good round journey, with strongly contrasted scenery.

Fox Bield

looking north

ASCENT FROM APPLETHWAITE
2700 feet of ascent : 3 miles

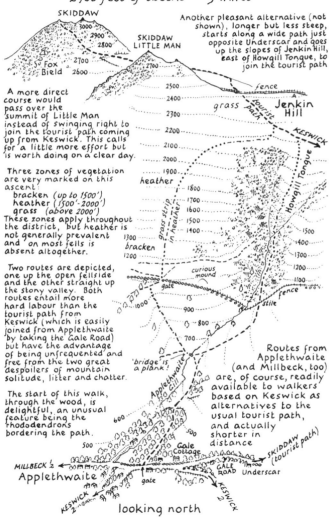

Another pleasant alternative (not shown), longer but less steep, starts along a wide path just opposite Underscar and goes up the slopes of Jenkin Hill, east of Howgill Tongue, to join the tourist path

A more direct course would pass over the summit of Little Man instead of swinging right to join the tourist path coming up from Keswick. This calls for a little more effort but is worth doing on a clear day.

Three zones of vegetation are very marked on this ascent:
bracken (up to 1500')
heather (1500'-2000')
grass (above 2000')
These zones apply throughout the district, but heather is not generally prevalent and on most fells is absent altogether.

Two routes are depicted, one up the open fellside and the other straight up the stony valley. Both routes entail more hard labour than the tourist path from Keswick (which is easily joined from Applethwaite by taking the Gale Road) but have the advantage of being unfrequented and free from the two great despoilers of mountain solitude, litter and chatter.

The start of this walk, through the wood, is delightful, an unusual feature being the rhododendrons bordering the path.

Routes from Applethwaite (and Millbeck, too) are, of course, readily available to walkers based on Keswick as alternatives to the usual tourist path, and actually shorter in distance

SKIDDAW

SKIDDAW LITTLE MAN

Fox Bield

fence

grass

Jenkin Hill

KESWICK

Howgill Tongue

heather

grass strip in heather

bracken

curious mound

gate

fence

stile

'bridge' is a plank!

Applethwaite Gill

Gale Cottage

SKIDDAW (tourist path)

MILLBECK ½

Applethwaite

GALE ROAD   Underscar

gate

KESWICK 2

KESWICK 2

looking north

ASCENTS FROM BASSENTHWAITE VILLAGE
AND HIGH SIDE

2800 feet of ascent : 4-4½ miles (from Bassenthwaite Village)

2700 feet
3¼-3¾ miles
(from High Side)

north top
SKIDDAW
south top

3000

North top

2900

Gibraltar Crag

North col

2800

Carlside col

2700
2600
2500
2400

plateau

2300
2200
2100
2000
1900
1800
1700
1600

ruined fold

Randel Crag

Lakeland is far removed from world events and it is unusual to find a 'foreign' name in use here. Gibraltar Crag must owe its title to an enthusiastic local patriot.

Buzzard Knott

1500

Southerndale

north-west ridge

sledgate

ULLOCK PIKE

1400

Southerndale Beck

1500

Great Knott

1300

The Edge

1400

Little Knott

1200

1300

Barkbethdale

1100

1200

Gibraltar Crag and Randel Crag are merely steep loose roughnesses. Neither would earn the name of crag in the Scafell area.

boulders (a little Stonehenge)

1000

fold

1100

1000

900

800

900

RAVENSTONE

intake wall

800

boulder

700

Barkbeth

farm road

600

gorse

500

High Side

←ORTHWAITE 1½

ruin

500

BASSENTHWAITE VILLAGE 1½ CASTLE INN 1½

MAIN ROAD KESWICK 6

The sledgates are wide grassy paths originally made for the passage of sledges (here probably bringing down stones for the walls). Nowadays their only use is as "drove roads" when sheep are being gathered.

Chapel Beck

Burthwaite

More details of the routes are given on the opposite page

Bassenthwaite Village

looking south-east

ASCENTS FROM BASSENTHWAITE VILLAGE
AND HIGH SIDE
continued

THE NORTH·WEST RIDGE: Ask a Barkbeth sheep what the north-west ridge of Skiddaw is like and it will reply without hesitation "C'est magnifique" (if it is French, which is unlikely) — which just shows how tastes differ, for most walkers, less easily satisfied, will consider it disappointing. Its one attribute is its peace and quietness. There is no path along it, no line of cairns, no litter, nothing to show that others may have passed this way. It is a low, gentle hump, entirely grassy (hence the enthusiastic rejoinder quoted above), rising between Southerndale and Barkbethdale and not too well defined until the ground steepens into Randel Crag; a few easy rocks here may be scrambled up or circumvented to give access to a grassy shelf, where the ridge proper ends. A tiny tarn here is shaped like a W. Rising ahead is the scree-slope falling from Skiddaw's top: this is vaster than it appears to be and much longer, but not unpleasant to ascend, the scree being a soft, yielding shale. The only interest here derives from an attempt to score a bulls-eye by 'hitting' the summit-cairn direct (it is out of sight until the last minute).

SOUTHERNDALE, too, is quiet and unfrequented although a clear-cut valley and useful for quick and easy progress, the final climb up to Carlside col giving less trouble than the approach to it suggests. A sledgate 'road' is a good help; when it ceases (close by an old and scattered cairn) a narrow trod continues to the sheepfold. At the col turn half-left up a scree-slope to the south top. Southerndale is dominated more by Long Side and Ullock Pike than by Skiddaw.

Neither of these routes, nor that via Barkbethdale, is to be compared as a way up Skiddaw from the north-west, in interest, views or grandeur, with the fine high-level traverse of Ullock Pike and Long Side; they are direct routes, however, and as such have a certain appeal.

Concave and convex slopes

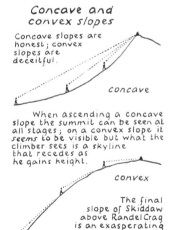

Concave slopes are honest; convex slopes are deceitful.

concave

When ascending a concave slope the summit can be seen at all stages; on a convex slope it seems to be visible but what the climber sees is a skyline that recedes as he gains height.

convex

The final slope of Skiddaw above Randel Crag is an exasperating example of convexity

Ullock Pike, from Randel Crag

ASCENTS FROM BASSENTHWAITE VILLAGE AND HIGH SIDE

2800 feet of ascent : 5 miles (from Bassenthwaite Village)
2700 feet
4¼ miles
(from High Side)

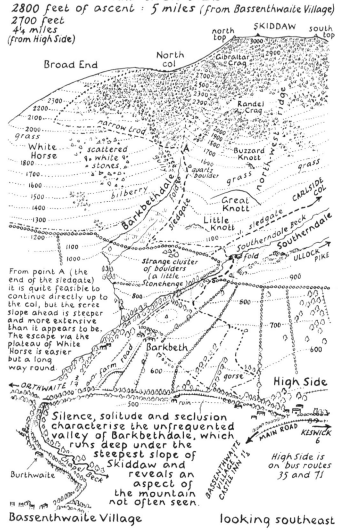

From point A (the end of the sledgate) it is quite feasible to continue directly up to the col, but the scree slope ahead is steeper and more extensive than it appears to be. The escape via the plateau of White Horse is easier but a long way round.

Silence, solitude and seclusion characterise the unfrequented valley of Barkbethdale, which runs deep under the steepest slope of Skiddaw and reveals an aspect of the mountain not often seen.

High Side is on bus routes 35 and 71

Bassenthwaite Village

looking southeast

Southerndale *from the gate in the intake wall above Barkbeth. Carlside col, Long Side and Ullock Pike on skyline.*

Barkbethdale *from Little Knott on the north-west ridge. Looking to Skiddaw; Randel Crag below on right.*

ASCENT FROM MELBECKS
2500 feet of ascent : 3 miles

This route is included only because of the insistence of the Ordnance Survey (repeated in various editions of their maps of 1" scale and upwards) in depicting a footpath from the road-corner near Melbecks up to the intake wall — which might attract the attention of walkers and lure them in search of it.

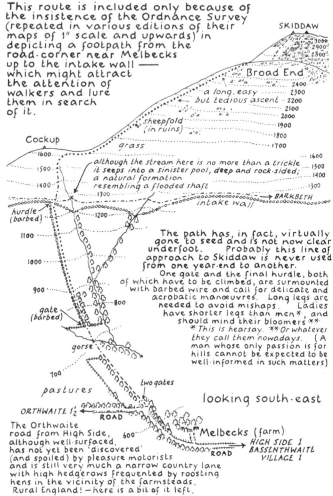

SKIDDAW

2400
2900
2800
Broad End
2400
a long, easy 2300
but tedious ascent ... 2200
2100
2000
sheepfold 1900
(in ruins) 1800
1700
Cockup
grass 1600
1600
although the stream here is no more than a trickle 1500
1500 it seeps into a sinister pool, deep and rock-sided;
a natural formation
1400 resembling a flooded shaft 1400
1300 BARKBETH
intake wall 1300
hurdle
(barbed) 1200

1100

1000

900
gate
(barbed) 800

gorse

700

pastures

ORTHWAITE 1½ ROAD

two gates

looking south-east

Melbecks (farm)
HIGH SIDE 1
BASSENTHWAITE
VILLAGE 1
600 ROAD

The path has, in fact, virtually gone to seed and is not now clear underfoot.   Probably this line of approach to Skiddaw is never used from one year-end to another.
    One gate and the final hurdle, both of which have to be climbed, are surmounted with barbed wire and call for delicate and acrobatic manoeuvres.   Long legs are needed to avoid mishaps.   Ladies have shorter legs than men*, and should mind their bloomers.**
    * This is hearsay. ** Or whatever they call them nowadays. (A man whose only passion is for hills cannot be expected to be well-informed in such matters)

The Orthwaite road from High Side, although well-surfaced, has not yet been 'discovered' (and spoiled) by pleasure motorists and is still very much a narrow country lane with high hedgerows frequented by roosting hens in the vicinity of the farmsteads. Rural England! — here is a bit of it left.

Of all ways up Skiddaw this is the least interesting.

ASCENT FROM THE ROAD TO SKIDDAW HOUSE
1800 feet of ascent : 2 miles from Dash Falls

2750 feet : 6 miles
from High Side or
Bassenthwaite Village

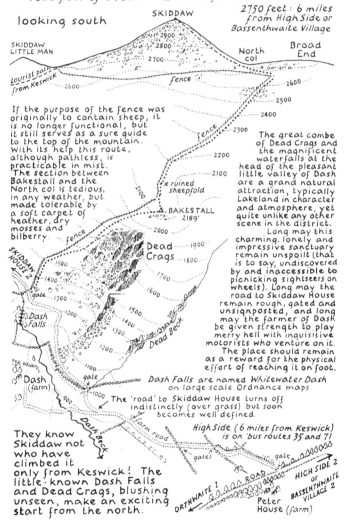

looking south

SKIDDAW

SKIDDAW
LITTLE MAN

2900
2800
2700

North col

Broad End

tourist path
from Keswick

fence

2600

2600

2500

2400

2300

fence

2200

2100

x ruined
sheepfold

2100

△ BAKESTALL
2189'

2000

fence

1900

1800

Dead
Crags

1500

1400

1300

1700

1600

1500

1400

1300

1200

1100

SKIDDAW
HOUSE 2

gate

Dash
Falls

Dead Beck

gate

1000

Dash
(farm)

Dash beck

farm road

900

High Side (6 miles from Keswick)
is on 'bus routes 35 and 71

ORTHWAITE 1

ROAD

gates

gate

HIGH SIDE 2
or
BASSENTHWAITE
VILLAGE 2

Peter
House (farm)

If the purpose of the fence was originally to contain sheep, it is no longer functional, but it still serves as a sure guide to the top of the mountain. With its help this route, although pathless, is practicable in mist. The section between Bakestall and the North col is tedious, in any weather, but made tolerable by a soft carpet of heather, dry mosses and bilberry.

The great combe of Dead Crags and the magnificent waterfalls at the head of the pleasant little valley of Dash are a grand natural attraction, typically Lakeland in character and atmosphere, yet quite unlike any other scene in the district. Long may this charming, lonely and impressive sanctuary remain unspoilt (that is to say, undiscovered by and inaccessible to picnicking sightseers on wheels). Long may the road to Skiddaw House remain rough, gated and unsignposted, and long may the farmer of Dash be given strength to play merry hell with inquisitive motorists who venture on it. The place should remain as a reward for the physical effort of reaching it on foot.

Dash Falls are named Whitewater Dash on large scale Ordnance maps

The 'road' to Skiddaw House turns off indistinctly (over grass) but soon becomes well defined.

They know Skiddaw not who have climbed it only from Keswick! The little-known Dash Falls and Dead Crags, blushing unseen, make an exciting start from the north.

ASCENT FROM SKIDDAW HOUSE
1600 feet of ascent : 2½ miles (via Sale How); 1700 feet,
3 miles (via Hare Crag)

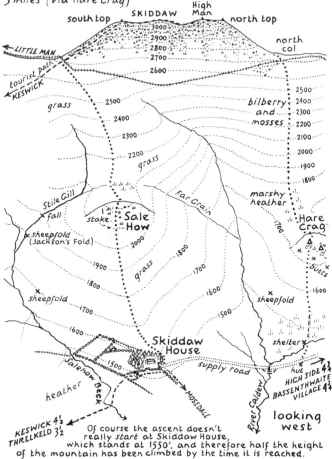

SKIDDAW
High Man
south top   north top
3000
2900
2800
2700
2600

LITTLE MAN
tourist path
KESWICK

north col

north

grass   2500
2400
2300
2200   grass

bilberry
and
mosses

2500
2400
2300
2200
2100
2000
1900
1800

Stile Gill
× fall
× stake
Sale How
× sheepfold
(Jackson's Fold)

Far Crain

marshy
heather

Hare
Crag

2000
1900
1800
1700

grass   1800
1700
1600
1500

△ △
× ×
butts

1600

× sheepfold

× sheepfold

shelter

Skiddaw
House

supply road

hut
HIGH SIDE 4½
BASSENTHWAITE
VILLAGE 4½

Salehow Beck

heather

MOSEDALE

River Calder

looking
west

KESWICK 4½
THRELKELD 3½

Of course the ascent doesn't
really *start* at Skiddaw House,
which stands at 1550', and therefore half the height
of the mountain has been climbed by the time it is reached.

The eastern slopes of Skiddaw are gently inclined, and
progress is smooth and simple. Two routes are given,
alike in having an intermediate height; the more direct,
by Sale How, is on dry grass; that by Hare Crag is rather
more interesting but wet initially. The Hare Crag route
follows the important Derwent-Eden watershed.

THE SUMMIT

looking south

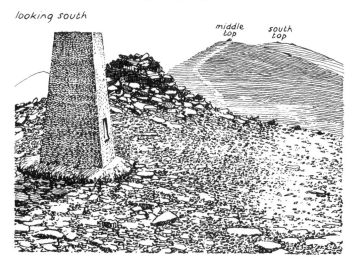

Some walkers, but not many, will be disappointed by the ease with which the summit of Skiddaw can be gained and the lack of exciting terrain during the ascent, especially if they have used the tourist path from Keswick, but the top itself is rough enough and airy enough to suit all tastes. It takes the form of a stony, undulating ridge exceeding 3000' throughout its length of almost half a mile and provides a glorious promenade high in the sky where one can enjoy a rare feeling of freedom and escape from a world far below, and, for a time, forgotten.

There is a south top and a north top, a middle top and a main top, all in line and connected by a pavement of slaty stones. In mist it is not uncommon to assume the middle top to be the highest point, there being a descent immediately following (when approached from the south, as is usual) but a final halt should not be made until the Ordnance Survey's triangulation column (S 1543) is reached: this is the true, the indisputable, summit.

A feature of the ridge is a series of roughly-erected wind shelters of stones, crescent-shaped to make them snug (they fail lamentably in this object) — these are only partially effective against cruel gales and useless as a protection in rain. The summit is completely exposed to the north and its weather can be fierce.

Skiddaw is often described as 'merely a grassy hill.' But its summit is the summit of a mountain.'

continued

THE SUMMIT

continued

DESCENTS

The few shaded areas (⫿⫿⫿) are rough: these apart, the summit may be left safely in any direction. The only continuous path is that to Keswick.

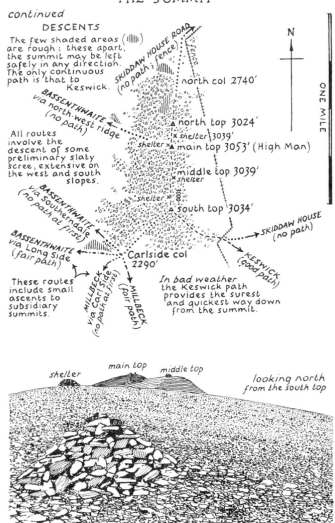

SKIDDAW HOUSE ROAD *(no path; fence)*

fence

north col 2740'

N

ONE MILE

BASSENTHWAITE *via north-west ridge (no path)*

△ north top 3024'
× *shelter* 3039'
shelter × main top 3053' (High Man)

All routes involve the descent of some preliminary slaty scree, extensive on the west and south slopes.

middle top 3039'
shelter

3000

BASSENTHWAITE *via Southerndale (no path at first)*

shelter × South top 3034'

→ SKIDDAW HOUSE *(no path)*

BASSENTHWAITE *via Long Side (fair path)*

Carlside col 2290'

→ KESWICK *(good path)*

These routes include small ascents to subsidiary summits.

MILLBECK *via Carl Side (no path at first)*

MILLBECK *(fair path)*

In bad weather the Keswick path provides the surest and quickest way down from the summit.

shelter   *main top*   *middle top*

looking north from the south top

RIDGE ROUTES

To SKIDDAW LITTLE MAN, 2837': 1 mile : S, then SSE
Depression at 2680'
190 feet of ascent
A good detour on the way down to Keswick

Use the Keswick path to the first fence, which follow to the right across a grassy furrowed depression to the stony cone now directly ahead.

To CARL SIDE, 2420':
1 mile : S, then SW
Depression at 2290'
160 feet of ascent
One unavoidably rough section

From the south top go bravely down the steepening slope of loose scree south-west, wasting no time looking for a path. Aim for the depression soon in view below, escaping to grass at the foot of the scree. The flat plateau of Carl Side rises directly beyond the two small tarns. This route is often used, every passage causing a fresh disturbance of the scree on the big slope and obliterating the incipient paths that would otherwise develop. If used less often, a path would survive!

To BAKESTALL, 2189': 1¼ miles : NNE
Depression at 2160': 40 feet of ascent
A good route, but only if aiming for the Skiddaw House road.

From the north top, go down to the col and across to the fence, which leads unerringly but tediously to the objective.

North top and Gibraltar Crag

THE VIEW

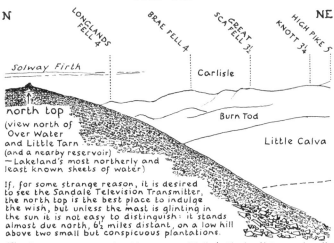

N — LONGLANDS FELL 4 — BRAE FELL 4 — GREAT SCA FELL 3½ — KNOTT 3¼ — HIGH PIKE 5 — NE

Solway Firth

Carlisle

north top
(view north of
Over Water
and Little Tarn
(and a nearby reservoir)
—Lakeland's most northerly and
least known sheets of water)

Burn Tod

Little Calva

If, for some strange reason, it is desired
to see the Sandale Television Transmitter,
the north top is the best place to indulge
the wish, but unless the mast is glinting in
the sun it is not easy to distinguish: it stands
almost due north, 6½ miles distant, on a low hill
above two small but conspicuous plantations.

The figures accompanying the names of fells indicate distances in miles

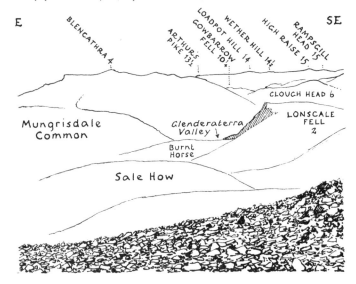

E — BLENCATHRA 4 — ARTHUR'S PIKE 13½ — GOWBARROW FELL 10* — LOADPOT HILL 14 — WETHER HILL 14½ — HIGH RAISE 15 — RAMPSGILL HEAD 15 — SE

CLOUGH HEAD 6

LONSCALE FELL 2

Mungrisdale Common

Glenderaterra Valley ↓

Burnt Horse

Sale How

THE VIEW

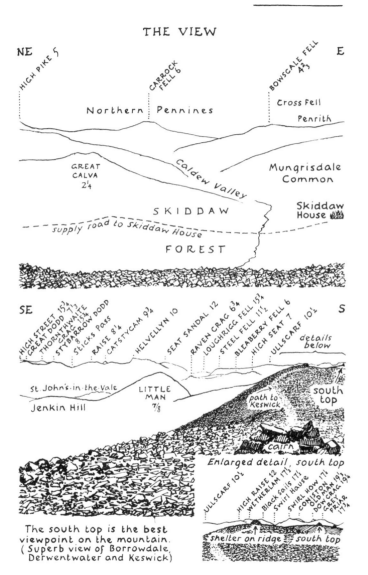

NE · E

HIGH PIKE 5

CARROCK FELL 6

BOWSCALE FELL 4¾

Northern Pennines

Cross Fell

Penrith

GREAT CALVA 2¼

Caldew Valley

Mungrisdale Common

SKIDDAW

Skiddaw House

supply road to Skiddaw House

FOREST

SE · S

HIGH STREET 15¼
GREAT DODD 7¾
THORNTHWAITE CRAG 15¼
STYBARROW DODD 8
STICKS PASS
RAISE 8¼
CATSTYCAM 9¾
HELVELLYN 10
SEAT SANDAL 12
RAVEN CRAG 6¾
LOUGHRIGG FELL 15¾
STEEL FELL 11½
BLEABERRY FELL 6
HIGH SEAT 7
ULLSCARF 10½

details below

St. John's-in-the-Vale

LITTLE MAN 7/8

Jenkin Hill

path to Keswick

south top

cairn

Enlarged detail, south top

ULLSCARF 10½
HIGH RAISE 12
WETHERLAM 17½
Black Sails 17½
SWIRL HOW 17½
Old Man 19½
CONISTON 19½
DOW CRAG 19¼
GREAT FRIAR 17¾

shelter on ridge · south top

The south top is the best
viewpoint on the mountain.
(Superb view of Borrowdale,
Derwentwater and Keswick)

THE VIEW

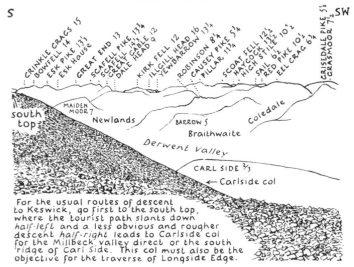

S — CRINKLE CRAGS 15, BOWFELL 14, ESK PIKE 13½, ESK HOUSE, GREAT END 13, SCAFELL PIKE 13¾, SCAFELL 14½, GREAT GABLE 12, DALE HEAD 9, KIRK FELL 12, ILLGILL HEAD 16, YEWBARROW 13¾, ROBINSON 8½, CAUSEY PIKE 5¾, PILLAR 11½, SCOAT FELL 12½, HAYCOCK 13½, HIGH STILE 10½, SAIL 6½, RED PIKE 10½, EEL CRAG 6¾, GRISEDALE PIKE 5½, GRASMOOR 7½ — SW

south top

MAIDEN MOOR 7

Newlands

BARROW 5

Braithwaite

Coledale

Derwent Valley

CARL SIDE ⅔

← Carlside col

For the usual routes of descent
to Keswick, go first to the south top,
where the tourist path slants down
half-left and a less obvious and rougher
descent *half-right* leads to Carlside col
for the Millbeck valley direct or the south
ridge of Carl Side. This col must also be the
objective for the traverse of Longside Edge.

W   NW

Solway Firth   Hills of Galloway

Cumberland coastal plain

SALE FELL 4
plantations
Bassenthwaite Lake

shelter

THE VIEW

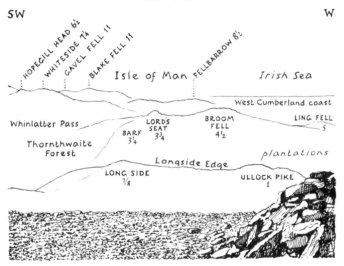

SW   W

HOPEGILL HEAD 6½
WHITESIDE 7¼
GAVEL FELL 11
BLAKE FELL 11
FELLBARROW 8½

Isle of Man   Irish Sea

West Cumberland coast

Whinlatter Pass   LORDS SEAT 3¾   BROOM FELL 4½   LING FELL 5

BARF 3¼

Thornthwaite Forest

plantations

Longside Edge

LONG SIDE 7/8   ULLOCK PIKE 1

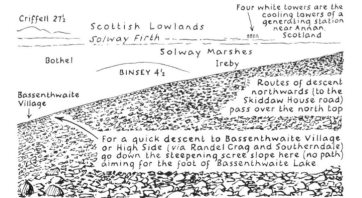

NW   N

Four white towers are the cooling towers of a generating station near Annan, Scotland

Criffell 27½   Scottish Lowlands

Solway Firth

Bothel   Solway Marshes

BINSEY 4½   Ireby

Bassenthwaite Village

Routes of descent northwards (to the Skiddaw House road) pass over the north top

For a quick descent to Bassenthwaite Village or High Side (via Randel Crag and Southerndale) go down the steepening scree slope here (no path) aiming for the foot of Bassenthwaite Lake

14 | Catbells

Book Six: The North Western Fells

Wainwright got his maps right because he was helped by the recently issued Ordnance Survey $2\frac{1}{2}$-inch maps, which are very detailed, and because he had walked every inch of the fells, taking notes. But what about his drawings? Can you rely on them too?

The ones showing pretty scenes, as in the first page of Catbells, are almost like watercolours, only in black and white, in pen and ink. The close-ups of rocks and crags, as on Catbells 3, look accurate enough, but did he use artistic licence?

The answer is that he used a camera. He made notes while out on the fells but never drew scenes *in situ*. Lakeland weather does not always allow pretty pictures to be drawn out of doors, and Wainwright had a strict schedule to follow. No time to hang about. But at home, during the winter, recollecting and reconstructing in tranquillity, he had time to produce detailed and very attractive illustrations, copying them from photographs he had taken.

If you look at Wainwright's drawing of himself which appears at the front of this book, you'll see that on the ground beside his knapsack there is a camera. It is hard to see its make, but he always had a fairly cheap camera with which he took fairly cheap photographs.

Around 1950, he had started taking his negatives to a proper professional photographer, Ken Shepherd, who lived in Kendal, hoping he would do a better job on the prints. After working on some very distinguished local newspapers, such as the *Carlisle Journal* – where I once had a holiday job – Ken had become a wedding and portrait photographer with his own darkroom. For almost the next forty years, Wainwright regularly got him to work on his snaps.

Wainwright would lay out a sequence of photographs, fitting them together to get the whole of a mountain range, or the entire view from the summit, then draw what he wanted. In pen and ink, he could highlight dark crevices, put more shadow on awesome crags, light up summits, insert the odd sheep, boulder or even tufts of grass, just to add interest and colour to the finished illustration. More often than not, he didn't do skies. In his main opening drawing, showing each new fell, he usually had the top silhouetted against a bare, white background. With Catbells, he adds a few strokes to suggest clouds.

On Catbells 5, in the bottom right-hand corner, he mentions that Hawes End is 'served by motor launch from Keswick (summer only)'. He doesn't say that the Keswick steamers – as they romantically prefer to call them, although they are just motor launches – also stop at Nichol End, High Brandelhow and Low Brandelhow, each one very useful for climbing Catbells, making it a round tour from Keswick, without having to go by car or bus.

Wainwright doesn't reveal whether, when doing this area of the North Western Fells, he himself used the Keswick motor launches. They go round and round Derwentwater, with seven stopping places in all, each with an attractive landing stage.

Wainwright's feelings about Catbells are clear. He calls it 'one of the great favourites, a family fell where grandmothers and infants can climb the heights together, a place beloved'. Below the fell, Derwentwater and the steamers are also a huge attraction, especially now they run all the year round. The winter service is not as frequent, but is still pretty good.

More and more people now come to the Lake District out of season. In 1984, only seven per cent of the total annual visitors to the Lakes came in January, February and March. Now it's 18 per cent. Despite Wainwright's worries, that things were growing worse, it's an example of things getting better: services improving, people being sensible, spreading out their Lakeland delights.

Catbells

1481'

Cat Bells
(two words)
on Ordnance maps

from Derwentwater

- Portinscale
- Keswick
- Stair
▲ CATBELLS
- Little Town
▲ MAIDEN MOOR
- Grange

MILES

0 1 2 3 4

from the Portinscale path

NATURAL FEATURES

Catbells is one of the great favourites, a family fell where grandmothers and infants can climb the heights together, a place beloved. Its popularity is well deserved: its shapely topknot attracts the eye, offering a steep but obviously simple scramble to the small summit; its slopes are smooth, sunny and sleek; its position overlooking Derwentwater is superb. Moreover, for stronger walkers it is the first step on a glorious ridge that bounds Borrowdale on the west throughout its length with Newlands down on the other side. There is beauty everywhere — and nothing but beauty. Its ascent from Keswick may conveniently, in the holiday season, be coupled with a sail on the lake, making the expedition rewarding out of all proportion to the small effort needed. Even the name has a magic challenge.

Yet this fell is not quite so innocuous as is usually thought, and grandmothers and infants should have a care as they romp around. There are some natural hazards in the form of a line of crags that starts at the summit and slants down to Newlands, and steep outcrops elsewhere. More dangerous are the levels and open shafts that pierce the fell on both flanks: the once-prosperous Yewthwaite Mine despoils a wide area in the combe above Little Town in Newlands, to the east the debris of the ill-starred Brandley Mine is lapped by the water of the lake, and the workings of the Old Brandley Mine, high on the side of the fell at Skelgill Bank, are in view on the ascent of the ridge from the north. A tragic death in one of the open Yewthwaite shafts in 1962 serves as a warning.

Words cannot adequately describe the rare charm of Catbells, nor its ravishing view. But no publicity is necessary: its mere presence in the Derwentwater scene is enough. It has a bold 'come hither' look that compels one's steps, and no suitor ever returns disappointed, but only looking back often. It has only to be seen from Friar's Crag — and a spell is cast. No Keswick holiday is consummated without a visit to Catbells.

from Yewthwaite Combe

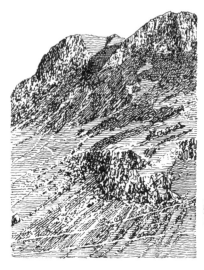

Crags and Caverns of Catbells

left: The crags of Mart Bield, below the summit on the Newlands side of the fell

right: A dangerous hole at Yewthwaite Mine. At the end of a rock cutting the adit suggests a level (horizontal tunnel) but in fact is the opening of a vertical shaft.

below: Workings at the Old Brandley Mine. A shaft with twin entrances, overhung by a tree, *left*, and a nearby level, *right*.

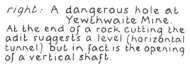

MAP

O: Old Brandley Mine
B: Brandlehow Mine
Y: Yewthwaite Mine
   (disused)

ONE MILE

The name Catbells might well be a corruption of *Cat Bields* (the shelter of the wild cat) although this has been disputed by authorities of repute. It is interesting to note, however, that the crags below the top on the west side have the name of Mart Bield (the shelter of the marten), which seems to lend support to the suggestion. Further, a place in the hills near Wasdale is still known as Cat Bields.

The alternative spellings of Brandelhow and Brandlehow are used indiscriminately nowadays. Both versions of the name are used by the Ordnance Survey. A tablet by the roadside states that Brandelhow Park was the first property in the Lake District to be acquired by the National Trust (1902)

ASCENT FROM HAWSE END
1250 feet of ascent : 1½ miles

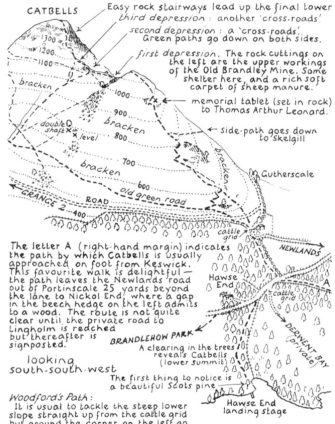

CATBELLS

Easy rock stairways lead up the final tower
third depression : another 'cross-roads'

*second depression : a 'cross-roads'.
Green paths go down on both sides.*

*first depression. The rock cuttings on
the left are the upper workings
of the Old Brandley Mine. Some
shelter here, and a rich soft
carpet of sheep manure.*

— memorial tablet (set in rock)
to Thomas Arthur Leonard.

← side-path goes down
to Skelgill

Gutherscale

bracken

double
shaft
level

bracken

bracken

old green road

GRANGE 2   ROAD

cattle
grid

NEWLANDS

Hawse
End

cattle
grid

DERWENT BAY (private)

BRANDLEHOW PARK

looking
south-south-west

The letter A (right-hand margin) indicates
the path by which Catbells is usually
approached on foot from Keswick.
This favourite walk is delightful—
the path leaves the Newlands road
out of Portinscale 25 yards beyond
the lane to Nickol End, where a gap
in the beech hedge on the left admits
to a wood. The route is not quite
clear until the private road to
Lingholm is reached
but thereafter is
signposted.

A clearing in the trees
reveals Catbells
(lower summit)

The first thing to notice is
a beautiful Scots pine

Hawse End
landing stage

Derwentwater

Hawse End is served
by motor-launch from
Keswick (summer only)

One of the very best
of the shorter climbs.
A truly lovely walk.

Woodford's Path:
It is usual to tackle the steep lower
slope straight up from the cattle grid
but around the corner on the left an
exquisite series of zigzags provides a
more enjoyable start to the ascent.
These zigzags leave the old green road
80 yards along it: watch for the first.
The direct route joins in at the top of
the series; another series is then
soon reached. *This path was engineered
by a Sir John Woodford, who lived near,
and his name deserves to be remembered
by those who use his enchanting stairway.*

ASCENT FROM GRANGE
1250 feet of ascent : 2 miles

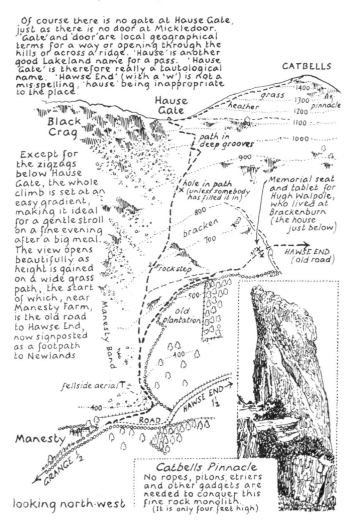

Of course there is no gate at Hause Gate, just as there is no door at Mickledoor. 'Gate' and 'door' are local geographical terms for a way or opening through the hills or across a ridge. 'Hause' is another good Lakeland name for a pass. 'Hause Gate' is therefore really a tautological name. 'Hawse End' (with a 'w') is not a mis-spelling, 'hause' being inappropriate to the place.

CATBELLS

Hause Gate

Black Crag

grass
heather
1400
1300   A pinnacle
1200
1100
1000
900

path in deep grooves

Except for the zigzags below Hause Gate, the whole climb is set at an easy gradient, making it ideal for a gentle stroll on a fine evening after a big meal. The view opens beautifully as height is gained on a wide grass path, the start of which, near Manesty Farm, is the old road to Hawse End, now signposted as a footpath to Newlands.

hole in path X (unless somebody has filled it in)

Memorial seat and tablet for Hugh Walpole, who lived at Brackenburn (the house just below)

800
bracken
700

HAWSE END (old road)

rock step

Manesty Band

500
old plantation

400

fellside aerial

400

HAWSE END 1½

ROAD

Manesty

GRANGE ½

looking north-west

Catbells Pinnacle
No ropes, pitons, etriers and other gadgets are needed to conquer this fine rock monolith. (It is only four feet high)

ASCENT FROM NEWLANDS

via SKELGILL
1200 feet of ascent : 1½ miles
from Stair

via LITTLE TOWN
950 feet of ascent : 1½ miles
from Little Town

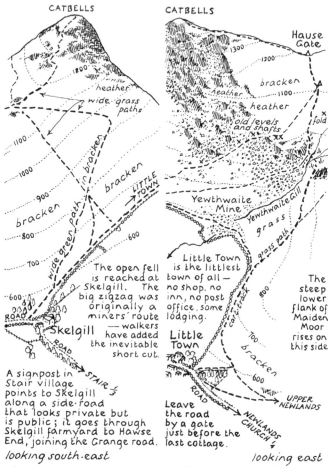

The open fell
is reached at
Skelgill. The
big zigzag was
originally a
miners' route
— walkers
have added
the inevitable
short cut.

Little Town
is the littlest
town of all —
no shop, no
inn, no post
office, some
lodging.

The
steep
lower
flank of
Maiden
Moor
rises on
this side

A signpost in
Stair village
points to Skelgill
along a side-road
that looks private but
is public; it goes through
Skelgill farmyard to Hawse
End, joining the Grange road.

Leave
the road
by a gate
just before the
last cottage.

looking south-east

looking east

Up one way and down the other is a nice idea

THE SUMMIT

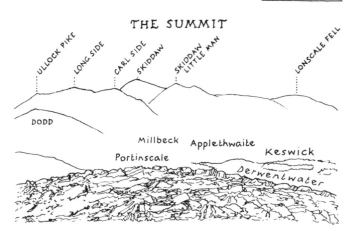

ULLOCK PIKE LONG SIDE CARL SIDE SKIDDAW SKIDDAW LITTLE MAN LONSCALE FELL

DODD

Millbeck Applethwaite Keswick

Portinscale

Derwentwater

The summit, which has no cairn, is a small platform of naked rock, light brown in colour and seamed and pitted with many tiny hollows and crevices that collect and hold rainwater — so that, long after the skies have cleared, glittering diamonds adorn the crown. Almost all the native vegetation has been scoured away by the varied footgear of countless visitors; so popular is this fine viewpoint that often it is difficult to find a vacant perch. In summer this is not a place to seek quietness. DESCENTS: Leave the top only by the ridge; lower down there is a wealth of choice. Keep clear of the craggy Newlands face.

RIDGE ROUTE

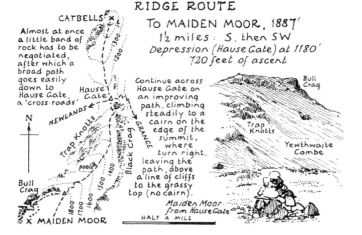

CATBELLS

Almost at once a little band of rock has to be negotiated, after which a broad path goes easily down to Hause Gate, a 'cross-roads'

Hause Gate

NEWLANDS

N

Trap Knotts

Black Crag

GRANGE

pools

Bull Crag

X MAIDEN MOOR

To MAIDEN MOOR, 1887'

1½ miles : S. then SW
Depression (Hause Gate) at 1180'
720 feet of ascent

Continue across Hause Gate on an improving path, climbing steadily to a cairn on the edge of the summit, where turn right, leaving the path, above a line of cliffs to the grassy top (no cairn).

Maiden Moor from Hause Gate

HALF A MILE

Bull Crag

Trap Knotts

Yewthwaite Combe

THE VIEW

Scenes of great beauty unfold on all sides, and they are scenes in depth to a degree not usual, the narrow summit permitting downward views of Borrowdale and Newlands within a few paces. Nearby valley and lake attract the eye more than the distant mountain surround, although Hindscarth and Robinson are particularly prominent at the head of Newlands and Causey Pike towers up almost grotesquely directly opposite. On this side the hamlet of Little Town is well seen down below, a charming picture, but it is to Derwentwater and mid-Borrowdale that the captivated gaze returns again and again.

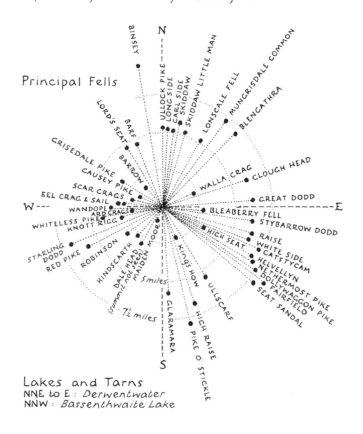

Principal Fells

Lakes and Tarns
NNE to E : Derwentwater
NNW : Bassenthwaite Lake

Hindscarth and Robinson from Catbells

15 | Grasmoor
Book Six: The North Western Fells

By getting up early and catching the 8.30am bus from Kendal, Wainwright could usually start walking up his chosen fell, even in the Northern and North Western Fells, by 10.30. Then he'd walk till nine at night in summer, when it is still perfectly light in the Lake District. In 1978, he boasted to me that he had never missed the bus home in thirteen years. 'I was always at the road end twenty minutes before the bus was due, just in case my watch had gone wrong during the day. The slower the bus, the better I liked it. There's nothing more restful than a stopping bus.'

Being out so long, he inevitably ran into lousy weather on many occasions. So what did he do? Got wet, is the obvious answer. He had no fancy all-weather gear. He didn't even have a waterproof rucksack. His knapsack, from the look of it in the drawing opposite, was flimsy and soft, as most small ones were in those days. His opinion of elaborate walking gear was summed up in his book *Fellwanderer*. 'If sheep didn't have such good manners, they would laugh their heads off.'

What Wainwright normally wore for the fells were his ordinary clothes. Not his best clothes, his suit, which he wore to work, but clothes that had become too shabby for the office. He did often walk in an old tweed suit, complete with collar and tie. There's a photo of him in this outfit, out on the fells. Not a sight you ever see today. On his feet, he normally wore a stout pair of walking shoes, although he eventually did have leather boots. In the drawing on Grasmoor 15, he is wearing nothing on his head, but elsewhere – in the self-portrait shown opposite, from Book Seven, Yewbarrow 9, the very last fell – he is wearing a cap, and has the sheep poking fun at his expense, wondering if he is going bald.

I think even today, Wainwright would have gone walking in ordinary outdoor clothes. Walking is very simple, he always said. One foot in front of the other. That's all you need to know.

Although Wainwright described Grasmoor as 'a favourite for discerning West Cumbrians', it didn't make it into his top six fells. It is in *The Best of Wainwright* because of its size and position, its commanding views over Crummock Water, and also – perhaps most of all – because I happen to look out on it from all front windows at our Loweswater home. In fact our house is named after it. So what better reason?

Wainwright dressed for walking

Grasmoor

2791'

from Lanthwaite Hill

NATURAL FEATURES

The culminating point of the North Western Fells occurs overlooking Crummock Water, where the massive bulk of Grasmoor towers above the threshold of the Buttermere valley, showing its full height to great advantage from the shores of the lake. As Nature has arranged matters this particular aspect of the fell, facing west, is also the finest: a steep pyramid of rocky ribs and broken crags suspended far above the road along its base, the road that carries travellers to Buttermere — and few go this way who do not look upwards rather fearfully to the cliffs poised overhead, seeming to threaten safe passage. Yet familiarity with this monstrous monolith dispels fear and the brackeny hollows below, adjoining the unfenced road, harbour summer migrants in the shape of campers, motorists and caravanners: it is a favourite picnic and recreation ground for discerning West Cumbrians. Apart from the two dark clefts on this face, there are no continuous courses to attract rockclimbers; the only crags of any size circle an upland combe on the north flank and rim the edge of the summit. On the south side are the most extensive scree-slopes in the district: a colourful but arid desert of stones. Eastwards there is a high link with Eel Crag and a fine ridge descending into Newlands. But probably most visitors to Grasmoor will remember the fell for a summit-plateau remarkable both for its extent and its luxurious carpet of mossy turf, close-cropped by the resident sheep who range these broad acres. In structure the fell assumes a simple form, the only unorthodoxy being a ramp down the middle of the south slope curving round into the heathery spur of Lad House, now known as Lad Hows. The streams bounding Grasmoor occupy the stony side-valleys of Gasgale Gill and Rannerdale Beck. It has no tarns.

Braithwaite ●
● Scale Hill Road End
▲ WHITESIDE
● Loweswater
GRASMOOR ▲   ▲ EEL CRAG
WANDOPE ▲
▲
WHITELESS PIKE
● Buttermere
MILES
0 1 2 3 4

The name of the fell is commonly mis-spelt as Grassmoor, even in print, by writers who would never dream of mis-spelling Grasmere Grassmere. There is only one 's'. The gras derives from grise — wild boar — as in so many Lakeland names e.g. Grisedale.

MAP

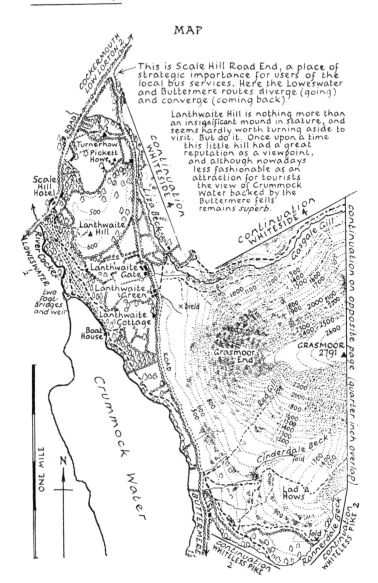

This is Scale Hill Road End, a place of strategic importance for users of the local bus services. Here the Loweswater and Buttermere routes diverge (going) and converge (coming back).

Lanthwaite Hill is nothing more than an insignificant mound in stature, and seems hardly worth turning aside to visit. But do it. Once upon a time this little hill had a great reputation as a viewpoint, and although nowadays less fashionable as an attraction for tourists the view of Crummock Water backed by the Buttermere fells remains superb.

ONE MILE

N

MAP

The natural boundaries of mountains tend to be obscured by man's lines of communications. It is not the valley roads that define the limits of a mountain but the main watercourses. Here is a case in point (opposite page). The road along the bases of Whiteside and Grasmoor appears to terminate their slopes, but these fells are divided by Liza Beck (Gasgale Gill higher up), which, instead of completing the severance neatly by a direct cut into Crummock Water, turns north to join the River Cocker beyond the outflow of the lake and thereby claims for Grasmoor a wedge of low country that, to a casual observer, would seem to belong to Whiteside. Thus Lanthwaite Hill is Grasmoor's cub although it sits at the feet of Whiteside.

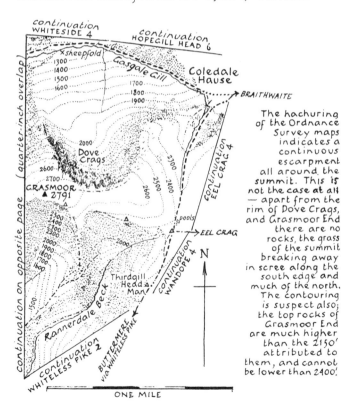

The hachuring of the Ordnance Survey maps indicates a continuous escarpment all around the summit. This is not the case at all — apart from the rim of Dove Crags, and Grasmoor End there are no rocks, the grass of the summit breaking away in scree along the south edge and much of the north. The contouring is suspect also; the top rocks of Grasmoor End are much higher than the 2150' attributed to them, and cannot be lower than 2400!

ASCENT FROM LANTHWAITE GREEN
VIA DOVE CRAGS
2300 feet of ascent : 2 miles

GRASMOOR

Dove Crags

2700
2600
2500
2400
2300

grass

grass

Grasmoor End

- 2200
- 2100
- 2000

rock slab

grassy arete

grassy basin at 1900'

- 1800
- 1700
- 1600
- 1500
- 1400
- 1300
- 1200
- 1100

heather

One of the natural wonders of Grasmoor is the profound hollow scooped out of its north flank and encircled by Dove Crags. The floor of this amphitheatre is a grassy basin, surrounded on all sides by higher ground. It seems an obvious site for a tarn, yet is dry, although clearly all the drainage from the crags must be received there. Because of the raised edge of the hollow there is no issuing stream, nor indeed are there any watercourses within it. All this is very odd. What happens to all the water falling within the area of the combe? The explanation can only be that the screes below the crags act as soakaways and absorb all moisture from above as it falls, releasing it to the basin so slowly that evaporation and not accumulation takes place.

Many sheep tracks are crossed during the early stages of the climb from the valley. One of these (at about 1500') is a particularly clear trail (it is used by shepherds also): it traverses the fellside and links with the terrace on the direct route.

x bield

1000

Gasgale Gill

usual path to Coledale Hause

This old walkers' path on the Grasmoor side of the gill now serves only for sheep. It is rough but still fairly clear

900

2 latches

800

DIRECT ROUTE

Gasgale Gill is a narrow V-shaped cutting, no wider than the bed of the stream. On the north side Whiteside rises even more steeply than Grasmoor on the south side.

Nature never uses straight lines in her designs, but has come remarkably close to doing so in fashioning this arete and the approach to it from the gill along the edge of the scree. A plumb-line dropped from the summit to the valley would lie over the route almost exactly. This is very noticeable from the top of Whiteside.

bracken

falls

bracken

700

600

water cut

grassy

600

weir

There are no difficulties in this ascent. The rock slab is set at an easy gradient but is greasy and needs care. The views down the crags from the arete are tremendous.

cattle grid

The route can be identified from the road. Looking up the valley of Gasgale Gill, it is the skyline ridge rising smoothly to the right, the one roughness on it being the rock slab.

ROAD

Lanthwaite Green

Lanthwaite Gate

LORTON 3½

looking south-south-east

ASCENT FROM LANTHWAITE GREEN DIRECT

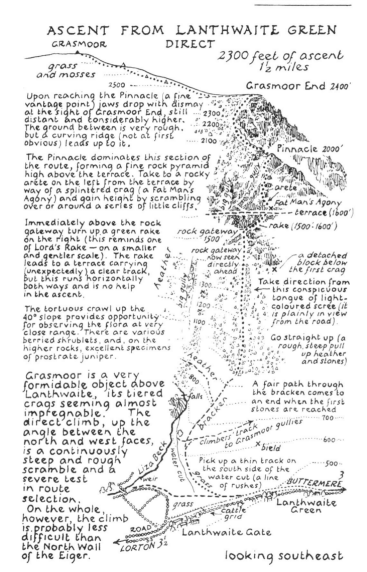

GRASMOOR

grass and mosses

2500

2300 feet of ascent
1½ miles

Grasmoor End 2400'

2300
2200
2100

Pinnacle 2000'

Upon reaching the Pinnacle (a fine vantage point) jaws drop with dismay at the sight of Grasmoor End, still distant and considerably higher. The ground between is very rough, but a curving ridge (not at first obvious) leads up to it.

The Pinnacle dominates this section of the route, forming a fine rock pyramid high above the terrace. Take to a rocky arête on the left from the terrace by way of a splintered crag (a Fat Man's Agony) and gain height by scrambling over or around a series of little cliffs.

arête

Fat Man's Agony

terrace (1600')

rake (1500'-1600')

Immediately above the rock gateway turn up a green rake on the right (this reminds one of Lord's Rake — on a smaller and gentler scale). The rake leads to a terrace carrying (unexpectedly) a clear track, but this runs horizontally both ways and is no help in the ascent.

rock gateway 1500'

rock gateway now seen directly ahead

a detached block below the first crag

Take direction from this conspicuous tongue of light-coloured scree (it is plainly in view from the road).

The tortuous crawl up the 40° slope provides opportunity for observing the flora at very close range. There are various berried shrublets, and, on the higher rocks, excellent specimens of prostrate juniper.

big gully

1300
1200
1100

Go straight up (a rough, steep pull up heather and stones)

Grasmoor is a very formidable object above Lanthwaite, its tiered crags seeming almost impregnable. The direct climb, up the angle between the north and west faces, is a continuously steep and rough scramble and a severe test in route selection.

On the whole, however, the climb is probably less difficult than the North Wall of the Eiger.

900

800

falls

bracken

A fair path through the bracken comes to an end when the first stones are reached

700

climbers' track to Grasmoor gullies

bield

600

Pick up a thin track on the south side of the water cut (a line of rushes)

500

Liza Beck

water cut

weir

grass

BS

BUTTERMERE

Lanthwaite Green

grass

cattle grid

ROAD

LORTON 3½

Lanthwaite Gate

looking southeast

ASCENT FROM RANNERDALE
2430 feet of ascent : 1¼ miles

via **RED GILL**

Grasmoor End

top of south spur

GRASMOOR

GRASMOOR

2700
2600
2500
2400
2300

2200
2100
2000
1900
1800
1700

spur

heather

Red Gill

path alongside scree

bracken

1500

1400

1300

1200

Preferably, ignore this escape from the gill to the spur (steep heather) and continue ahead to the skyline, there making the short detour left (grass) to Grasmoor End, a fine viewpoint.

Red Gill is named after the colour of its scree. It has no stream.

The route to the ridge is remarkably straight and unobstructed. Looking back, the starting-point is always in view.

sheep tracks

patch of heather (cross it)

thin track in bracken

low crag

marshy patch

It needs an experienced eye fully to appreciate, from the foot of the slope, the length of the scree run in Red Gill. Most observers will seriously under-estimate both its length and steepness.

800

bracken

700

600

500

Fall Crag

400

bracken

ROAD

LANTHWAITE

distinct grass path in bracken

common

bracken

500

GRASMOOR via LAD HOWS

Cinderdale Beck

The climb starts at an open common (a popular halt for motors and campers) and every step is up, without respite.

looking north-east

Crummock Water

From the road, the route is in full view to the skyline 2000' above — it is a very obvious line of ascent, and indeed the only practicable one in sight.

Rannerdale Farm

BUTTERMERE 1½

ASCENT FROM RANNERDALE
2450 feet of ascent : 1¾ miles

VIA LAD HOWS

looking east-north-east

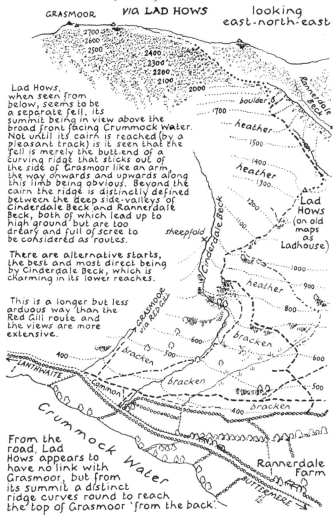

GRASMOOR

2700
2600
2500
2400
2300
2200
2100
2000

Rannerdale Beck

boulder

1700

heather

1500

1400

heather

1300

1200

Lad Hows
(on old maps as Ladhouse)

1100

sheepfold

1000

GRASMOOR VIA RED GILL

heather

900

800

heather

bracken

600

500

bracken

400

bracken

600

500

bracken

LANTHWAITE

Common

400

Crummock Water

Rannerdale Farm

BUTTERMERE

Lad Hows,
when seen from below, seems to be a separate fell, its summit being in view above the broad front facing Crummock Water. Not until its cairn is reached (by a pleasant track) is it seen that the fell is merely the butt-end of a curving ridge that sticks out of the side of Grasmoor like an arm the way onwards and upwards along this limb being obvious. Beyond the cairn the ridge is distinctly defined between the deep side-valleys of Cinderdale Beck and Rannerdale Beck, both of which lead up to high ground but are too dreary and full of scree to be considered as routes.

There are alternative starts, the best and most direct being by Cinderdale Beck, which is charming in its lower reaches.

This is a longer but less arduous way than the Red Gill route and the views are more extensive.

From the road, Lad Hows appears to have no link with Grasmoor, but from its summit a distinct ridge curves round to reach the top of Grasmoor 'from the back'.

The Scafell group

from Grasmoor

ASCENT FROM COLEDALE HAUSE
850 feet of ascent
1¼ miles

looking southeast

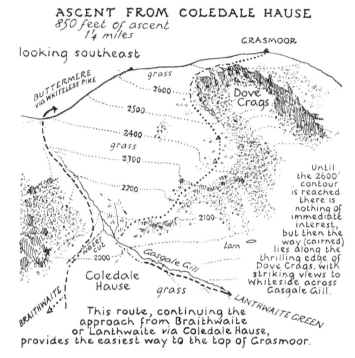

Until the 2600' contour is reached there is nothing of immediate interest, but then the way (cairned) lies along the thrilling edge of Dove Crags, with striking views to Whiteside across Gasgale Gill.

This route, continuing the approach from Braithwaite or Lanthwaite via Coledale Hause, provides the easiest way to the top of Grasmoor.

RIDGE ROUTE

To EEL CRAG, 2749': 1¼ miles: generally E
Depression at 2350': 400 feet of ascent
A long moorland tramp, excellent underfoot

The first half-mile is the easiest walking to be found anywhere; keep left for a sight of Dove Crags. After crossing the depression, bear right for a look down into Addacomb Hole. These are the only excitements.

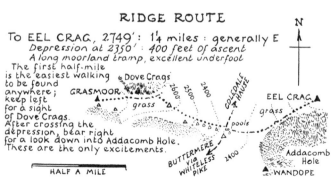

HALF A MILE

THE SUMMIT

There are many cairns at various stations on the broad top, but no mistaking the highest of all, which is a huge heap of stones divided into shelter compartments, open to the sky, designed to give protection from wind (but not wet) coming from any direction. Some skill and much labour has gone into its construction (where did the stones come from?) and visitors should feel a sense of responsibility for keeping it in repair. It stands a score of yards only from the edge of the south face, and a smaller wind-shelter perched here on the brink marks a better viewpoint. The summit has a covering of shale hereabouts, but elsewhere a soft mossy turf is a pleasure to walk upon.

The top of the fell is a long plateau coming up from the east and is generally broad but midway it narrows to a waist a hundred yards wide, the north side of this section being rimmed by the top rocks of Dove Crags. This scene, and the exciting scaffold of Grasmoor End (which should be visited if time permits) are the finest topographical features of an otherwise rather dull summit.

DESCENTS: Generally, ways off lie along the plateau eastwards whatever the destination, but Red Gill is a quick and safe way down to Crummock Water for Buttermere, and the left edge of Dove Crags is a practicable route down to Gasgale for Lanthwaite and Loweswater. Grasmoor End leads only to trouble. In mist, go east for half a mile, descending very little, to the good path through the grassy hollow between Grasmoor and Eel Crag, and here turn left for Coledale Hause, right for Buttermere.

PLAN OF SUMMIT

THE VIEW

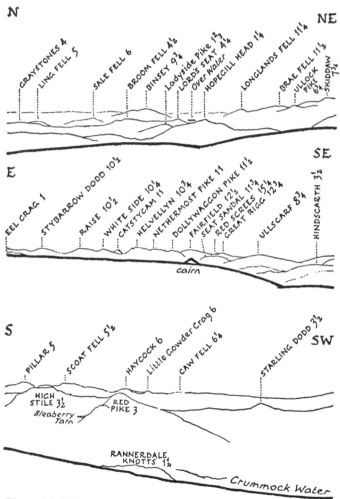

The thick line marks the visible boundaries
of the summit from the cairn

THE VIEW

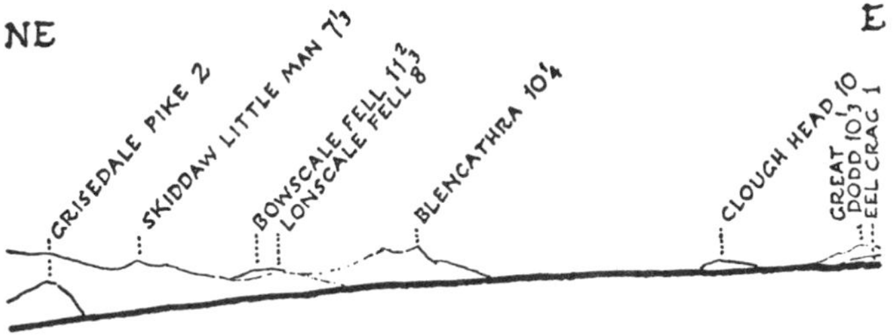
NE
E
GRISEDALE PIKE 2
SKIDDAW LITTLE MAN 7⅓
BOWSCALE FELL 11⅔
LONSCALE FELL 8
BLENCATHRA 10¼
CLOUGH HEAD 10
GREAT DODD 10⅓
EEL CRAG 1

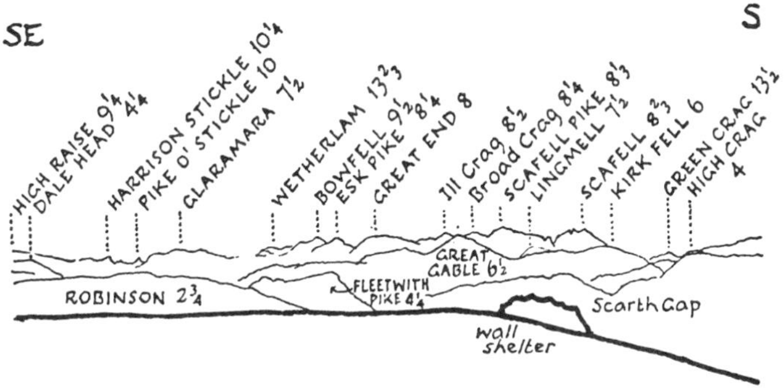
SE
S
HIGH RAISE 9¼
DALE HEAD 4¼
HARRISON STICKLE 10¼
PIKE O' STICKLE 10
GLARAMARA 7½
WETHERLAM 13⅔
BOWFELL 9½
ESK PIKE 8¼
GREAT END 8
Ill Crag 8½
Broad Crag 8¼
SCAFELL PIKE 8⅓
LINGMELL 7½
SCAFELL 8⅔
KIRK FELL 6
GREEN CRAG 13½
HIGH CRAG 4
GREAT GABLE 6½
ROBINSON 2¾
FLEETWITH PIKE 4¼
Scarth Gap
wall shelter

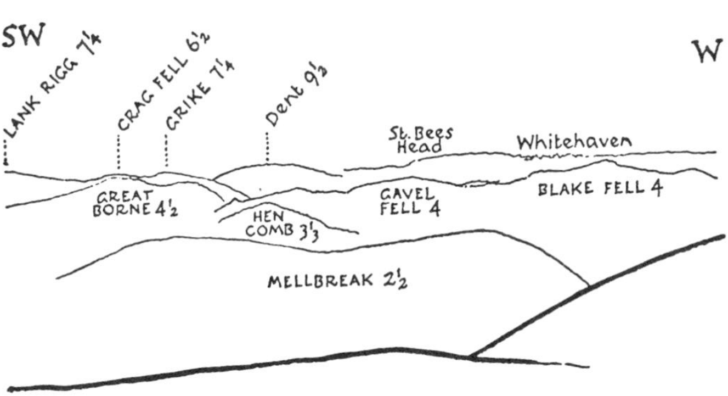
SW
W
LANK RIGG 7¼
CRAG FELL 6½
GRIKE 7¼
Dent 9⅓
St. Bees Head
Whitehaven
GREAT BORNE 4½
HEN COMB 3⅓
GAVEL FELL 4
BLAKE FELL 4
MELLBREAK 2½

The figures accompanying the names of fells indicate distances in miles

continued

THE VIEW
continued

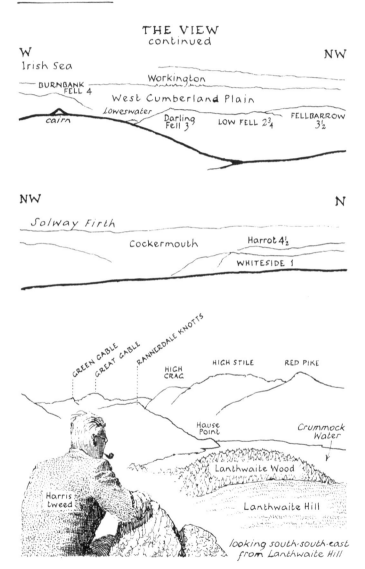

W

Irish Sea

NW

Workington

BURNBANK
FELL 4

West Cumberland Plain

Loweswater

cairn

Darling
Fell 3^9

LOW FELL 2$\frac{3}{4}$

FELLBARROW
3$\frac{1}{2}$

NW

N

Solway Firth

Cockermouth

Harrot 4$\frac{1}{2}$

WHITESIDE 1

GREEN GABLE

GREAT GABLE

RANNERDALE KNOTTS

HIGH
CRAG

HIGH STILE

RED PIKE

Hause
Point

Crummock
Water

Lanthwaite Wood

Harris
tweed

Lanthwaite Hill

looking south-south-east
from Lanthwaite Hill

Cinderdale Beck : a favourite stream, well known (but not by name) to the many motorists and campers who enjoy the freedom of the open fell alongside the road to Buttermere at the base of Grasmoor.

Dove Crags

Grasmoor End
from Crummock Water

16 | Great Gable

Book Seven: The Western Fells

Wainwright preferred to travel and walk alone. Most travel writers do, although not for the same reasons as him. On your own, you are open to offers, excitements, conversations, meetings, changes of plan, which means you pick up more copy. But Wainwright wanted to be left on his own so he could concentrate on what he had already planned to do, and not get deflected. He was appalled if any stranger approached him, which happened quite regularly by Book Seven. If accosted directly, he would deny who he was.

At the end of Book Two, in his Personal Notes, he had thanked those who had written to him. 'There have been offers of hospitality, of transport (I have no car nor any wish for one), of company and of collaboration, and of financial help – all of which I have declined as gracefully as I could ... I have set myself this task and I am pigheaded enough to want to do it without help.'

By the time he got to Book Seven, *The Western Fells*, he was beginning to find it more and more awkward to get to places like Ennerdale and Wastwater and back in one day. Normally, he tried to do his main walking on a Saturday, spending the Sunday writing, but on several occasions he had to stay somewhere overnight. From his letters, it looks as if he sometimes stayed at the Kirkstile Inn at Loweswater, from where he could cover quite a few local fells, like Mellbreak and Red Pike, and also get across to Ennerdale.

Great Gable is one of the grandest of the Western Fells – 'everybody's favourite', Wainwright called it – and he included it in his top six fells. When he climbed it for Book Seven, he was not, in fact, alone, as his private letters later revealed. He went up with Harry Firth, Printing Manager of the Westmorland Gazette, who had been involved with the Guides from the beginning, helping to print and sell them. On that day, Harry had driven him there and back – so Wainwright had broken two of his self-imposed rules.

But this was rare. He was almost always alone. In his description of Great Gable – on Great Gable 9, bottom of the page – he suggests that 'nagging wives should be left to paddle their feet in Styhead Tarn', although it might be all right to take 'well-behaved women'.

At this stage in his life, he had recently met Betty McNally and was conducting a secret relationship with her. Up on the Western Fells, a lot of his thoughts were about Betty. We know from a letter he wrote her that he did not get to the summit of Great Gable on the day he was covering it for *The Western Fells*. It seems he had lingered too long in a sheltered hollow into which he had turned in order to read a letter from Betty, and had then fallen to dreaming. The following weekend, when he did reach its summit, he sat on the top looking towards Ireland which, of course, you can't see. Dublin just happened to be where Betty was that weekend, and naturally he was thinking of her.

Doing the Western Fells, which needed longer days and nights away, gave him a good excuse to meet Betty – which they often did in a café in Keswick, travelling there separately. They couldn't meet in Kendal as nosey parkers would be bound to spot the Borough Treasurer with someone not his wife and start spreading rumours.

Betty offered to drive him on his journeys to the last of his Western Fells, as she had her own car, but he didn't think it wise. Later on, when their relationship was more established and he was researching the Pennine Way, he allowed her to drive him to the beginning of his walk, drop him off, then pick him up later at an appointed place on the map. She soon grew bored with having to hang around, and would sometimes follow him at a safe distance behind. Eventually, he did allow her on his walks, on one condition. 'As long as you don't talk…'

Great Gable

2949'

from Wastwater

NATURAL FEATURES

Great Gable is a favourite of all fellwalkers, and first favourite with many. Right from the start of one's apprenticeship in the hills, the name appeals magically. It is a good name for a mountain, strong, challenging, compelling, starkly descriptive, suggesting the pyramid associated with the shape of mountains since early childhood. People are attracted to it because of the name. There is satisfaction in having achieved the ascent and satisfaction in announcing the fact to others. The name has status, and confers status... Yes, the name is good, simple yet subtly clever. If Great Gable were known only as Wasdale Fell fewer persons would climb it.

continued

from Great End

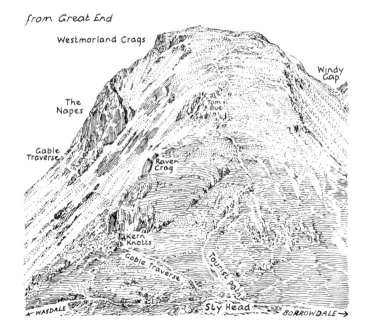

Westmorland Crags

Windy Gap

The Napes

Tom Blue

Gable Traverse

Raven Crag

Kern Knotts

Gable Traverse

Tourist Path

← WASDALE

Sty Head

BORROWDALE →

NATURAL FEATURES

continued

In appearance, too, Great Gable has the same appealing attributes. The name fits well. This mountain is strong yet not sturdy, masculine yet graceful. It is the undisputed overlord of the group of hills to which it belongs, and its superior height is emphasised tremendously by the deep gulf separating it from the Scafells and allowing an impressive view that reveals the whole of its half-mile altitude as an unremitting and unbroken pyramid: this is the aspect of the fell that earned the name. From east and west the slender tapering of the summit as seen from the south is not in evidence, the top appearing as a massive square-cut dome. From the north, where the build-up of height is more gradual, the skyline is a symmetrical arc.

continued

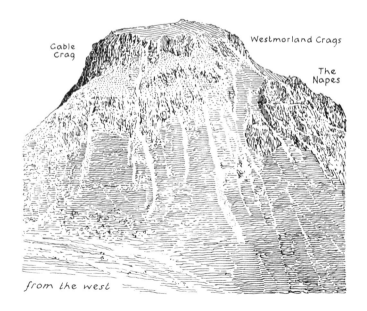

Gable Crag

Westmorland Crags

The Napes

from the west

NATURAL FEATURES

continued

Great Gable is a desert of stones. Vegetation is scanty, feeding few sheep. Petrified rivers of scree scar the southern slopes, from which stand out the bony ribs of the Napes ridges; the whole fell on this side is a sterile wilderness, dry and arid and dusty. The north face is a shadowed precipice, Gable Crag. Slopes to east and west are rough and stony. In some lights, especially in the afterglow of sunset, Great Gable is truly a beautiful mountain, but it is never a pretty one.

The view from the top is far-reaching, but not quite in balance because of the nearness of the Scafells, which, however, are seen magnificently. The aerial aspect of Wasdale is often described as the finest view in the district, a claim that more witnesses will accept than will dispute.

continued

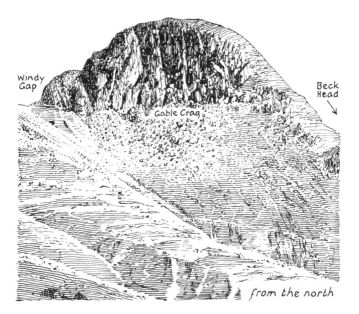

Windy Gap

Gable Crag

Beck Head

from the north

NATURAL FEATURES
continued

The failing of Great Gable is that it holds few mysteries, all its wares being openly displayed. The explorer, the man who likes to look around corners and discover secrets and intimacies, may be disappointed, not on a first visit, which cannot fail to be interesting, but on subsequent occasions. There are no cavernous recesses, no hidden tarns, no combes, no hanging valleys, no waterfalls, no streams other than those forming the boundaries.

Yet walkers tread its familiar tracks again and again, almost as a ritual, and climbers queue to scale its familiar rocks. The truth is, Great Gable casts a spell. It starts as an honourable adversary and becomes a friend. The choice of its summit as a war memorial is testimony to the affection and respect felt for this grand old mountain.

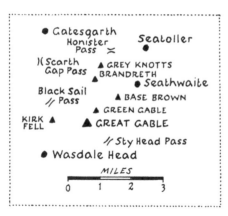

• Gatesgarth
Honister
Pass ✕   Seatoller •
)(Scarth
Gap Pass   ▲ GREY KNOTTS
▲ BRANDRETH
• Seathwaite
Black Sail
// Pass   ▲ BASE BROWN
▲ GREEN GABLE
KIRK
FELL ▲   ▲ GREAT GABLE
// Sty Head Pass
• Wasdale Head

MILES
0   1   2   3

Dry Tarn

This is a tarn that Nature fashioned and forgot. It is invariably bone-dry although mossy stones indicate the former presence of water. Dry Tarn is almost unknown, yet is within sight of the main path up Great Gable from Sty Head, being situated at 2100 feet on a grass shelf: it is more likely to be seen when descending.
This is Great Gable's only tarn.

MAP

Crags and other features are shown in greater detail, and named, on the larger-scale maps and diagrams appearing elsewhere in this chapter.

A curious thing about Great Gable is that, although of commanding height and so far overtopping the supporting fells as to seem to rise in isolation, it is really a huge cone resting on a high land-mass. Great Gable overlooks many valleys and waters three, yet it has no roots in any except Wasdale; even here its foothold is ineffectual, being a mile beyond the true head of the valley in a side-opening. On all other flanks, it is a mountain hoisted on the shoulders of supporters that have direct valley links and take over the function of principal buttresses.

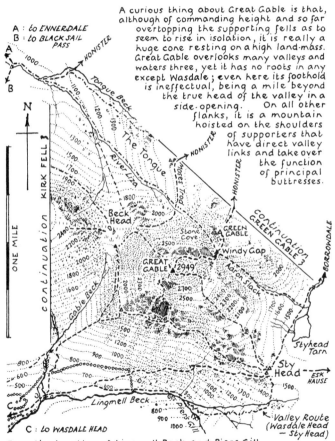

A : to ENNERDALE
B : to BLACK SAIL PASS

C : to WASDALE HEAD

From the junction of Lingmell Beck and Piers Gill the summit is two-thirds of a mile north in lateral distance and the difference in altitude is 2,200 feet, a gradient of 1 in 1⅓. This is the longest slope in the district of such continuous and concentrated steepness.

Moses' Trod

In the years before the construction of the gravitation tramways to convey slate from Dubs and the upper Honister quarries, when man-handled sledges were the only means of negotiating the steep slopes to the road below, it was more convenient to transport supplies destined for South Cumberland and the port of Ravenglass by packhorse directly across the high fells to Wasdale, a practice followed until the primitive highway through Honister Pass was improved for wheeled traffic. This high-level route, cleverly planned to avoid steep gradients and rough places, can still be traced almost entirely although it has had no commercial use since about 1850. Because of the past history and legend connected with it the early tourists in the district were well aware of its existence, and the path is kept in being today by discerning walkers who appreciate the easy contours, fast travel, glorious scenery and superb views.

In places, the original line of the path is in doubt. The earlier Ordnance Survey maps indicated a wide divergence from the present footpath in the vicinity of Dubs Beck, but this may have been a rare error of cartography, for there are now no signs of it and it would have involved an obviously unnecessary descent and re-ascent. Traces are also missing on both sides of the Brandreth fence, but beyond the way is clear to the west ridge of Great Gable above Beck Head, where again the path is indistinct for a short distance until it starts the descent to Wasdale Head.

Honister Quarries

Dubs Quarry

old footpath

Drum House (foundations)

old tramway

HONISTER PASS 1700

1800

1900

Dubs Beck

2000

ENNERDALE

2000

2100

2200

BRANDRETH

GREAT GABLE

Brin Crag

springs

2100

2000

Tongue Beck

sheepfold

2000

2100

2200

xxxxx : line of original path, according to Ordnance maps.

ooooooo : suggested links between present walkers' path and Moses' Trod. (In mist, the second (2) is better)

SCALE OF MAP: Three inches = one mile

N

Unaccountably the greater part of the centuries-old Moses' Trod (ie. from Brandreth almost to Wasdale Head) was omitted from O maps until 1963!

continued on next page

Moses' Trod

continued on previous page

Moses is a well-established figure in local tradition, which describes him as a Honister quarryman who, after his day's work, illegally made whisky from the bog-water on Fleetwith at his quarry hut, smuggling this potent produce to Wasdale with his pony-loads of slate. There is now no evidence of his family name, or even that he ever lived, but no reason either for doubting the existence of a man of whom so many legends still survive in the district.

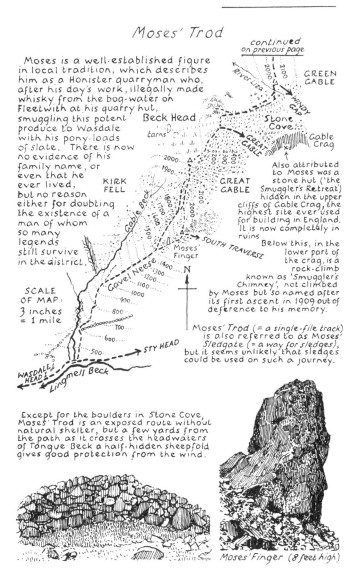

SCALE OF MAP:
3 inches = 1 mile

Also attributed to Moses was a stone hut ('the Smuggler's Retreat') hidden in the upper cliffs of Gable Crag, the highest site ever used for building in England. It is now completely in ruins

Below this, in the lower part of the crag, is a rock-climb known as 'Smuggler's Chimney', not climbed by Moses but so named after its first ascent in 1909 out of deference to his memory.

Moses' Trod (= a single-file track) is also referred to as Moses' Sledgate (= a way for sledges), but it seems unlikely that sledges could be used on such a journey.

Except for the boulders in Stone Cove, Moses' Trod is an exposed route without natural shelter, but a few yards from the path as it crosses the headwaters of Tongue Beck a half-hidden sheepfold gives good protection from the wind.

Moses' Finger (8 feet high)

The Gable Girdle
(linking the South Traverse and the North Traverse)

Originally a track for a privileged few (i.e. the early rock-climbers) the South Traverse, rising across the flank of Great Gable from Sty Head, has now become a much-fancied way for lesser fry (i.e. modern hikers). The North Traverse passes immediately below the base of Gable Crag, and although still largely the province of climbers is equally accessible to walkers.   The two traverses can be linked on the west by tracks over the scree above Beck Head; to the east the North Traverse is continued by the regular path down Aaron Slack to Sty Head. It is thus possible for walkers to make a full circuit of the mountain through interesting territory with fairly distinct tracks underfoot the whole way.

This is the finest mountain walk in the district that does not aim to reach a summit.

It is not level going: the route lies between 1500' and 2500', with many ups and downs. There are rough places to negotiate and nasty scree to cross and climb, but no dangers or difficulties. It is a doddle compared with, say, Jack's Rake or even Lord's Rake. Here one never has the feeling that the end is nigh.

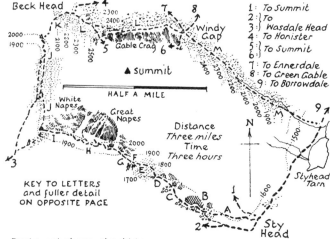

1: To Summit
2: To
3: Wasdale Head
4: To Honister
5: To Summit
6:
7: To Ennerdale
8: To Green Gable
9: To Borrowdale

Beck Head

Windy Gap

Gable Crag

▲ Summit

HALF A MILE

White Napes

Great Napes

Distance
Three miles
Time
Three hours

N

Styhead Tarn

KEY TO LETTERS
and fuller detail
ON OPPOSITE PAGE

Sty Head

Boots, not shoes, should be worn, and they must have soles with a firm grip, or there will be trouble on the boulders. There are few sections where the splendid views may be admired while walking: always stop to look around. The route is almost sheep-free, and dogs may be taken. So may small children, who are natural scramblers, and well-behaved women — but nagging wives should be left to paddle their feet in Styhead Tarn. The journey demands and deserves concentration.

The Gable Girdle

The South Traverse leaves Sty Head near the stretcher box, by a distinct stony path slanting left of the direct route up the mountain. There has been a big change here in the last twenty years. At one time, when the Traverse was the exclusive preserve of climbers, the commencement at Sty Head was deliberately kept obscure, so that walkers bound for the summit direct would not be beguiled along a false trail. But now the start is clearer than the start of the direct route, and many walkers enter upon it in the belief that it will lead them to the top of the mountain. It won't, not without a lot of effort.

KEY TO THE MAP ON THE OPPOSITE PAGE:

High
Kern
Knotts

Sty Head to Kern Knotts:
- **A :** Undulating path over grassy alps to bouldery depression and stony rise to the base of the crag.
- **B :** Huge boulders to be negotiated along the base of the crag. [A simpler variation passes below these boulders (good shelter here) and climbs roughly up the far side]

Kern Knotts to Great Hell Gate:
- **C :** Horizontal track over boulders leads to easier ground. A small hollow is skirted (boulders again) after which there is a short rise to a rocky corner.
- **D :** A cave on the right provides a trickle of water (the last until Aaron Slack). A short scramble up rocky steps follows.
- **E :** An easy rising path on scree.
- **F :** The head of two gullies is crossed on rocky slabs.
- **G :** Easy rising path to Great Hell Gate (a scree shoot). Tophet Wall in view ahead.

Great Hell Gate to Little Hell Gate:
- **H :** A section of some confusion, resolved by referring to the next page following.

Little Hell Gate to Beck Head:
- **I :** The scree-shoot of Little Hell Gate is crossed and a track picked up opposite: this trends downwards to a cairn at the angle of the south and west faces. Here endeth the South Traverse. [A scree-path goes down to Wasdale Head at this point]
- **J :** Around the grassy corner a thin trod contours the west slope and joins a clear track rising to Beck Head (cairn on a boulder).

The water-hole (D)

Beck Head to Windy Gap:
- **K :** Skirt the marshy ground ahead to a slanting scree-path rising to the angle of the north and west faces. [Moses'Trod goes off to the left here by a small pool]
- **L :** The steep loose scree of the north-west ridge is climbed for 100 yds. Watch closely for two cairns forming a 'gateway' (illustrated on page 27). Here commenceth the North Traverse. A track runs along the base of Gable Crag, descending to round the lowest buttress and then rising across scree to Windy Gap.

Windy Gap to Sty Head :
- **M :** A popular tourist path descends Aaron Slack to Styhead Tarn, where, if women are found paddling their feet, a greeting may be unwise.

The Great Napes

Rock climbers have played a much greater part than walkers in the selection of identifying names for natural features. All the names of the Great Napes are attributable to those who carried out the first exploration of the crags. Fortunately their choice was always appropriate, descriptive, and often inspired.

A : Sphinx Ridge
B : Arrowhead Ridge
C : Eagle's Nest Ridge
D : Needle Ridge
E : Tophet Bastion

F : Arrowhead Gully
G : Eagle's Nest Gully
H : Needle Gully
I : Dress Circle

J : rock island
K : Hell Gate Pillar

The Great Napes is a rocky excrescence high on the southern flank of Great Gable. Unlike most crags, which buttress and merge into the general slope of a mountain, the Great Napes rises like a castle above its surroundings so that there is not only a front wall of rock but side walls and a back wall too. This elevated mass is cut into by gullies to form four ridges, three of slender proportions and the fourth, and most easterly, broadly based and of substantial girth. The steepest rock occurs in the eastern part, the ground generally becoming more broken to the west. The front of the ridges, facing Wasdale, springs up almost vertically, but the gradient eases after the initial steepness to give grassy ledges in the higher reaches; the gullies, too, lose their sharp definition towards the top. Gradually the upper extremities of the Napes rise to a common apex, and here, at this point only, the Napes is undefended and a simple, grassy, and quite delightful ridge links with the main body of the fell. Here a climber may walk off the Napes and a walker may enter, with care, upon the easier upper heights. From the link ridge wide channels of scree pour down both sides of the Napes, thus defining the area clearly.

Across the westerly scree-channel the rocky tower of the White Napes emphasises the angle of the south and west faces of the mountain but has no notable crags and little of interest.

The Great Napes

continued

The South Traverse reaches its highest elevation in the section of about 250 yards between the two Hell Gates and beneath the Great Napes, but it does not venture to the base of the wall of crags, preferring an easier passage 50-80 yards lower down the slope, where it maintains a horizontal course on the 2000'contour. The intervening ground is steep and rocky, especially in the vicinity of the Needle, and its exploration calls for care. The Needle is in full view from the Traverse 'but does not seem its usual self (as usually seen in illustrations) and on a dull day is not easily distinguished from its background of rock. To visit it, take the rising branch-path from the Traverse into Needle Gully, and go up this to the base of the pinnacle; a scrambling track *opposite* climbs up to a ledge known as the Dress Circle, the traditional balcony for watching the ascent of the Needle. From this ledge a higher traverse can be made along the base of the crags, going below the Cat Rock into Little Hell Gate, but there is a tricky section initially and this is no walk for dogs, small children, well behaved women and the like.

Napes Needle

definitely not the author! ←

Midway between the two Hell Gates Needle Gully and a branch gully, full of scree, cut across the South Traverse, which otherwise hereabouts is mainly a matter of rounding little buttresses. Another bifurcation leads off to Little Hell Gate at a higher level, near the Cat Rock. If proceeding west (i.e. from Sty Head) the two rising branch-paths may be followed by mistake without realising that the Traverse has been left, they being the more distinct, a circumstance that does not arise when proceeding east.

ROUTES TO THE SUMMIT FROM THE SOUTH TRAVERSE

It is no uncommon thing for walkers to venture upon the South Traverse, from Sty Head, in the fond hope that it will lead them in due course to the summit of Great Gable. This hope is dashed when the Napes is reached, for here the path becomes uncertain and the rocks are an impassable obstacle. The clue to further ascent is provided when it is remembered that 'gate' is a local word for 'way' and that the Napes is bounded by the two Hell Gates. Either of these will conduct the walker safely upwards, but both are chutes for loose stones and steep and arduous to climb. (In Little Hell Gate it is possible, with care, to scramble off the scree onto Sphinx Ridge at several points). The two routes converge at the little ridge below Westmorland Crags, which are rounded on the left by a good track that winds up to the summit plateau.

The Cat Rock

The Sphinx Rock

This is the same pinnacle, shown here from the two angles that have given the two names

The Great Napes

left:
Tophet Bastion, as seen from the South Traverse on the approach from Sty Head.

The scree of Great Hell Gate runs down to the bottom left.

below:
looking steeply down on Tophet Bastion and the upper wall of the Napes, with the scree of Great Hell Gate running down to the left, from Westmorland Cairn.

The Great Napes

Eagle's Nest Gully

Eagle's Nest Ridge
(lower part known as
Abbey Buttress)

looking upwards
from just above
the South Traverse

Needle Gully

Needle Ridge

Napes Needle

rock island

Westmorland Crags

looking up Little Hell Gate

Tophet Bastion

Hell Gate Pillar

looking up Great Hell Gate

ASCENT FROM SEATHWAITE
2700 feet of ascent
2¼ miles

GREAT GABLE

2800
2700
2600

Gable Crag

Windy Gap

Stone Cove

GREEN GABLE

Mitchell Cove

HONISTER

2300
2200
2100
2000
1900
1800
1700

BASE BROWN

2100

2000

grass

1600

Gillercomb

Hanging Stone

1500

1400

Sour Milk Gill

1300
1200
1100

gap

900
800
700
600

Seathwaite Slabs

500

lane

ROAD

R. Derwent

SEATOLLER

Seathwaite

looking south-west

Although this cannot rank as a direct ascent, Green Gable having to be surmounted first, it is to be preferred to the traditional route from Seathwaite via Stockley Bridge and Sty Head because of its greater interest, greater attractiveness, and *quietness*.

With little extra effort the journey may be improved by adding Base Brown to the day's summits. For details of the ascent, see page Base Brown 6.

The dogs of Seathwaite are friendly, and grand companions on the hills, but they must NOT be encouraged to join the party. They have work to do.

At 1400' the view opens up ahead. To the right is Grey Knotts, across the hollow of Gillercomb, half-right is Brandreth, and straight in front is Green Gable.

The big crag here is known to climbers as Gillercomb Buttress.

The hardest work comes at once, on the steep attractive climb by Sour Milk Gill. The usual path is on the south bank, has a mild scramble on rock, and leads to a gap in the cross-wall. The track on the north bank has several variations, is rather easier, and ends at a hurdle in the corner of the wall, beyond which the stream must be crossed, the fording being best done 50 yards above the wall.

Leave Seathwaite under the arch of the farm buildings, but if travelling on foot from Seatoller, bypass the hamlet by taking the river-bank path at a gate alongside Seathwaite Bridge after three-quarters of a mile on the road.

ASCENT FROM STY HEAD
1350 feet of ascent : 1 mile
(from Wasdale Head : 2750 feet : ¾ miles
from Seathwaite : 2600 feet : 3¼ miles)

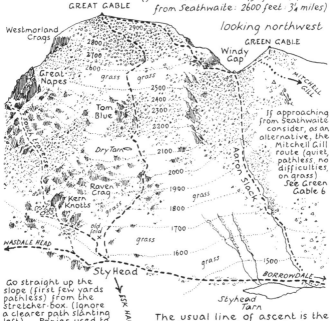

GREAT GABLE

looking northwest

Westmorland Crags

GREEN GABLE

Windy Gap

MITCHELL GILL

Great Napes

2900
2800
2700
2600
grass   grass
2500
2400
2300
2200

Tom Blue

If approaching from Seathwaite consider, as an alternative, the Mitchell Gill route (quiet, pathless, no difficulties, on grass) See Green Gable 6

Dry Tarn

2100

2000

Aaron Slack

Raven Crag

1900

grass

Kern Knotts

grass

1800

old fold
×

grass

1700

WASDALE HEAD

grass

1600

grass

1500

Sty Head

BORROWDALE

ESK HAUSE

Styhead Tarn

Go straight up the slope (first few yards pathless) from the stretcher-box. (Ignore a clearer path slanting left). Ponies used to be taken up to the grass shelf at 2500', but the path was then in a better state!

The usual line of ascent is the original tourist path (also known as the Breast Route) from Sty Head. It is abundantly cairned, safe in mist, but very bad underfoot (loose scree) on the steep rise by Tom Blue, where clumsy walkers have utterly ruined the path. The Aaron Slack route gives a rather firmer footing.

There are good walkers and bad walkers, and the difference between them has nothing to do with performances in mileage or speed. The difference lies in the way they put their feet down.

A good walker is a *tidy* walker. He moves quietly, places his feet where his eyes tell him to, on beaten tracks treads firmly, avoids loose stones on steep ground, disturbs nothing. He is, by habit, an improver of paths.

A bad walker is a *clumsy* walker. He moves noisily, disturbs the surface and even the foundations of paths by kicking up loose stones, tramples the verges until they disintegrate into debris. He is, by habit, a maker of bad tracks and a spoiler of good ones.

A good walker's special joy is zigzags, which he follows faithfully. A bad walker's special joy is in shortcutting and destroying zigzags.

All fellwalking accidents are the result of clumsiness.

ASCENT FROM HONISTER PASS
1950 feet of ascent : 3 miles

GREAT GABLE

Windy Gap
GREEN GABLE

Gable Crag

looking south

2500
2500
2400

2400

Stone Cove

2000

Beck Head

2300

River Liza

2200

The Tongue

Tongue Beck

2100

Gillercomb Head

Moses Trod

BRANDRETH

2200

2200

2100

grass

2000

→ ENNERDALE

GREY KNOTTS

2100

The usual route follows the path over Green Gable, descends to Windy Gap and climbs left of Gable Crag: a well-blazed trail with a large population on any fine day.

Human beings can be avoided and the ascent made more direct (omitting Green Gable) by switching over to Moses' Trod at the Brandreth west fence (to join the Trod, aim across grass south for 200 yards). Follow the Trod into Stone Cove, where either (a) turn left up to Windy Gap, there rejoining the main path, or (b) continue along the Trod to the bluff above Beck Head and there turn up scree to the summit. If returning to Honister, use (b), and come back by the path over Green Gable.

An initially more strenuous alternative follows the line of fenceposts behind the quarry buildings, passing over the summits of Grey Knotts and Brandreth.
There is no path (although the 1963 1" Ordnance Survey map shows one) until the usual route is joined at Gillercomb Head but the line of posts is an impeccable guide in any sort of weather; at a junction of fences on Grey Knotts keep to the right.

grass

1900

1800

1700

→ DUBS QUARRY

foundations of Drum House

1600

sleepers

old tramway

For additional notes relating to this walk and its surroundings consult Brandreth 4
Fleetwith Pike 5
Great Gable 7
Green Gable 4
Grey Knotts 7

rock cutting

1300

1200

quarry buildings

signpost

PRIVATE

Youth Hostel

quarry road

BUTTERMERE

SEATOLLER
1½

ROAD
Honister Pass
(or Hause)

This is an excellent route for motorists, who may abandon their cars on the Pass with a height of 1190 feet already achieved, and experience the wind on the heath, brother, for the next five hours with no thought of gears and brakes and clutches and things, and feel all the better for exercising his limbs as nature intended.

ASCENT FROM GATESGARTH
2800 feet of ascent : 4 miles

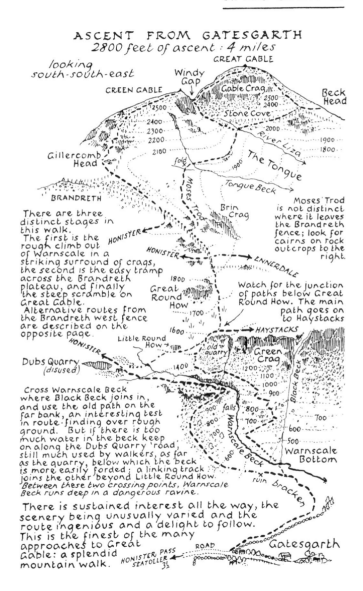

looking
south-south-east

GREAT GABLE

CREEN GABLE   Windy
              Gap

Cable Crag,   Beck
               Head

2500
2400

Stone Cove

2500

2400
2300
2200

2100

Gillercomb
Head

2000

River Liza

1900
1800

The Tongue

900

fold

Tongue Beck

Moses Trod

BRANDRETH

Brin
Crag

Moses' Trod
is not distinct
where it leaves
the Brandreth
fence; look for
cairns on rock
outcrops to the
right.

There are three
distinct stages in
this walk.
The first is the
rough climb out
of Warnscale in a
striking surround of crags,
the second is the easy tramp
across the Brandreth
plateau, and finally
the steep scramble on
Great Gable.
Alternative routes from
the Brandreth west fence
are described on the
opposite page.

HONISTER

HONISTER

ENNERDALE

1800

Great
Round
How

Watch for the junction
of paths below Great
Round How. The main
path goes on
to Haystacks

1700

HAYSTACKS

1600

Little Round
How

old
quarry

Green
Crag

HONISTER

Dubs Quarry
(disused)

1400

1200
1100
1000
900

Black Beck

Cross Warnscale Beck
where Black Beck joins in,
and use the old path on the
far bank, an interesting test
in route-finding over rough
ground. But if there is too
much water in the beck keep
on along the Dubs Quarry 'road',
still much used by walkers, as far
as the quarry, below which the beck
is more easily forded; a linking track
joins the other beyond Little Round How.
Between these two crossing points, Warnscale
Beck runs deep in a dangerous ravine.

900   falls   800
900   700
              700

Warnscale Beck

600

Too

500

Warnscale
Bottom

ruin   bracken

There is sustained interest all the way, the
scenery being unusually varied and the
route ingenious and a delight to follow.
This is the finest of the many
approaches to Great
Gable: a splendid
mountain walk.

ROAD

Gatesgarth

HONISTER, PASS
SEATOLLER
3½

ASCENT FROM ENNERDALE
(BLACK SAIL YOUTH HOSTEL)
2000 feet of ascent : 2¼ miles

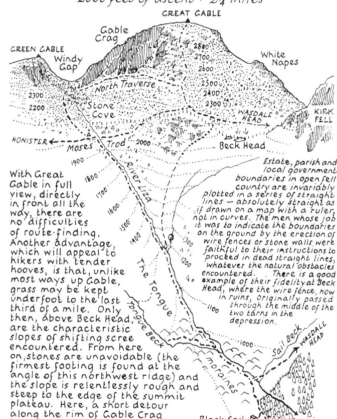

GREAT GABLE

Gable Crag

GREEN GABLE

Windy Gap

White Napes

2800
2700
2600
2500
2400
2300

North Traverse

2300
2200

Stone Cove

WASDALE HEAD

KIRK FELL

HONISTER ←— Moses Trod —→ 2000

Beck Head

1900
1800
1700
1600
1500
1400
1300
1200

River Liza

The Tongue

1100

Tongue Beck

1000

moraines

Sail Beck

WASDALE HEAD

Black Sail Youth Hostel

ENNERDALE

SCARTH GAP

looking southeast

With Great Gable in full view, directly in front all the way, there are no difficulties of route-finding. Another advantage, which will appeal to hikers with tender hooves, is that, unlike most ways up Gable, grass may be kept underfoot to the last third of a mile. Only then, above Beck Head, are the characteristic slopes of shifting scree encountered. From here on, stones are unavoidable (the firmest footing is found at the angle of this northwest ridge) and the slope is relentlessly rough and steep to the edge of the summit plateau. Here, a short detour along the rim of Gable Crag is more rewarding in scenery and views than a direct course for the top cairn.

Estate, parish and local government boundaries in open fell country are invariably plotted in a series of straight lines — absolutely straight as if drawn on a map with a ruler, not in curves. The men whose job it was to indicate the boundaries on the ground by the erection of wire fences or stone walls were faithful to their instructions to proceed in dead straight lines, whatever the natural obstacles encountered. There is a good example of their fidelity at Beck Head, where the wire fence, now in ruins, originally passed through the middle of the two tarns in the depression.

Difficulties of access to the lonely head of Ennerdale for walkers based elsewhere make this ascent almost the exclusive preserve of those privileged by Y.H.A. membership to stay at the hostel.

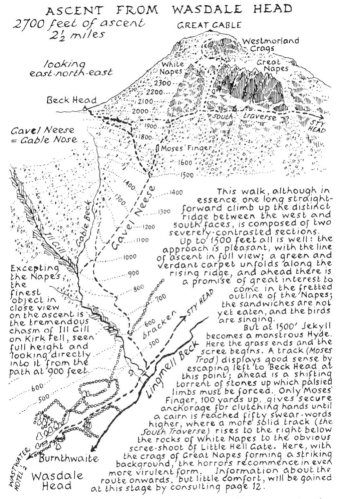

ASCENT FROM WASDALE HEAD

2700 feet of ascent
2½ miles

looking
east-north-east

GREAT GABLE

Westmorland Crags

White Napes

Great Napes

Beck Head

STY HEAD

Gavel Neese = Gable Nose

south traverse

Moses' Finger

Gavel Neese

Gable Beck

Ill Gill

STY HEAD

bracken

Lingmell Beck

WASTWATER HOTEL 2

Burnthwaite

Wasdale Head

Excepting the Napes, the finest object in close view on the ascent is the tremendous chasm of Ill Gill on Kirk Fell, seen full height and looking directly into it from the path at 900 feet.

This walk, although in essence one long straight-forward climb up the distinct ridge between the west and south faces, is composed of two severely-contrasted sections. Up to 1500 feet all is well: the approach is pleasant, with the line of ascent in full view; a green and verdant carpet unfolds along the rising ridge, and ahead there is a promise of great interest to come in the fretted outline of the Napes; the sandwiches are not yet eaten, and the birds are singing.

But at 1500' Jekyll becomes a monstrous Hyde. Here the grass ends and the scree begins. A track (Moses Trod) displays good sense by escaping left to Beck Head at this point; ahead is a shifting torrent of stones up which palsied limbs must be forced. Only Moses' Finger, 100 yards up, gives secure anchorage for clutching hands until a cairn is reached fifty swear-words higher, where a more solid track (the South Traverse) rises to the right below the rocks of White Napes to the obvious scree-shoot of Little Hell Gate. Here, with the crags of Great Napes forming a striking background, the horrors recommence in even more virulent form. Information about the route onwards, but little comfort, will be gained at this stage by consulting page 12.

From Wasdale Head this route is clearly seen to be the most direct way to the summit. It is also the most strenuous. (Its conquest is more wisely announced at supper, afterwards, than at breakfast, in advance).

THE SUMMIT

Great Gable's summit is held in special respect by the older generation of fellwalkers, because here, set in the rocks that bear the top cairn, is the bronze War Memorial tablet of the Fell and Rock Climbing Club, dedicated in 1924, and ever since the inspiring scene of an annual Remembrance Service in November. It is a fitting place to pay homage to men who once loved to walk on these hills and gave their lives defending the right of others to enjoy the same happy freedom, for the ultimate crest of Gable is truly characteristic of the best of mountain Lakeland: a rugged crown of rock and boulders and stones in chaotic profusion, a desert without life, a harsh and desolate peak thrust high in the sky above the profound depths all around.

Gable, tough and strong all through its height, has here made a final gesture by providing an outcrop of rock even in its last inches, so that one must climb to touch the cairn (which, being hallowed as a shrine by fellwalkers everywhere, let no man tear asunder lest a thousand curses accompany his guilty flight!). On three sides the slopes fall away immediately, but to the north there extends a small plateau, with a little vegetation, before the summit collapses in the sheer plunge of Gable Crag. The rim of this precipice, and also the top of Westmorland Crags to the south, should be visited for their superlative views.

There are few days in the year when no visitors arrive on the summit. Snow and ice and severe gales may defy those who aspire to reach it in winter, but in the summer months there is a constant parade of perspiring pedestrians across the top from early morning to late evening.

To many fellwalkers this untidy bit of ground is Mecca.

continued

THE SUMMIT

continued

DESCENTS : All ways off the summit are paved with loose stones and continue so for most of the descent. Allied to roughness is steepness, particularly on the Wasdale side, and care is needed to avoid involuntary slips. In places, where scree-runners have bared the underlying ground, surfaces are slippery and unpleasant. Never descend Gable in a mad rush!

In fine weather there should be no trouble in distinguishing the various cairned routes; in mist their direction is identified by the memorial tablet, which faces north overlooking the path to Windy Gap. Not all cairns can be relied upon; some are not route-markers but indicators of viewpoints and rock-climbs. Generally, however, the principal traffic routes are well-blazed by boots.

In bad conditions the safest line is down the breast of the mountain to Sty Head. Care is needed in locating the descent to Beck Head, which keeps closely to the angle of the north and west faces and does not follow any of the inviting scree-runs on the west side, which end in fields of boulders. Caution is also advised in attempting direct descents of the Wasdale face if the topography of the Napes is not already familiar.

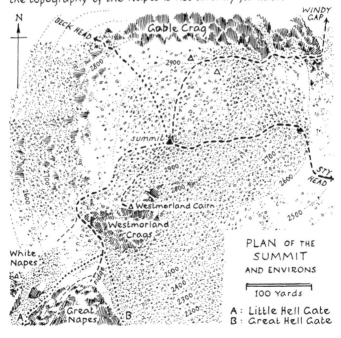

PLAN OF THE
SUMMIT
AND ENVIRONS

100 Yards

A: Little Hell Gate
B: Great Hell Gate

THE VIEW

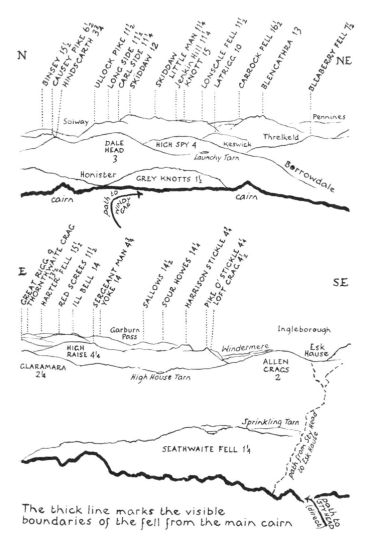

N

BINSEY 15½
CAUSEY PIKE 6¾
HINDSCARTH 3¾
ULLOCK PIKE 11½
LONG SIDE 11½
CARL SIDE 11½
SKIDDAW 12*
SKIDDAW 11¼
LITTLE MAN 11¼
JENKIN HILL 11¼
KNOTT 15
LONSCALE FELL 11½
LATRIGG 10
CARROCK FELL 16½
BLENCATHRA 13
BLEABERRY FELL 7½

NE

Solway   Pennines

Threlkeld

DALE HEAD 3   HIGH SPY 4   Keswick

Launchy Tarn

Honister   GREY KNOTTS 1½

Borrowdale

cairn   path to WINDY GAP   cairn

E

GREAT RIGG 9
THORNTHWAITE CRAG 13½
HARTER FELL 15½
RED SCREES 11½
ILL BELL 14
SERGEANT MAN 4¾
YOKE 14
SALLOWS 14½
SOUR HOWES 14¼
HARRISON STICKLE 4¾
PIKE O' STICKLE 4¾
LOFT CRAG 4½

SE

Garburn Pass   Ingleborough

HIGH RAISE 4¼   Windermere   Esk Hause

CLARAMARA 2¼   High House Tarn   ALLEN CRAGS 2

Sprinkling Tarn

path from Sty Head to Esk House

SEATHWAITE FELL 1¼

path to STY HEAD (direct)

The thick line marks the visible
boundaries of the fell from the main cairn

THE VIEW

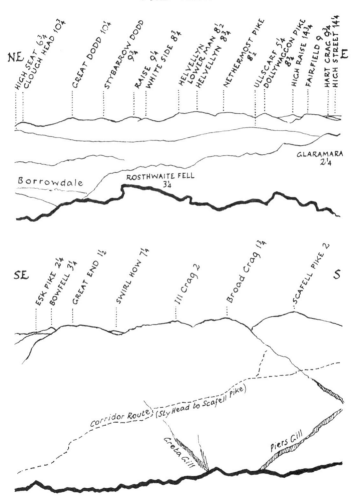

NE

HIGH SEAT 6¾
CLOUGH HEAD 10¾
GREAT DODD 10¼
STYBARROW DODD 9¾
RAISE 9¼
WHITE SIDE 8¾
HELVELLYN LOWER MAN 8½
HELVELLYN 8¾
NETHERMOST PIKE 8½
ULLSCARF 5¼
DOLLYWAGGON PIKE 8½
HIGH RAISE 14¾
FAIRFIELD 9
HART CRAG 9¾
HIGH STREET 14¼

E

GLARAMARA 2¼

Borrowdale

ROSTHWAITE FELL 3¼

SE

ESK PIKE 2¼
BOWFELL 3¼
GREAT END 1½
SWIRL HOW 7¼
Ill Crag 2
Broad Crag 1¾
Scafell Pike 2

S

Corridor Route (Sty Head to Scafell Pike)

Greta Gill

Piers Gill

The figures accompanying the names of fells indicate distances in miles

THE VIEW

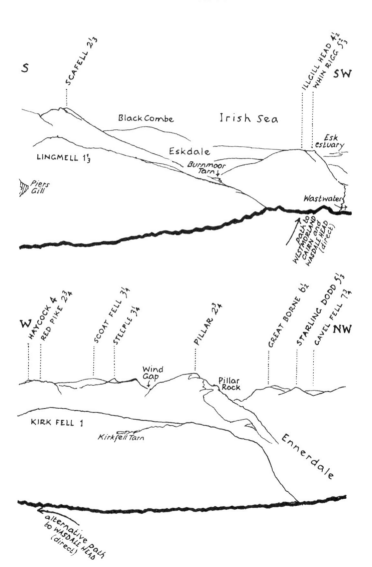

THE VIEW

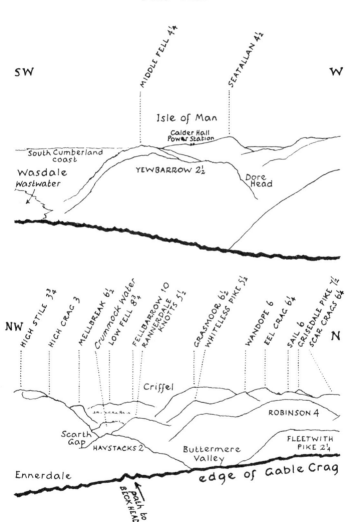

RIDGE ROUTES

To GREEN GABLE, 2603': NNE, then E and NNE: ½ mile
Depression (Windy Gap) at 2460'
150 feet of ascent
Rough and stony all the way

The best that can be said for the path is that it is clearly defined throughout, which is as well, there being unseen precipices in the vicinity. One section, where Gable Crag is rounded to reach Windy Gap, is particularly objectionable and needs care on smooth rocky steps.

To KIRK FELL, 2630': NW, then W and SW: 1⅓ miles
Depression (Beck Head) at 2040'   700 feet of ascent.
A passing from the sublime to the less sublime, better done the other way.

Pick a way carefully down the north-west ridge, avoiding false trails that lead only to boulder slopes and keeping generally near the angle of the ridge, where the footing is firmest. When a line of fence posts is joined, the remainder of the route is assured, the posts leading across the depression of Beck Head, up the steep facing slope of Rib End, and visiting first the lower and then the top summit of Kirk Fell across a wide grassy plateau.

A place to remember.......

Some quite ordinary patches of fellside have extraordinary significance when they indicate important route junctions occurring in rough terrain and not clearly defined by paths on the ground. The best example is the upper exit of Lords Rake on Scafell, and there are many others.

GREEN GABLE
Windy Gap
line of North Traverse
Stone Cove
scree and boulders
Gable Crag

Illustrated here is the place where the North Traverse leaves the northwest ridge to cross below Gable Crag to Windy Gap.

Pass between the two cairns and the track comes into view

Westmorland Cairn

Erected in 1876 by two brothers of the name of Westmorland to mark what they considered to be the finest mountain viewpoint in the district, this soundly-built and tidy cairn is wellknown, to climbers and walkers alike, and has always been respected. The cairn has maintained its original form throughout the years quite remarkably; apart from visitors who like to add a pebble, it has suffered neither from the weather nor from human despoilers. It stands on the extreme brink of the south face, above steep crags, and overlooks Wasdale. Rocky platforms around make the place ideal for a halt after climbing Great Gable. The cairn is not in sight from the summit but is soon reached by walking 150 yards across the stony top in the direction of Wastwater.

17 | Pillar

Book Seven: The Western Fells

Wainwright had it in for the Forestry Commission for having planted millions of uniform trees. Especially on Pillar, one of his top six fells, 'a fine bold mountain overtopping all else around'. On Pillar 3, he fairly savaged what had happened in Ennerdale: '...a dark and funereal shroud of foreign trees, an intrusion that nobody who knew Ennerdale of old can ever forgive, the former charm of the valley having been destroyed thereby. We condemn vandalism and sanction this mess!'

Complaining about acts of man in the Lake District has a long history. One of Wordsworth's moans was about people painting their cottages white. He maintained it ruined the landscape, spoiled the views. He wanted them left bare stone or slate, as nature intended. He also hated all the new houses being built around him in Grasmere by the *nouveaux riches* from Lancashire. He called one of the houses an 'abomination' – until he and his family moved into it, fed up with the damp and the cold in Dove Cottage.

In the illustration on Pillar 3, Wainwright has a neat reference to Wordsworth. 'Ten thousand saw I at a glance.' Meaning, of course, the dratted fir trees, not daffodils. This criticism of the Forestry Commission was common in the 1960s and much earlier. The Forestry Commission had first started planting Norway spruce in Ennerdale in 1926 – so Wainwright himself never quite saw 'Ennerdale of old'. It was part of a post-First-World-War plan to build up a reserve of wood in case of another war.

Many Lakelanders before and after Wainwright have criticised the Forestry Commission and it now varies new plantings, putting in deciduous trees alongside conifers, staggering rows, avoiding straight lines, and they are less secretive, more sensitive to public opinion.

In Ennerdale, some of the monster forests have now been felled, and, in addition, the Forestry Commission has created numerous trails and paths. They have also worked hard on their public car park at Bowness Point on Ennerdale Water. It even has award-winning lavatories, ever so artistic, very handy for all Ennerdale walkers. Elsewhere in the Lake District, at Grizedale Forest and at Whinlatter, the Forestry Commission has created tasteful visitor attractions with walks, displays, boards and forest sculptures.

I agree with Wainwright that a forest of identical fir trees can look ugly and menacing, but I'm not sure I agree that what was underneath, 'the old desolation of boulder and bog', was necessarily better. When fir forests are cut down, the land beneath is usually revealed to be barren, steep and boulder-strewn. I quite like trees and foliage on rough stony ground, as long as it is pretty, varied stuff like heather, rowan, birch and oak. But it is true that a forest of trees does tend to obliterate the shape of a fell.

Black Sail Youth Hostel, which is shown on many of Wainwright's maps of the area, is still active, and still a YHA hostel, and since you can't get to it by car, it remains the most inaccessible hostel in the Lake District, if not England. You still can't drive beyond the Bowness Point car park, which means Ennerdale Water is still the only road-free lake in the Lake District.

Ennerdale has been protected and remains one of the wildest valleys in Lakeland – though perhaps not as wild as in 1799 when Coleridge visited it with Wordsworth. A farmer told them that two eagles had just stolen one of his live geese, 'a full-fed harvest goose'. One eagle had lifted it up, carrying it away, then when it was exhausted, the other eagle took over. No eagles today in Ennerdale, but look out for buzzards, sparrowhawks and peregrine falcons. And, of course, fearsome fir trees.

Pillar

2927'

from Brin Crag, Brandreth

NATURAL FEATURES

Great Gable, Pillar and Steeple are the three mountain names on Lakeland maps most likely to fire the imagination of youthful adventurers planning a first tour of the district, inspiring exciting visions of slim, near-vertical pinnacles towering grandly into the sky.

Great Gable lives up to its name, especially if climbed from Wasdale; Pillar has a fine bold outline but is nothing like a pillar; Steeple is closely overlooked by a higher flat-topped fell and not effectively seen.

Pillar, in fact, far from being a spire of slender proportions, is a rugged mass broadly based on half the length of Ennerdale, a series of craggy buttresses supporting the ridge high above this wild north face; and the summit itself, far from being pointed, is wide and flat. The name of the fell therefore clearly derives from a conspicuous feature on the north face directly below the top, the most handsome crag in Lakeland, originally known as the Pillar Stone and now as Pillar Rock. The Rock, despite a remote and lonely situation, had a well-established local notoriety and fame long before tourists called wider attention to it, and an object of such unique appearance simply had to be given a descriptive name, although, at the time, one was not yet needed to identify the mountain of which it formed part. *The Pillar* was an inspiration of shepherds. Men of letters could not have chosen better.

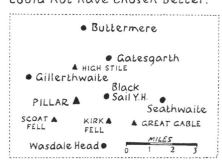

The north face of the fell has a formidable aspect. Crags and shadowed hollows, scree and tumbled boulders, form a wild, chaotic scene, a setting worthy of a fine mountain.

continued

NATURAL FEATURES

continued

Pillar is the highest mountain west of Great Gable, from which it is sufficiently removed in distance to exhibit distinctive slopes on all sides. It dominates the sunset area of Lakeland superbly, springing out of the valleys of Mosedale and Ennerdale, steeply on the one side and dramatically on the other, as befits the overlord of the western scene. A narrow neck of land connects with a chain of other grand fells to the south, and a depression forms the east boundary and is crossed by Black Sail Pass at 1800', but elsewhere the full height of the fell from valley level is displayed. Some of the streams flow west *via* Ennerdale Water and some south *via* Wast Water, but their fate, discharge into the Irish Sea from the coast near Seascale, is the same, only a few miles separating the two outlets.

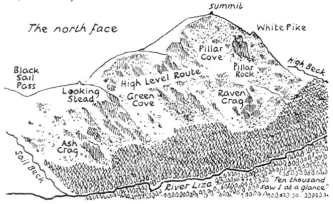

The north face

summit · White Pike · Pillar Cove · Pillar Rock · High Beck · Black Sail Pass · High Level Route · Looking Stead · Green Cove · Raven Crag · Ash Crag · Sail Beck · River Liza · "Ten thousand saw I at a glance"

Afforestation in Ennerdale has cloaked the lower slopes on this side in a dark and funereal shroud of foreign trees, an intrusion that nobody who knew Ennerdale of old can ever forgive, the former charm of the valley having been destroyed thereby. We condemn vandalism and sanction this mess! Far better the old desolation of boulder and bog when a man could see the sky, than this new desolation of regimented timber shutting out the light of day. It is an offence to the eyes to see Pillar's once-colourful fellside now hobbled in such a dowdy and ill-suited skirt, just as it is to see a noble animal caught in a trap. Yet, such is the majesty and power of this fine mountain that it can shrug off the insults and indignities, and its summit soars no less proudly above. It is the admirers of this grand pile who feel the hurt.

A Pillar Rock
portfolio

from the east

Pillar 5

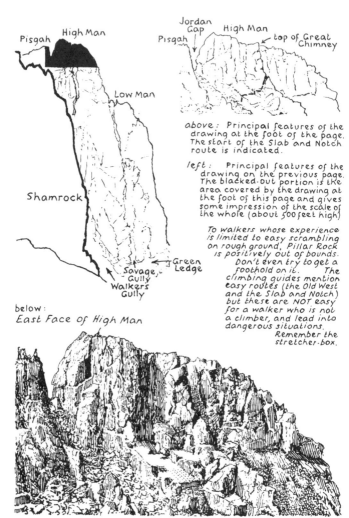

Pisgah · High Man

Low Man

Shamrock

Green Ledge

Savage Gully
Walkers Gully

below:
East Face of High Man

Jordan Gap · High Man
Pisgah · top of Great Chimney

above: Principal features of the drawing at the foot of the page. The start of the Slab and Notch route is indicated.

left: Principal features of the drawing on the previous page. The blacked-out portion is the area covered by the drawing at the foot of this page and gives some impression of the scale of the whole (about 500 feet high)

To walkers whose experience is limited to easy scrambling on rough ground, Pillar Rock is positively out of bounds. Don't even try to get a foothold on it. The climbing guides mention easy routes (the Old West and the Slab and Notch) but these are NOT easy for a walker who is not a climber, and lead into dangerous situations.
Remember the stretcher-box.

as seen from the Shamrock Traverse.

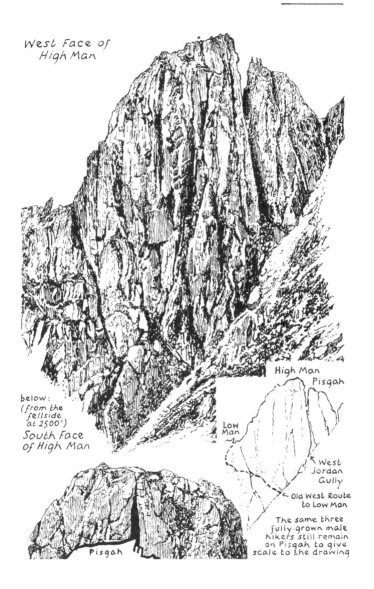

West Face of
High Man

below:
(from the
fellside
at 2500')
South Face
of High Man

Pisgah

High Man

Pisgah

Low
Man

West
Jordan
Gully

Old West Route
to Low Man

The same three
fully-grown male
hikers still remain
on Pisgah to give
scale to the drawing

MAP

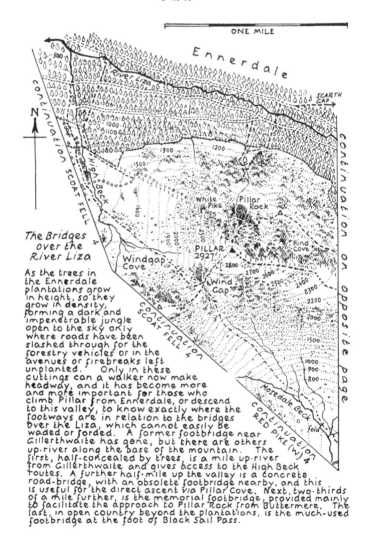

The Bridges over the River Liza

As the trees in the Ennerdale plantations grow in height, so they grow in density, forming a dark and impenetrable jungle open to the sky only where roads have been slashed through for the forestry vehicles or in the avenues or firebreaks left unplanted. Only in these cuttings can a walker now make headway, and it has become more and more important for those who climb Pillar from Ennerdale, or descend to this valley, to know exactly where the footways are in relation to the bridges over the Liza, which cannot easily be waded or forded. A former footbridge near Gillerthwaite has gone, but there are others up-river along the base of the mountain. The first, half-concealed by trees, is a mile up-river from Gillerthwaite and gives access to the High Beck routes. A further half-mile up the valley is a concrete road-bridge, with an obsolete footbridge nearby, and this is useful for the direct ascent via Pillar Cove. Next, two-thirds of a mile further, is the memorial footbridge, provided mainly to facilitate the approach to Pillar Rock from Buttermere. The last, in open country beyond the plantations, is the much-used footbridge at the foot of Black Sail Pass.

MAP

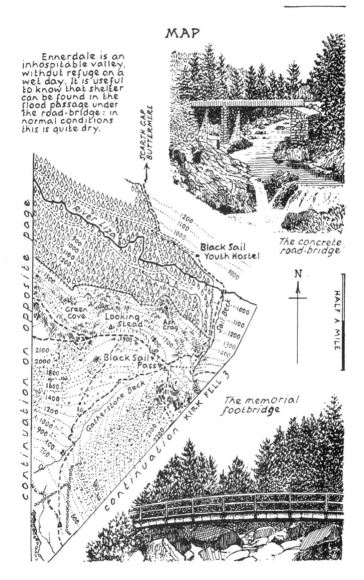

Ennerdale is an inhospitable valley, without refuge on a wet day. It is useful to know that shelter can be found in the flood passage under the road-bridge: in normal conditions this is quite dry.

SCARTH GAP BUTTERMERE

The concrete road-bridge

River Liza

Black Sail Youth Hostel

Green Cove

Looking Stead

Black Sail Pass

Gatherstone Beck

continuation on opposite page

continuation KIRK FELL 3

N

HALF A MILE

The memorial footbridge

ASCENT FROM WASDALE HEAD
2700 feet of ascent
4½ miles via Black Sail Pass
3¼ miles via Wind Gap

PILLAR

Wind Gap

2800

2700

2600

2500

2400

2300

2200

2100

2000

1900

1800

1700

1600

1500

1400

1300

1200

1100

1000

900

800

700

Wistow Crags

grass

The short cut is not really a time-saver in ascent, the better plan being to go on to the top of the Pass and do the whole ridge.

looking north

At this point the High Level route goes off to the right (see next page)

Looking Stead

Black Sail Pass

grass

tarn

short cut

1500

1600

last water on the ascent

Indistinct track on a rising tongue of grass

Gatherstone Beck

bield
×

c. grass

Wind Gap

scree shoot

bracken

fold

If using the Wind Gap route, be careful to identify the Gap correctly from the valley. It is clearly in sight and identifiable by its long scree-run. But note that the Gap is not the true head of the valley, this being Blackem Head away to the left, where Mosedale Beck has its source.

Mosedale Beck

800

700

pen

The usual route (via Black Sail Pass and the ridge) is an excellent walk and the easiest way to any of the Wasdale summits. A good walker will do it nonstop. The more direct Wind Gap route is out of favour, being more confined, less attractive in its views, and damned by an unpleasant and unavoidable scree-run.

Mosedale

The Wind Gap route turns (indistinctly) from the Black Sail path at the cairn at 500'.

600

500

400

300

Don't go wrong at the very start! The way lies NOT over the bridge but through the yard of Row Head (the last building up the lane from the Wastwater Hotel)

Wasdale Head

Row Head

Hotel

ASCENT FROM ENNERDALE
(BLACK SAIL YOUTH HOSTEL)
2000 feet of ascent : 2¾ miles
(2100 feet, 3 miles by High Level Route)

The main ridge, from Black Sail Pass to the summit, is a pleasant walk without difficulty, three stony rises being succeeded by splendid turf. A line of iron posts accompanies the ridge but the path, in many places, deviates to the left.

The High Level route is a traverse across the fellside (aiming for Pillar Rock), not a way to the summit, although the two can be connected (see next page). This is a fine pedestrian way, highly recommended, rough but not difficult.

Originally the High Level Route had an awkward start. A new variation avoids the difficulty.

PILLAR

Great Doup

stretcher box

Hind Cove

Pillar Rock

gross

Green Cove

Robinson's Cairn

High Level Route

← detail →

2700
2600
2500
2400
2300

Looking Stead

1900

WASDALE HEAD
← direct route

tarn

WASDALE HEAD

1800

Black Sail Pass

1700

There is a gate at the top of the pass but only a fanatical purist would think of using it.

1600

The path avoids the actual top of Looking Stead, but walkers should not. It is an excellent viewpoint for a survey, both of the High Level route and of Ennerdale.

Main ridge :
1 : zigzag path
2 : direct path
High Level route :
3 : original start
4 : new variation
Main ridge :
5 : from Black Sail

1
2
3
4
5

Ash Crag

1500
1400
1300
1200

River Liza

Sojourners at the hostel are fortunate in having Pillar on their doorstep, and can enjoy one of the best days of their young lives by climbing it.

Sail Beck

1100

1000

Black Sail Y.H.

moraines

looking west

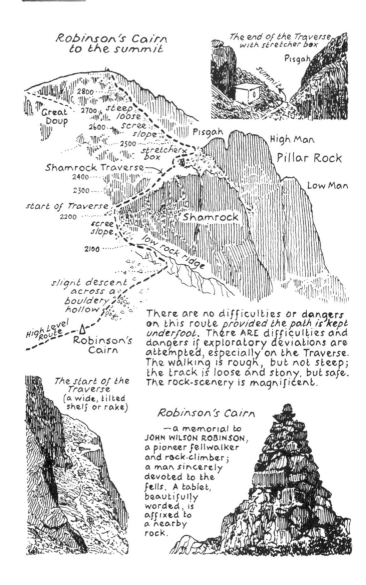

Robinson's Cairn to the summit

2800
Great Doup
2700 *steep loose scree slope*
2600
2500
Pisgah
stretcher box
Shamrock Traverse
2400
2300
start of Traverse
2200
scree slope
2100
low rock ridge
Shamrock

High Man
Pillar Rock
Low Man

slight descent across a bouldery hollow

High Level Route
△ Robinson's Cairn

The end of the Traverse, with stretcher box
Pisgah
summit

The start of the Traverse (a wide, tilted shelf or rake)

There are no difficulties or dangers on this route *provided the path is kept underfoot.* There ARE difficulties and dangers if exploratory deviations are attempted, especially on the Traverse. The walking is rough, but not steep; the track is loose and stony, but safe. The rock-scenery is magnificent.

Robinson's Cairn

—a memorial to JOHN WILSON ROBINSON, a pioneer fellwalker and rock-climber; a man sincerely devoted to the fells. A tablet, beautifully worded, is affixed to a nearby rock.

ASCENT FROM ENNERDALE
(HIGH GILLERTHWAITE)
2500 feet of ascent
3¼ miles (A) : 2¾ miles (B)

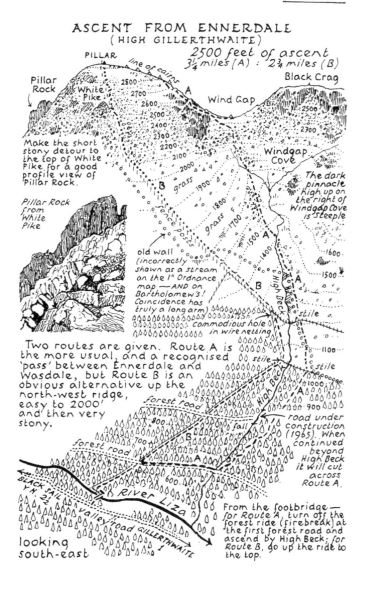

PILLAR

line of cairns

A

Wind Gap

Black Crag

Pillar
Rock

White
Pike

2800
2700
2600
2500
2400
2300
2200
2100
2000

2500

2300

Make the short
stony detour to
the top of White
Pike for a good
profile view of
Pillar Rock.

Windgap
Cove

The dark
pinnacle
high up on
the right of
Windgap Cove
is Steeple

Pillar Rock
from
White
Pike

B

grass

1900

1800

grass

1700

A

1500

1400

1600

1500

old wall
(incorrectly
shewn as a stream
on the 1" Ordnance
map — AND on
Bartholomew's!
Coincidence has
truly a long arm)

High Beck

B

A

stile

Commodious hole
in wire netting

1100

Two routes are given. Route A is
the more usual, and a recognised
'pass' between Ennerdale and
Wasdale, but Route B is an
obvious alternative up the
north-west ridge,
easy to 2000'
and then very
stony.

stile

stile

forest road

High Beck

A

1000

900

800

road under
construction
(1965). When
continued
beyond
High Beck
it will cut
across
Route A.

fall

B

700

A

forest road

600

River Liza

BLACK SAIL
Y.H. 2½

valley road GILLERTHWAITE

looking
south-east

From the footbridge—
for Route A, turn off the
forest ride (firebreak) at
the first forest road and
ascend by High Beck; for
Route B, go up the ride to
the top.

ASCENT FROM ENNERDALE
(direct from THE MEMORIAL FOOTBRIDGE)

2250 feet of ascent
1¼ miles

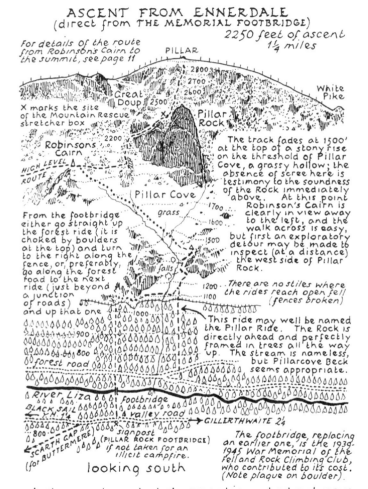

For details of the route
from Robinson's Cairn to
the summit, see page 11

PILLAR

2800
2700
2600
2500

White
Pike

Great
Doup

X marks the site
of the Mountain Rescue
stretcher box

2200

Pillar
Rock

Robinson's
Cairn

HIGH LEVEL
ROUTE

Pillar Cove

grass

1700
1600
1500

The track fades at 1500'
at the top of a stony rise
on the threshold of Pillar
Cove, a grassy hollow; the
absence of scree here is
testimony to the soundness
of the Rock immediately
above.   At this point
Robinson's Cairn is
clearly in view away
to the left, and the
walk across is easy,
but first an exploratory
detour may be made to
inspect (at a distance)
the west side of Pillar
Rock.

From the footbridge
either go straight up
the forest ride (it is
choked by boulders
at the top) and turn
to the right along the
fence, or, preferably,
go along the forest
road to the next
ride (just beyond
a junction
of roads)
and up that one

falls

1200
1100

1000
900
800
forest road

There are no stiles where
the rides reach open fell
(fences broken)

This ride may well be named
the Pillar Ride. The Rock is
directly ahead and perfectly
framed in trees all the way
up. The stream is nameless,
but Pillarcove Beck
seems appropriate.

River Liza   footbridge
BLACK SAIL
K.H. 1¼   valley road   →GILLERTHWAITE 2¼
800
←SCARTH GAP   signpost
(for BUTTERMERE) (PILLAR ROCK FOOTBRIDGE)
if not taken for an
illicit campfire.

looking south

The footbridge, replacing
an earlier one, is the 1939-
1945 War Memorial of the
Fell and Rock Climbing Club,
who contributed to its cost.
(Note plaque on boulder.)

A steep and rough, but romantic and adventurous
climb in magnificent surroundings: the finest way
up the mountain. Pillar Rock grips the attention
throughout. Unfortunately the route is somewhat
remote from tourist centres, but strong walkers can
do it from Buttermere via Scarth Gap.

ASCENT FROM BUTTERMERE

Most walkers when planning to climb a mountain aim to avoid any downhill section between their starting-point and the summit, and if the intermediate descent is considerable the extra effort of regaining lost height may rule out the attempt altogether. A good example is Great Gable from Langdale, where the descent from Esk Hause to Sty Head is a loss of height of 700 feet and a double loss of this amount if returning to Langdale. Plus the 3000' of effective ascent, this is too much for the average walker. Distance is of less consequence. The same applies to ascent of Pillar from Buttermere. This is a glorious walk, full of interest, but it cannot be done without first climbing the High Stile range (at Scarth Gap) and then descending into Ennerdale before setting foot on Pillar. If returning to Buttermere, Ennerdale and the High Stile range will have to be crossed again towards the end of an exhausting day. There is no sadder sight than a Buttermere-bound pedestrian crossing Scarth Gap on his hands and knees as the shadows of evening steal o'er the scene. *The route is therefore recommended for strong walkers only.*

The most thrilling line of ascent of Pillar is by way of the memorial footbridge, this being very conveniently situated for the Buttermere approach ('the bridge was, in fact, provided to give access to Pillar from this direction). A slanting route down to the footbridge leaves the Scarth Gap path some 150 yards on the Ennerdale side of the pass. The bifurcation is not clear, but the track goes off to the right above the plantation, becoming distinct and crossing the fences by three stiles. The climb from the bridge is described on the opposite page. A less arduous route of ascent is to keep to the Scarth Gap path into Ennerdale and climb out of the valley by Black Sail Pass to its top, where follow the ridge on the right — but this easier way had better be reserved for the return when energy is flagging.

To find the slanting path from Scarth Gap look for the rocky knoll, with tree (illustrated) and turn right on grass above it

Via the footbridge :   3550 feet of ascent :   5¼ miles
Via Black Sail Pass :   3250 feet of ascent :   6¼ miles

Pillar Rock, from the north

The Pillar Ride

THE SUMMIT

As in the case of many fells of rugged appearance, the summit is one of the smoothest places on Pillar, and one may perambulate within a 50-yard radius of the cairn without being aware of the declivities on all sides. There are stones, but grass predominates. The number of erections, including two wind-shelters and a survey column, testifies to the importance of the summit in the esteem of fellwalkers and map-makers.

DESCENTS :

To Wasdale Head: In fair weather or foul, there is one royal road down to Wasdale Head, and that is by the eastern ridge to join Black Sail Pass on its journey thereto. The views are superb, and the walking is so easy for the most part that they can be enjoyed while on the move. There should be no difficulty in following the path in mist — only in one cairned section is it indistinct — but the fence-posts are there in any event as a guide to the top of the Pass. Ten minutes can be saved by the short cut going down from the side of Looking Stead. The route into Mosedale via Wind Gap is much less satisfactory, and no quicker although shorter. Another way into Mosedale sometimes used is the obvious scree-gully opening off the ridge opposite the head of Great Doup, but why suffer the torture of a half-mile of loose stones when the ridge is so much easier and pleasanter?

To Ennerdale : If bound for Black Sail Hostel, follow the eastern ridge to the pass, and there turn left on a clear path. If bound for Gillerthwaite or places west, follow the fence-posts northwest for White Pike and its ridge, which has a rough section of boulders below the Pike ; but in stormy weather prefer the route joining High Beck from Wind Gap.

To Buttermere : In clear weather, the direct route climbing up out of Ennerdale may be reversed ; at the forest road beyond the memorial footbridge walk up the valley for 120 yards, then taking a slanting path through the plantation on the left to Scarth Gap. In bad conditions, it is safer to go round by Black Sail Pass.

To any of the above destinations via Robinson's Cairn
Leave the summit at the north wind-shelter. Pillar Rock comes into view at once, and a rough loose track slithers down to the point where the first of its buttresses (Pisgah) rises from the fellside. Here turn right, by the stretcher-box (an excellent landmark) and along the Traverse to easy ground and the Cairn. *On no account descend the hollow below the stretcher-box:* this narrows to a dangerous funnel of stones and a sheer drop into a gully. (This is known as Walker's Gully, NOT because it is a gully for walkers, but because a man of this name fell to his death here).

PLAN OF THE SUMMIT

100 YARDS

Pillar Rock as seen from the north shelter

RIDGE ROUTES

To SCOAT FELL, 2760′: 1¼ miles : WSW
Depression at 2480′ (Wind Gap): 300 feet of ascent
A fine little journey in spectacular scenery.

After an indefinite start, a line of
cairns leads down to Wind Gap, the
last stage of the descent being
steep and rough, but not
difficult. Beyond the
Gap a clear path goes
up the facing slope
into the boulders
preceding the easy
grassy promenade
along the top above
Black Crag. Then follows a slight loss of height before
the final rise to Scoat Fell, the summit wall of which
is joined in a chaotic pile of boulders.

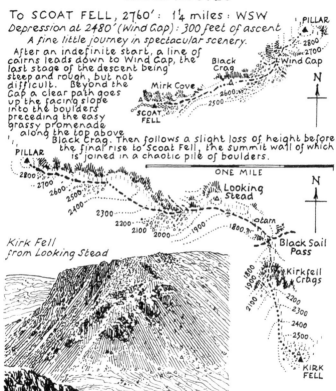

To KIRK FELL, 2630′: 2½ miles : ESE, then S
Depression at 1800′ (Black Sail Pass): 850 feet of ascent
Excellent views, both near and far; a good walk

The Ennerdale fence (what is left of it) links the two tops,
and the route never ventures far from it. The eastern ridge
of Pillar offers a speedy descent, the path being clear except
on one grassy section, which is, however, well cairned. At
the Pass, the crags of Kirk Fell look ferocious and hostile, but
a thin track goes off bravely to tackle them and can be relied
upon to lead to the dull top of Kirk Fell after providing a minor
excitement where a high rock step needs to be surmounted.

THE VIEW

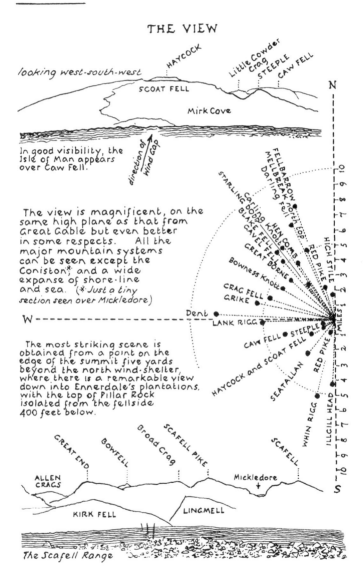

looking west-south-west

HAYCOCK · Little Cowder Crag · STEEPLE · CAW FELL

SCOAT FELL

Mirk Cove

N

In good visibility, the Isle of Man appears over Caw Fell.

direction of Wind Gap

The view is magnificent, on the same high plane as that from Great Gable but even better in some respects. All the major mountain systems can be seen except the Coniston* and a wide expanse of shore-line and sea. (* *Just a tiny section seen over Mickledore*)

The most striking scene is obtained from a point on the edge of the summit five yards beyond the north wind-shelter, where there is a remarkable view down into Ennerdale's plantations, with the top of Pillar Rock isolated from the fellside 400 feet below.

FELLBARROW
MELLBREAK above COP
Darling Fell

STARLING DODD
CARLING KNOTT
HEN COMB
BLAKE FELL
GAVEL FELL
GREAT BORNE

HIGH STILE
RED PIKE

10
9
8
7
6
5
4
3
2
1

Bowness Knott

CRAG FELL
GRIKE

W

Dent

LANK RIGG

CAW FELL · STEEPLE

HAYCOCK and SCOAT FELL

SEATALLAN

WHIN RIGG

ILLGILL HEAD

RED PIKE

1 2 MILES
3
4
5
6
7
8
9
10

S

GREAT END
BOWFELL
Broad Crag
SCAFELL PIKE
SCAFELL

ALLEN CRAGS

Mickledore

KIRK FELL

LINGMELL

The Scafell Range

THE VIEW

Principal Fells

Lakes and Tarns

SSE: *Eel Tarn*
SSE: *Burnmoor Tarn*
WNW: *Ennerdale Water*
NNW: *Loweswater*

Innominate Tarn on Haystacks, ENE, is brought in the view by walking 10 yards from the column eastwards

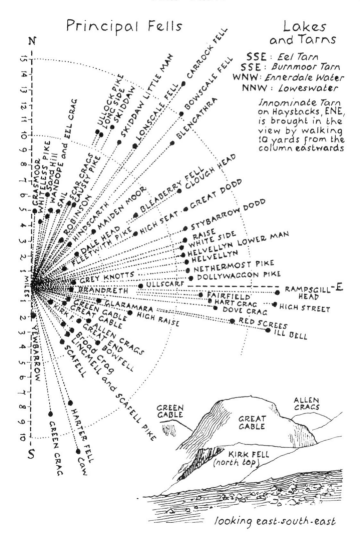

looking east-south-east

18 | Haystacks

Book Seven: The Western Fells

Wainwright decided he couldn't put Haystacks in his top six fells, the names of which he finally reveals at the end of Book Seven – Scafell Pike, Bowfell, Pillar, Great Gable, Blencathra and Crinkle Crags. The top six he chose were all roughly 1000 ft higher. On Haystacks 10, however, he makes it very clear it is his favourite: 'for beauty, variety and interesting detail, for sheer fascination and unique individuality, the summit-area of Haystacks is supreme. This is in fact the best fell-top of all.'

He didn't at this stage disclose that he had decided to pay Haystacks the final accolade – that it was where he wanted his ashes to be scattered. He let out this information not long afterwards, in 1966, with the publication of *Fellwanderer*.

All I ask for, at the end, is a last long resting place by the side of Innominate Tarn on Haystacks, where the water gently laps the gravelly shore and the heather blooms and Pillar and Gable keep unfailing watch. A quiet place, a lonely place. I shall go to it for the last time, and be carried: someone who knew me in life will take me there and empty me out of a little box and leave me there alone.

And if you, dear reader, should get a bit of grit in your boots as you are crossing Haystacks in the years to come, please treat it with respect. It might be me.

Two months after his death, on 22 March 1991, Betty, his widow, did as Wainwright requested, accompanied by Percy Duff, one of his oldest friends and colleagues. They were each in their seventieth year by then, so they asked Percy's two sons to go with them as pos-

Innominate Tarn, Haystacks

sible stretcher bearers, so Percy said, in case he collapsed. They'd waited for signs of spring to arrive to make the going easier, the day more clement.

They left Kendal at six in the morning and headed for Honister Pass, one of the ascents described by Wainwright. By seven o'clock they were at the old Honister quarry. An hour and a half later, they had reached Innominate Tarn – so named because it has never had a proper name. Betty scattered the ashes near a cairn, the precise location of which she never revealed – just as Beatrix Potter's shepherd never revealed where he had scattered her ashes. The sun came out. Not another soul was around. Then Betty and the little party came back down Haystacks the way they had come.

Not long afterwards, Allerdale Council, one of Cumbria's four District Councils, was approached to re-christen Innominate Tarn in

The plaque in honour of Wainwright in St James Church, Buttermere

Wainwright's honour and call it Wainwright Tarn. It passed through various stages, until, at the last moment, someone (obviously not quite as expert as Wainwright at reading maps) realised that the tarn was in fact in Copeland, the next-door district. The proposal was then dropped. In any case, it turns out that permission to change the name of Innominate Tarn lies with the owner of the land, Willie Richardson of Gatesgarth, Buttermere, not the council. I put the question to him. 'Hmm, I quite like the name Innominate Tarn. And I don't like change. But there is another tarn on the very top of Haystacks, a bit smaller, which hasn't got a name. That could be called Wainwright Tarn. But I'll have to think about it. And I'd have to ask my mother what she thinks…'

After you have climbed Haystacks and have made sure you have not picked up any grit, you can honour Wainwright's name by visiting the little church in Buttermere. There you will see a plaque to his memory. Wainwright was not a church-goer, but all followers of Wainwright will find it a soothing, peaceful, perfect place of worship. Through the window above the memorial you can look out and see Haystacks, and remember him.

Haystacks

properly
Hay Stacks
(two words)
as on
Ordnance maps

from Gamlin End, High Crag

Gatesgarth
HIGH
CRAG
HAYSTACKS

Black●Sail Y.H.
MILES
0   1   2

NATURAL FEATURES

Haystacks stands unabashed and unashamed in the midst of a circle of much loftier fells, like a shaggy terrier in the company of foxhounds, some of them known internationally, but not one of this distinguished group of mountains around Ennerdale and Buttermere can show a greater variety and a more fascinating arrangement of interesting features. Here are sharp peaks in profusion, tarns with islands and tarns without islands, crags, screes, rocks for climbing and rocks not for climbing, heather tracts, marshes, serpentine trails, tarns with streams and tarns with no streams.   All these, with a background of magnificent landscapes, await every visitor to Haystacks but they will be appreciated most by those who go there to linger and explore.   It is a place of surprises around corners, and there are many corners.   For a man trying to get a persistent worry out of his mind, the top of Haystacks is a wonderful cure.

The fell rises between the deep hollow of Warnscale Bottom near Gatesgarth, and Ennerdale: between a valley familiar to summer motorists and a valley reached only on foot. It is bounded on the west by Scarth Gap, a pass linking the two. The Buttermere aspect is the better known, although this side is often dark in shadow and seen only as a silhouette against the sky: here, above Warnscale, is a great wall of crags. The Ennerdale flank, open to the sun, is friendlier but steep and rough nevertheless.

Eastwards, beyond the tangle of tors and outcrops forming the boundary of Haystacks on this side, a broad grass slope rises easily and unattractively to Brandreth on the edge of the Borrowdale watershed; beyond is Derwent country.

The spelling of Haystacks as one word is a personal preference of the author (and others), and probably arises from a belief that the name originated from the resemblance of the scattered tors on the summit to stacks of hay in a field. If this were so, the one word *Haystacks* would be correct (as it is in *Haycock*).

But learned authorities state that the name derives from the Icelandic 'stack', meaning 'a columnar rock', and that the true interpretation is *High Rocks*. This is logical and appropriate. *High Rocks* is a name of two words and would be wrongly written as *Highrocks*.

The summit tarn

Big Stack,
looking east from a point
near the path to the
summit from
Scarth Gap.

In the picture below
Big Stack appears on
the extreme right.

The north crags,
looking west from the
slopes of Green Crag.

The path is seen
skirting the cliff
on the left.

MAP

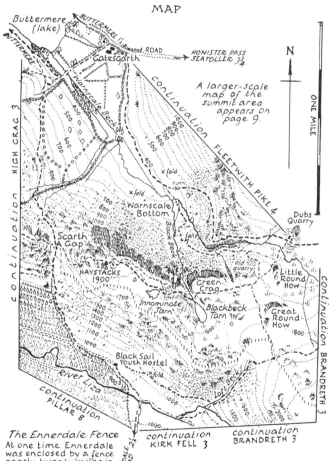

A larger-scale map of the summit area appears on page 9.

The Ennerdale Fence

At one time Ennerdale was enclosed by a fence nearly twenty miles in length, running along both watersheds and around the head of the valley. The fence was mainly of post and wire and only the posts now survive, with omissions, but part of the southern boundary was furnished with a stone wall, which is still in fair condition. In general, the line of the fence followed parish boundaries but on Haystacks there is considerable deviation. Here the series of cairns built around iron stakes (erected to mark the boundary of the Lonsdale estate) coincides with the parish boundary, but the fence keeps well to the south of this line.

ASCENT FROM GATESGARTH
1550 feet of ascent : 1¼ miles

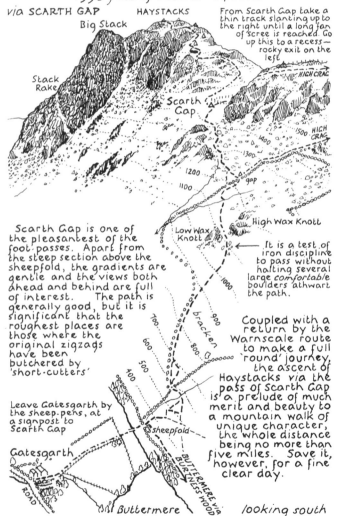

via SCARTH GAP   HAYSTACKS
Big Stack

From Scarth Gap take a thin track slanting up to the right until a long fan of scree is reached. Go up this to a recess—rocky exit on the left

Stack Rake

HIGH CRAG

Scarth Gap

1500 HIGH CRAG

1400

1300

1200

1100

gap

High Wax Knott

Low Wax Knott

It is a test of iron discipline to pass without halting several large *comfortable* boulders athwart the path.

Scarth Gap is one of the pleasantest of the foot-passes. Apart from the steep section above the sheepfold, the gradients are gentle and the views both ahead and behind are full of interest. The path is generally good, but it is significant that the roughest places are those where the original zigzags have been butchered by 'short-cutters'

1000

900

bracken

800

700

600

500

400

Coupled with a return by the Warnscale route to make a full 'round' journey, the ascent of Haystacks via the pass of Scarth Gap is a prelude of much merit and beauty to a mountain walk of unique character, the whole distance being no more than five miles. Save it, however, for a fine clear day.

Leave Gatesgarth by the sheep-pens, at a signpost to Scarth Gap

sheepfold

Gatesgarth

BUTTERMERE VIA BURTNESS WOOD

ROAD

Buttermere

looking south

ASCENT FROM GATESGARTH
via WARNSCALE

1600 feet of ascent : 2¾ miles

HAYSTACKS

looking south

A : Stack Gill
B : Warn Gill
C : The Y Gully
D : Toreador Gully
E : Green Crag Gully
F : Little Round How
G : Great Round How
H : Blackbeck Tarn
I : Innominate Tarn

grass

Green Crag

old quarry

dead trees

DUBS

FLEETWITH PIKE rises steeply on this side

DUBS QUARRY and HONISTER PASS

ravine

falls

fall

quarry road (not used on this ascent)

ruin

bracken

old fold

Warnscale Bottom

x *circular sheepfold*

Cross the stream near the confluence (easier said than done). Try a little higher where it runs in two channels.

excavated water via artificial cut

Two paths climb out of Warnscale Bottom. On the left, in a great loop, rises a wellknown quarry road (this is an excellent route to Honister). On the right, across the beck, is an old 'made' path, originally serving a quarry: this is now little used but is still well-cairned, and it provides a fascinating stairway of zigs and zags over rough ground with impressive views of the wall of crags above; this is the path to take. (It is possible to scramble up the only breach in the crags, alongside Black Beck, but this is not recommended.)
The grassy upland is reached directly opposite Great Round How, the path at this point being joined by another from Dubs Quarry. Full of variety and interesting situations, it swings right, passing Blackbeck and Innominate Tarns, to the top of the fell. Or, before reaching Innominate Tarn, a track on the right may be taken: this skirts the rim of the crags and crowds more thrills into the walk.

easy level walking

Gatesgarth used to be served by buses, but isn't now.

Gatesgarth

SCARTH GAP

ROAD

Gatesgarthdale Beck

HONISTER PASS SEATOLLER 3¾

BUTTERMERE 1½

For sustained interest, impressive crag scenery, beautiful views, and a most delightful arrangement of tarns and rocky peaks, this short mountain excursion ranks with the very best.

ASCENT FROM HONISTER PASS
1050 feet of ascent : 2¼ miles

A note of explanation is required.   This ascent-route does not conform to the usual pattern, being more in the nature of an upland cross-country walk than a mountain climb : there are two pronounced descents before foot is set on Haystacks. The wide variety of scene and the fascinating intricacies of the path are justification for the inclusion of the route in this book.

If returning to Honister, note the path to Brandreth just below Innominate Tarn. By using this until it joins the Great Gable path and then swinging left around Dubs Bottom, the Drum House can be regained without extra effort or time.

After traversing the back of Green Crag the path drops to the outlet of Blackbeck Tarn, rising stonily therefrom with a profound abyss on the right. This section is the highlight of the walk. An alternative way to the top, turning off opposite the Brandreth junction, follows closely the edge of the crags.

HAYSTACKS

tarn   1800

Innominate Tarn

BRANDRETH

Blackbeck Tarn

Green Crag

Great Round How   1600

Little Round How   grass

WARNSCALE BOTTOM

1500   1400

Dubs Bottom

1500

WARNSCALE BOTTOM

1600

Dubs Quarry (disused)

looking west

BRANDRETH GREAT GABLE

1700

foundations of Drum House

1700

1600

old tramway

1500

1400   rock cutting

1300

1200   quarry road

quarry buildings

BUTTERMERE

Honister Pass 1190'

From the hut at Dubs Quarry leave the path and go down to the stream, crossing it (somehow) where its silent meanderings through the Dubs marshes assume a noisy urgency.

From the top of Honister Pass Haystacks is nowhere in sight, and even when it comes into view, after crossing the shoulder of Fleetwith Pike at the Drum House, it is insignificant against the towering background of Pillar, being little higher in altitude and seemingly remote across the wide depression of Dubs Bottom. But, although the route here described is not a natural approach, the elevation of Honister Pass, its car-parking facilities, and the unerring pointer of the tramway make access to Haystacks particularly convenient from this point.

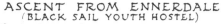

ASCENT FROM ENNERDALE
(BLACK SAIL YOUTH HOSTEL)

970 feet of ascent
1¼ miles

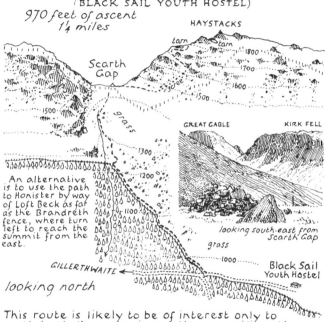

HAYSTACKS

tarn   tarn

1800
1700
1600

Scarth
Gap

1500

grass

1500

1300

1200

GREAT GABLE   KIRK FELL

An alternative
is to use the path
to Honister by way
of Loft Beck as far
as the Brandreth
fence, where turn
left to reach the
summit from the
east.

1100

1000

looking south-east from
Scarth Gap

grass

GILLERTHWAITE

1000

Black Sail
Youth Hostel

looking north

This route is likely to be of interest only to
youth hostellers staying at the magnificently
situated Black Sail Hut. Other mortals, denied
this privilege, cannot conveniently use Ennerdale
Head as a starting point for mountain ascents.

formerly a
shepherd's
hut,.....

Black Sail Youth Hostel

THE SUMMIT

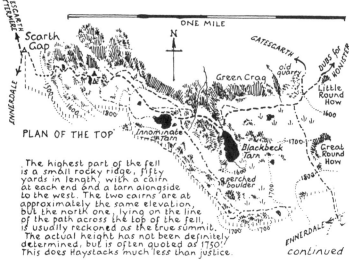

ONE MILE

N

GATESGARTH
BUTTERMERE

Scarth
Gap

ENNERDALE

PLAN OF THE TOP

GATESGARTH

old quarry

DUBS for HONISTER

Green Crag

Little
Round
How

1600

1800

1600

Innominate
Tarn

Blackbeck
Tarn

1700

Great
Round
How

1600

perched
boulder

1700

1800

1700

1700

ENNERDALE

The highest part of the fell
is a small rocky ridge, fifty
yards in length, with a cairn
at each end and a tarn alongside
to the west. The two cairns are at
approximately the same elevation,
but the north one, lying on the line
of the path across the top of the fell,
is usually reckoned as the true summit.
The actual height has not been definitely
determined, but is often quoted as 1750.
This does Haystacks much less than justice.

continued

THE SUMMIT

continued

Haystacks fails to qualify for inclusion in the author's "best half-dozen" only because of inferior height, a deficiency in vertical measurement. Another thousand feet would have made all the difference.

But for beauty, variety and interesting detail, for sheer fascination and unique individuality, the summit-area of Haystacks is supreme. This is in fact the best fell-top of all — a place of great charm and fairyland attractiveness. Seen from a distance, these qualities are not suspected: indeed, on the contrary, the appearance of Haystacks is almost repellent when viewed from the higher surrounding peaks: black are its bones and black is its flesh. With its thick covering of heather it is dark and sombre even when the sun sparkles the waters of its many tarns, gloomy and mysterious even under a blue sky. There are fierce crags and rough screes and outcrops that will be grittier still when the author's ashes are scattered here.

Yet the combination of features, of tarn and tor, of cliff and cove, the labyrinth of corners and recesses, the maze of old sheepwalks and paths, form a design, or a lack of design, of singular appeal and absorbing interest. One can forget even a raging toothache on Haystacks.

perched boulder
on a rock platform

Note the profile
in shadow.
Some women
have faces
like that.

On a first visit, learn thoroughly the details of the mile-long main path across the top, a magnificent traverse, because this serves as the best introduction to the geography of the fell.

Having memorised this, several interesting deviations may be made: the parallel alternative above the rim of the north face, the scramble onto Big Stack, the 'cross-country' route around the basin of Blackbeck Tarn, the walk alongside the fence, and so on.

typical summit tors

DESCENTS: Leave the top of Haystacks only by a recognisable route. It is possible to make rough descents in the vicinity (left bank) of Black Beck and Green Crag gully, but more advisable to regard the whole of the north edge as highly dangerous. The only advice that can be given to a novice lost on Haystacks in mist is that he should kneel down and pray for safe deliverance.

THE VIEW

This is not a case of distance lending enchantment to the view, because apart from a glimpse of Skiddaw above the Robinson-Hindscarth depression and a slice of the Helvellyn range over Honister, the scene is predominantly one of high mountains within a five-mile radius. And really good they look — the enchantment is close at hand. Set in a tight surround, they are seen in revealing detail: a rewarding study deserving leisurely appreciation.

Principal Fells

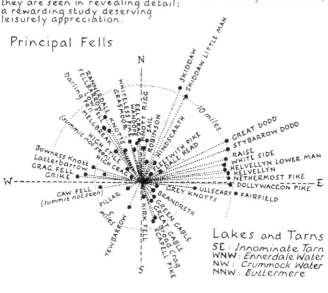

Lakes and Tarns
SE: Innominate Tarn
WNW: Ennerdale Water
NW: Crummock Water
NNW: Buttermere

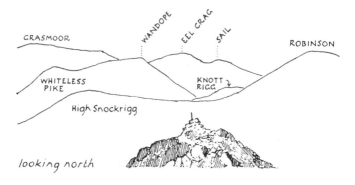

looking north

RIDGE ROUTES

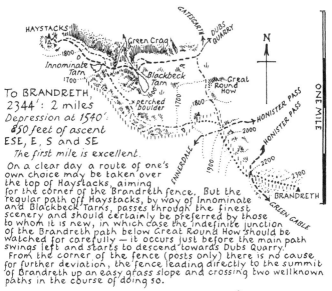

TO BRANDRETH,
2344': 2 miles
Depression at 1540'
850 feet of ascent
ESE, E, S and SE

The first mile is excellent.

On a clear day a route of one's own choice may be taken over the top of Haystacks, aiming for the corner of the Brandreth fence. But the regular path off Haystacks, by way of Innominate and Blackbeck Tarns, passes through the finest scenery and should certainly be preferred by those to whom it is new, in which case the indefinite junction of the Brandreth path below Great Round How should be watched for carefully — it occurs just before the main path swings left and starts to descend towards Dubs Quarry. From the corner of the fence (posts only) there is no cause for further deviation, the fence leading directly to the summit of Brandreth up an easy grass slope and crossing two well-known paths in the course of doing so.

TO HIGH CRAG, 2443'
1¼ miles : W, then NW
Depression at 1425' (Scarth Gap)
1100 feet of ascent
A fine walk in spite of scree

Follow faithfully the thin track trending west from the summit, a delightful game of ins and outs and ups and downs although the scree to which it leads is less pleasant: at the foot slant right to Scarth Gap. More scree is encountered across the pass on the climb to

High Crag, from Scarth Gap

Seat; then a good ridge follows to the final tower of High Crag: this deteriorates badly into slippery scree on the later stages of the ascent.

HALF A MILE

Postscript

In his Personal Notes in Conclusion at the end of *The Western Fells*, the seventh and last of the original series of Pictorial Guides to the Lakeland Fells, A. Wainwright wrote as follows:

.... So this is farewell to the present series of books.

The fleeting hour of life of those who love the hills is quickly spent, but the hills are eternal. Always there will be the lonely ridge, the dancing beck, the silent forest ; always there will be the exhilaration of the summits. These are for the seeking, and those who seek and find while there is yet time will be blessed both in mind and body.

I wish you all many happy days on the fells in the years ahead.

There will be fair winds and foul, days of sun and days of rain. But enjoy them all.

Good walking! And don't forget — watch where you are putting your feet.

AW.

Christmas, 1965.

The Wainwright Society

The primary aim of the Wainwright Society is to keep alive the things A. Wainwright promoted through the guide books and the many other publications that were the 'labour of love' of a large portion of his life. The inaugural meeting was held on 9 November 2002 at Ambleside Youth Hostel, followed by a walk to the summit of Dove Crag.

Details of the Society's activities, which include a programme of fell walks, a quarterly magazine, an annual landscape photography competition and an annual Wainwright Memorial Lecture are to be found on the Wainwright Society website: www.wainwright.org.uk.

Index

Entries in **bold** indicate the main fells. Page numbers in *italic* refer to illustration captions.

Walker's log

Fell	Dates walked	Ascent/s used

Remarks

Fell	Dates walked	Ascent/s used

Remarks

Books by A. Wainwright available from Frances Lincoln Ltd

The Pictorial Guides

Book One: The Eastern Fells | ISBN 0 7112 2227 4
Book Two: The Far Eastern Fells | ISBN 0 7112 2228 2
Book Three: The Central Fells | ISBN 0 7112 2229 0
Book Four: The Southern Fells | ISBN 0 7112 2230 4
Book Five: The Northern Fells | ISBN 0 7112 2231 2
Book Six: The North Western Fells | ISBN 0 7112 2232 0
Book Seven: The Western Fells | ISBN 0 7112 2233 9

Also:

Outlying Fells of Lakeland | ISBN 0 7112 2234 7

In the same series:

A Coast to Coast Walk | ISBN 0 7112 2236 3
Pennine Way Companion | ISBN 0 7112 2235 5
The Walker's Log Book (Volume One) | ISBN 0 7112 2389 0
The Walker's Log Book (Volume Two) | ISBN 0 7112 2390 4
Walks in Limestone Country | ISBN 0 7112 2237 1
Walks on the Howgill Fells | ISBN 0 7112 2238 X

The Lakeland Sketchbooks

A Lakeland Sketchbook | ISBN 0 7112 2333 5
A Second Lakeland Sketchbook | ISBN 0 7112 2334 3
A Third Lakeland Sketchbook | ISBN 0 7112 2335 1
A Fourth Lakeland Sketchbook | ISBN 0 7112 2336 X
A Fifth Lakeland Sketchbook | ISBN 0 7112 2337 8

Wainwright Boxed Set

The Pictorial Guides:
Books One to Seven | ISBN 0 7112 2281 9